Th. Jefferson

Other Books on Jefferson by Saul K. Padover

DEMOCRACY BY JEFFERSON
JEFFERSON [*a biography*]
THE COMPLETE JEFFERSON
THOMAS JEFFERSON AND THE NATIONAL CAPITAL

Also by the same author

THE REVOLUTIONARY EMPEROR: JOSEPH II
SECRET DIPLOMACY
THE LIFE AND DEATH OF LOUIS XVI
WILSON'S IDEALS
EXPERIMENT IN GERMANY
LA VIE POLITIQUE DES ÉTATS-UNIS
FRANCE: SETTING OR RISING STAR
PSYCHOLOGICAL WARFARE
EUROPE'S QUEST FOR UNITY
FRENCH INSTITUTIONS
THE LIVING U. S. CONSTITUTION
THE COMPLETE MADISON
THE WASHINGTON PAPERS

A JEFFERSON PROFILE

AS REVEALED IN HIS LETTERS

SELECTED AND ARRANGED
WITH AN INTRODUCTION
BY

Saul K. Padover

THE JOHN DAY COMPANY
NEW YORK

CONTENTS

PART THREE   MINISTER TO FRANCE   1784–1789

1796

1797

PART SIX VICE-PRESIDENT 1797–1801

1797

1798

1799

1800

1812

1813

1814

1815

INTRODUCTION

THE 180 letters in this book represent, in the editor's opinion, the essence of Jefferson. They were selected from the vast mass of the Jefferson correspondence—which runs to an astonishing total of 18,000 letters—with a view to portraying his extraordinary personality. These letters make up, in sum, Jefferson's intellectual portrait, as painted by himself.

The book is designed neither for Jefferson scholars nor for historians. Its aim is more modest. It hopes to give pleasure to the general reader and to help Americans make or renew the acquaintance of an exciting historic figure whose stature is increasing with the years. Here are lively and often moving letters of Jefferson the father and lover, student and statesman, artist and scientist, philosopher and inventor, educator and champion of democracy. Here we have Jefferson in his intimacy, writing letters generally not intended for the public eye. The over-all effect of these highly personal letters is a remarkably fresh picture of one whom Franklin D. Roosevelt once admiringly described as the "many-sided man."

The editor has taken a few small liberties in the presentation and arrangement of the letters. First, he has modernized the spelling and tried to make it consistent throughout the text. This was necessary because Jefferson, like his contemporaries in general, was inconsistent; sometimes he would spell a name or word differently in the same paragraph or letter. Secondly, the editor has written out in full Jefferson's ampersands and abbreviations; this was done for the sake of readability and clarity, without essentially sacrificing the spirit of the original text.

Some of the letters are here given in a somewhat abbreviated form. Others carry brief explanatory notes. In a few instances Greek quotations have been eliminated from the original text.

These minor editorial interventions were needed to give co-
herence and modern meaning to letters written many generations ago under special circumstances and for private purposes.
In this regard the editor cannot do better than quote from a
note on "Editing Letters," written by Samuel Butler:

> It is a mistake to think you are giving letters most faithfully by
> printing as they were written without the smallest alteration, for
> you do not give the letters unless you reproduce their environment,
> and this cannot be done. He who undertakes to edit letters, under-
> takes to translate them from one set of surroundings to other very
> different ones. It is the essence of a private letter that the audience
> should be few and known to the writer. It is the essence, generally,
> of a published letter that the audience should be large and un-
> known to the writer. . . . Very little would have been allowed to
> stand without alteration if the writer had had any idea that his or
> her letter was going to be laid before the public.

It is a tribute to Jefferson that so little alteration or emendation has been necessary to make his letters readable, timely, and
challenging. For among his other abundant gifts, Jefferson was
also a first-rate writer with a lucidity of phrase and range of
expression that accurately reflected his immense learning. On
occasion, indeed, he could rise to great literary heights. Let
him who doubts this try to improve on the prose of the Declaration of Independence, or the Bill for Establishing Religious
Freedom, or the Revised Code of Virginia.

How Jefferson found time to write so much and about so
many things is a mystery until one realizes that he was in the
habit of rising with the sun, working methodically until late
into the night, and not wasting any time. By vocation and avo-
cation he was both a practicing farmer and an active politician.
His livelihood was derived from his large plantation in Virginia and from the many public offices which he occupied for
a period of nearly forty years. He was a member of the Virginia
Legislature and of the Continental Congress, Governor of his
State, Minister to France, United States Secretary of State, Vice

President of the United States, and President of the United States twice. After retirement from the Presidency, in March 1809, he spent the last seventeen years of his life farming his extensive acres, building and organizing the University of Virginia, experimenting with agriculture and mechanics, supervising a growing family of grandchildren, entertaining hosts of visitors, reading philosophy and the classics in the original, receiving letters from all over America and Europe, and trying conscientiously to answer the flood of mail which all but inundated him. No fewer than 25,000 letters written to Jefferson have been preserved.

In 1816, at the age of 73, he wrote from Monticello:

My greatest oppression is a correspondence afflictingly laborious, the extent of which I have been long endeavoring to curtail. This keeps me at the drudgery of the writing-table all the prime hours of the day, leaving for the gratifications of my appetite for reading, only what I can steal from the hours of sleep. Could I reduce this epistolary corvée within the limits of my friends and affairs, and give the time redeemed from it to reading and reflection, to history, ethics, mathematics, my life would be as happy as the infirmities of age would admit.

But he could not escape the "epistolary corvée." The flood of letters continued to pour into Monticello. Although in retirement from public life, his fame continued to grow and to attract increasing attention. The author of the Declaration of Independence and the collaborator of the revered George Washington, Jefferson, in his later years, loomed larger and larger as one of the heroes of the American Revolution. The robust republic which he had helped to build would not—could not—ignore the Sage of Monticello. People kept on writing and writing to him. The pile of letters, coupled with the large numbers of visitors who climbed up the hill to steal a glance at the patriarch, disturbed the tranquillity of his old age. In his eightieth year, Jefferson wrote to his friend John Adams a letter of near-despair about "this distress" of the mail burden:

I do not know how far you may suffer, as I do, under the persecution of letters, of which every mail brings a fresh load. They are
letters of inquiry, for the most part, always of good will, sometimes
from friends whom I esteem, but much oftener from persons whose
names are unknown to me, but written kindly and civilly, and to
which, therefore, civility requires answers. . . . I happened to turn to
my letter-list some time ago, and a curiosity was excited to count
those received in a single year. It was the year before the last [1820].
I found the number to be one thousand two hundred and sixty-
seven, many of them requiring answers of elaborate research, and
all to be answered with due attention and consideration. Take an
average of this number for a week or a day, and I will repeat the
question . . . Is this life? At best it is but the life of a mill-horse,
who sees no end to his circle but in death. To such a life, that of a
cabbage is paradise.

He was unable to reply to all the letters, even though he tried
to use a copying machine; but he answered enough to form a
permanent treasury. Many of Jefferson's letters are classic contributions to American political thought, especially the philosophy of freedom and democracy. Others—notably the letter
to Dr. Walter Jones, written on January 2, 1814, describing the
character of George Washington—are literary gems. For Jefferson at his best was a literary craftsman acutely aware, as he said,
that "the most valuable of all talents [is] that of never using
two words where one will do." He was sensitive to the nuances
of Anglo-Saxon prose as he was to the beauties of English
poetry; he did, indeed, once write a learned essay on prosody.
His sensitivity to style was one reason why, although himself a
brilliant and successful lawyer, he did not like his profession.
The legal jargon of his fellow attorneys alternately repelled and
amused him. In a letter to Joseph C. Cabell, written in 1817
and enclosing a bill for a public-education system in Virginia,
Jefferson quipped:

I dislike the verbose and intricate style of the modern English
statutes. You, however, can easily correct this bill to the taste of

my brother lawyers by making every other word "said" or "aforesaid" and saying everything over two or three times, so that nobody but we of the craft can untwist the diction, and find out what it means; and that not too plainly but that we may conscientiously divide, one half on each side.

In this collection of letters, readers will find Jefferson at his literary and intellectual best. They will have the pleasure of discovering Jeffersonian phrases and comments that still sparkle and illuminate after a century and a half or more. Others, who know of Jefferson only as a statesman and Founding Father, will be delighted to see a new side of him here:

. . . a lively and lasting sense of filial duty is more effectually impressed on the mind . . . by reading King Lear, than by all the dry volumes of ethics.

A lady who has been seen as a sloven or slut in the morning, will never efface the impression she then made, with all the dress and pageantry she can afterwards involve herself in.

Give up money, give up fame, give up science, give up the earth itself and all it contains, rather than do an immoral act.

. . . a malady of either body or mind once known is half cured.

. . . the tax which will be paid for this purpose [public education], is not more than the thousandth part of what will be paid to kings, priests, and nobles, who will rise up among us if we leave the people in ignorance.

. . . were it left to me to decide whether we should have a government without newspapers, or newspapers without a government, I should not hesitate a moment to prefer the latter.

. . . a little rebellion, now and then, is a good thing, and as necessary in the political world as storms in the physical.

No vice is so mean as the want of truth, and at the same time so useless.

. . . it gives much more pain to the mind to be in debt, than to do without any article whatever which we may seem to want.

No race of kings has ever presented above one man of common sense in twenty generations.

The tree of liberty must be refreshed from time to time, with the blood of patriots and tyrants. It is its natural manure.

A man's moral sense must be unusually strong if slavery does not make him a thief.

. . . our country is a new creation . . . , because it is made on an improved plan. Europe is a first idea, a crude production, before the maker knew his trade.

The Jefferson who emerges in these pages is the very human philosopher of freedom and happiness. The child of the Virginia frontier has become, in the course of the years, one of the towering figures of history, a teacher who voiced mankind's aspirations to liberty, dignity, and self-expression. Above all it was Jefferson's brilliant formulation and championship of the idea of freedom that makes him timeless. His importance, indeed, exceeds national frontiers. Freedom, he wrote, "is the most sacred cause that ever man was engaged in." Without the "precious blessing" of liberty, he said, life had no sense and no dignity.

And he had faith that man everywhere—and not only in America—would achieve freedom and happiness.

SAUL K. PADOVER

PART ONE

Pre-Political

(1760–1771)

THOMAS JEFFERSON *was born at Shadwell in Virginia on April 13, 1743, and he entered William and Mary College in March, 1760, when he was hardly seventeen. He remained at college for two years and then studied law under the famous George Wythe, later a fellow-signer of the Declaration of Independence. At the age of twenty-four, Jefferson began to practice law. He was, in those days, not active in politics. His main preoccupations were legal, philosophic, and literary.*

The first letter in this collection was written when Jefferson was in his seventeenth year.

To John Harvey

Sir, I was at Colonel Peter Randolph's about a fortnight ago, and my schooling falling into discourse, he said he thought it would be to my advantage to go to the college, and was desirous I should go, as indeed I am myself for several reasons. In the first place as long as I stay at the mountains the loss of one-fourth of my time is inevitable, by company's coming here and detaining me from school. And likewise my absence will in a great measure put a stop to so much company, and by that means lessen the expenses of the estate in house-keeping. And on the other hand by going to the college I shall get a more universal acquaintance, which may hereafter be serviceable to me; and I suppose I can pursue my studies in the Greek and Latin as well there as here, and likewise learn something of the mathematics. I shall be glad of your opinion, and remain, sir, your most humble servant,

THOMAS JEFFERSON, JR.

To John Page *

Perfect happiness I believe was never intended by the deity to be the lot of one of his creatures in this world; but that he has very much put in our power the nearness of our approaches to it, is what I have steadfastly believed. The most

---

* Page (1743-1808) was Jefferson's boyhood friend and later Governor of Virginia.

fortunate of us, in our journey through life, frequently meet with calamities and misfortunes, which may greatly afflict us; and, to fortify our minds against the attacks of these calamities and misfortunes, should be one of the principal studies and endeavors of our lives. The only method of doing this is to assume a perfect resignation to the Divine will, to consider that whatever does happen, must happen; and that by our uneasiness, we cannot prevent the blow before it does fall, but we may add to its force after it has fallen. These considerations, and others such as these, may enable us in some measure to surmount the difficulties thrown in our way; to bear up with a tolerable degree of patience under this burthen of life; and to proceed with a pious and unshaken resignation, till we arrive at our journey's end, when we may deliver up our trust into the hands of him who gave it, and receive such reward as to him shall seem proportioned to our merit. Such, dear Page, will be the language of the man who considers his situation in this life, and such should be the language of every man who would wish to render that situation as easy as the nature of it will admit. Few things will disturb him at all: nothing will disturb him much. If this letter was to fall into the hands of some of our gay acquaintances, your correspondent and his solemn notions would probably be the subjects of a great deal of mirth and raillery, but to you I think I can venture to send it. It is in effect a continuation of the many conversations we have had on subjects of this kind; and I heartily wish we could continue these conversations face to face.

To William Fleming *

October, 1763   *Richmond* †

Dear Will, From a crowd of disagreeable companions, among whom I have spent three or four of the most tedious hours of my life, I retire into Gunn's bedchamber to converse in black and white with an absent friend. I heartily wish you were here that I might converse with a Christian once more before I die; for die I must this night unless I should be relieved by the arrival of some sociable fellow. But I will now endeavor to forget my present sufferings and think of what is more agreeable to both of us. Last Saturday I left Ned Carters where I had been happy in other good company, but particularly that of Miss Jenny Taliaferro: and though I can view the beauties of this world with the most philosophical indifference, I could not but be sensible of the justice of the character you had given me of her. She is in my opinion a great resemblance of Nancy Wilton, but prettier. I was vastly pleased with her playing on the spinnette and singing, and could not help calling to mind those sublime verses of the Cumberland genius

> Oh! how I was charmed to see
> Orpheus' music all in thee.

When you see Patsy Dandridge, tell her "God bless her." I do not like the ups and downs of a country life: today you are frolicking with a fine girl and tomorrow you are moping by yourself. Thank God! I shall shortly be where my happiness will be less interrupted. I shall salute all the girls below in your name, particularly S--y P--r [Suckey Potter]. Dear Will, I have thought of the cleverest plan of life that can be imagined. You exchange your land for Edgehill, or I mine for Fairfields, you

---

* Fleming (1729-1795) was a Virginia politician and soldier.
† The 20-year old Jefferson was on his way to Williamsburg, where he studied law.

marry S--y P--r, I marry R--a B--l [Rebecca Burwell] join and get
a pole chair and a pair of keen horses, practice the law in the
same courts, and drive about to all the dances in the country together. How do you like it? Well I am sorry you are at such a
distance I cannot hear your answer, but however you must let
me know it by the first opportunity, and all the other news in
the world which you imagine will affect me. I am, dear Will,
yours affectionately,

TH: JEFFERSON

To Robert Skipwith *

August 3, 1771   *Monticello*

    I sat down with a design of executing your request to
form a catalogue of books amounting to about £30 sterling,
but could by no means satisfy myself with any partial choice I
could make. Thinking therefore it might be as agreeable to
you, I have framed such a general collection as I think you
would wish, and might in time find convenient, to procure.
Out of this you will choose for yourself to the amount you
mentioned for the present year and may hereafter as shall be
convenient proceed in completing the whole. A view of the
second column in this catalogue would I suppose extort a smile
from the face of gravity. Peace to its wisdom! Let me not
awaken it. A little attention however to the nature of the human mind evinces that the entertainments of fiction are useful as well as pleasant. That they are pleasant when well
written, every person feels who reads. But wherein is its utility,
asks the reverend sage, big with the notion that nothing can be
useful but the learned number of Greek and Roman reading
with which his head is stored? I answer, every thing is useful
which contributes to fix us in the principles and practice of

---

* He was Jefferson's brother-in-law.

virtue. When any signal act of charity or of gratitude, for instance, is presented either to our sight or imagination, we are deeply impressed with its beauty and feel a strong desire in ourselves of doing charitable and grateful acts also. On the contrary, when we see or read of any atrocious deed, we are disgusted with its deformity and conceive an abhorrence of vice. Now every emotion of this kind is an exercise of our virtuous dispositions, and dispositions of the mind, like limbs of the body, acquire strength by exercise. But exercise produces habit, and in the instance of which we speak the exercise being of the moral feelings produces a habit of thinking and acting virtuously. We never reflect whether the story we read be truth or fiction. If the painting be lively, and a tolerable picture of nature, we are thrown into a reverie, from which if we awaken it is the fault of the writer. I appeal to every reader of feeling and sentiment whether the fictitious murder of Duncan by Macbeth in Shakespeare does not excite in him as great a horror of villainy, as the real one of Henry IV by Ravaillac as related by Davila? And whether the fidelity of Nelson and generosity of Blandford in Marmontel do not dilate his breast and elevate his sentiments as much as any similar incident which real history can furnish? Does he not in fact feel himself a better man while reading them, and privately covenant to copy the fair example? We neither know nor care whether Lawrence Sterne really went to France, whether he was there accosted by the Franciscan, at first rebuked him unkindly, and then gave him a peace offering; or whether the whole be not fiction. In either case we equally are sorrowful at the rebuke, and secretly resolve *we* will never do so. We are pleased with the subsequent atonement, and view with emulation a soul candidly acknowledging its fault and making a just reparation. Considering history as a moral exercise, her lessons would be too infrequent if confined to real life. Of those recorded by historians few incidents have been attended with such circumstances as to excite in any high degree this sympathetic emotion of virtue. We are therefore wisely framed to be as warmly interested for a fictitious as for

a real personage. The field of imagination is thus laid open to our use and lessons may be formed to illustrate and carry home to the heart every moral rule of life. Thus a lively and lasting sense of filial duty is more effectually impressed on the mind of a son or daughter by reading King Lear, than by all the dry volumes of ethics and divinity that ever were written. This is my idea of well written romance, of tragedy, comedy and epic poetry.

PART TWO

Member of Congress

(1775–1783)

IN THIS PERIOD *Jefferson served as a member of the Continental Congress in Philadelphia and Annapolis, as well as Governor of the State of Virginia. This epoch is marked by intensive creative intellectual activities. As a young member of the Virginia House of Burgesses on the eve of the American Revolution, he wrote the memorable* Summary View of the Rights of British America *(1774). Two years later he composed the Declaration of Independence. Soon afterwards he helped revise the Virginia code of laws and drew up the epoch-making Statute for Religious Freedom. He also wrote the* Notes on Virginia, *containing essays on a variety of subjects ranging from anthropology to zoology.*

To John Randolph *

Dear Sir, . . . I am sorry the situation of our country should render it not eligible to you to remain longer in it. I hope the returning wisdom of Great Britain will e'er long put an end to this unnatural contest. There may be people to whose tempers and dispositions contention is pleasing, and who therefore wish a continuance of confusion. But to me it is of all states, but one, the most horrid. My first wish is a restoration of our just rights; my second, a return of the happy period when, consistently with duty, I may withdraw myself totally from the public stage and pass the rest of my days in domestic ease and tranquillity, banishing every desire of afterwards ever hearing what passes in the world. Perhaps ardour for the latter may add considerably to the warmth of the former wish. Looking with fondness towards a reconciliation with Great Britain, I cannot help hoping you may be able to contribute towards expediting this good work. . . . I am sincerely one of those [who wish for a reunion with their parent country], and would rather be in dependence on Great Britain, properly limited, than on any nation upon earth, or than on no nation. But I am one of those, too, who rather than submit to the right of legislating for us assumed by the British parliament, and which late experience has shown they will so cruelly exercise, would lend my hand to sink the whole Island in the ocean.

---

* Randolph (1727-1784) was king's attorney in Virginia; at the outbreak of the Revolution he moved to England but remained a friend of Jefferson's.

To Giovanni Fabbroni

June 8, 1778   *Williamsburg*

If there is a gratification which I envy any people in this world it is to your country its music. This is the favorite passion of my soul, and fortune has cast my lot in a country where it is in a state of deplorable barbarism. From the [line] of life in which we conjecture you to be, I have for some time lost the hope of seeing you here. Should the event prove so, I shall ask your assistance in procuring a substitute who may be a proficient in singing and on the harpsichord. I should be contented to receive such an one two or three years hence, when it is hoped he may come more safely, and find here a greater plenty of those useful things which commerce alone can furnish. The bounds of an American fortune will not admit the indulgence of a domestic band of musicians. Yet I have thought that a passion for music might be reconciled with that economy which we are obliged to observe. I retain for instance among my domestic servants a gardener (Ortolano), weaver (Tessitore di lino e lan), a cabinet maker (Stipettaio) and a stonecutter (scalpellino lavorante in piano) to which I would add a Vigneron. In a country where, like yours, music is cultivated and practiced by every class of men I suppose there might be found persons of those trades who could perform on the French horn, clarinet or hautboy and bassoon, so that one might have a band of two French horns, two clarinets and hautboys and a bassoon, without enlarging their domestic expenses. A certainty of employment for a half dozen years, and at [the] end of that time to find them if they chose it a conveyance to their own country might induce [them] to come here on reasonable wages. Without meaning to give you trouble, perhaps it might be practicable for you in your ordinary intercourse with your people, to find out such men disposed to come to America. Sobriety and good nature would be desirable parts of their characters. If you think such a plan practicable, and will be so kind as to inform me what will be necessary to be done on my part, I will take care that it shall be done. The necessary expenses, when informed of them, I can remit before they are wanting, to any port in France with which country alone we have safe correspondence.

I am Sir with much esteem your humble servant.

T. J.

To Martha Jefferson *

November 28, 1783   *Annapolis*

My dear Patsy, After four days' journey, I arrived here without any accident and in as good health as when I left Philadelphia. The conviction that you would be more improved in the situation I have placed you than if still with me, has solaced me on my parting with you, which my love for you has rendered a difficult thing. The acquirements which I hope you will make under the tutors I have provided for you will render you more worthy of my love; and if they cannot increase it, they will prevent its diminution. Consider the good lady who has taken you under her roof, who has undertaken to see that you perform all your exercises, and to admonish you in all those wanderings from what is right or what is clever, to which your inexperience would expose you; consider her, I say, as your mother, as the only person to whom, since the loss with which Heaven has been pleased to afflict you, you can now look up; and that her displeasure or disapprobation, on any occasion, will be an immense misfortune, which should you be so unhappy as to incur by any unguarded act, think no concession too much to regain her good will. With respect to the distribution of your time, the following is what I should approve:

---

* Martha was Jefferson's oldest child. She was born in 1772 and died in 1836.

From eight to ten, practice music.

From ten to one, dance one day and draw another.

From one to two, draw on the day you dance, and write a letter next day.

From three to four, read French.

From four to five, exercise yourself in music.

From five till bed-time, read English, write, and so forth.

Communicate this plan to Mrs. Hopkinson, and if she approves of it, pursue it. As long as Mrs. Trist * remains in Philadelphia, cultivate her affection. She has been a valuable friend to you, and her good sense and good heart make her valued by all who know her, and by nobody on earth more than me. I expect you will write me by every post. Inform me what books you read, what tunes you learn, and inclose me your best copy of every lesson in drawing. Write also one letter every week, either to your Aunt Eppes, your Aunt Skipwith, your Aunt Carr, or the little lady from whom I now inclose a letter, and always put the letter you so write under cover to me. Take care that you never spell a word wrong. Always before you write a word, consider how it is spelt, and, if you do not remember it, turn to a dictionary. It produces great praise to a lady to spell well. I have placed my happiness on seeing you good and accomplished; and no distress which this world can now bring on me would equal that of your disappointing my hopes. If you love me, then strive to be good under every situation, and to all living creatures, and to acquire those accomplishments which I have put in your power, and which will go far towards ensuring you the warmest love of your affectionate father,

TH: JEFFERSON

P. S. Keep my letters and read them at times, that you may always have present in your mind those things which will endear you to me.

---

* See Jefferson's letter to her, written on August 18, 1785.

To Martha Jefferson

December 11, 1783   *Annapolis*

I hope you will have good sense enough to disregard those foolish predictions that the world is to be at an end soon. The Almighty has never made known to anybody at what time he created it; nor will he tell anybody when he will put an end to it, if he ever means to do it. As to preparations for that event, the best way is for you to be always prepared for it. The only way to be so is, never to say or do a bad thing. If ever you are about to say anything amiss, or to do anything wrong, consider beforehand. You will feel something within you which will tell you it is wrong, and ought not to be said or done. This is your conscience, and be sure to obey it. Our Maker has given us all this faithful internal monitor; and if you always obey it, you will always be prepared for the end of the world; or for a much more certain event, which is death. This must happen to all: it puts an end to the world as to us; and the way to be ready for it is never to do a wrong act.

To Martha Jefferson

December 22, 1783   *Annapolis*

I omitted in that letter to advise you on the subject of dress, which I know you are a little apt to neglect. I do not wish you to be gaily clothed at this time of life, but that what you wear should be fine of its kind. But above all things, and at all times, let your clothes be clean, whole, and properly put on. Do not fancy you must wear them till the dirt is visible to the eye. You will be the last who will be sensible of this. Some ladies think they may, under the privileges of the déshabillé, be loose and negligent of their dress in the morning. But be you, from the moment you rise till you go to bed, as cleanly and properly dressed as at the hours of dinner or tea. A lady who has been seen as a sloven or slut in the morning, will never efface the impression she then made, with all the dress and pageantry she can afterwards involve herself in. Nothing is so disgusting to our sex as a want of cleanliness and delicacy in yours. I hope, therefore, the moment you rise from bed, your first work will be to dress yourself in such a style, as that you may be seen by any gentleman without his being able to discover a pin amiss, or any other circumstance of neatness wanting.

PART THREE

Minister to France

(1784–1789)

JEFFERSON *spent nearly six years in Europe as American Minister to Paris. During this time he traveled to England, Holland, Germany, and Italy. He was also in intimate contact with some of the figures, notably Lafayette, who were active in the French Revolution. He moved in the highest circles of French society, and among his friends were distinguished people like Count Buffon, Baron Grimm, Marmontel, and Necker. It was a new and exciting world for the "savage of the mountains of America," as Jefferson described himself whimsically, and his letters reflect the multiplicity of his interests and the excitement of his observations.*

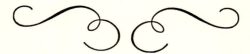

To Charles Thomson *

November 11, 1784   *Paris*

Dear Sir, I am to acknowledge the receipt of your favour of June 18. You will learn by the letters . . . which go in this packet that this world is all going to war. Thank God ours is out of their vortex. Holland and the Emperor [Joseph II] are the only powers which appear as yet, but I have no doubt that the spring will lead France, Prussia, and the Porte into the field on one side, and Russia on the other. England will probably be neutral, from impotence and domestic disturbance—but "what have you or I with peace or war to do" says the song, and say I.

I send you a pamphlet on the subject of animal magnetism, which has disturbed the nerves of prodigious numbers here. I believe this report will allay the evil. I also send you Roberts' last aerial voyage. There has been a lamp called the cylinder lamp, lately invented here. It gives a light equal, as is thought, to that of six or eight candles. It requires olive oil, but its consumption is not great. The improvement is produced by forcing the wick into a hollow cylinder so that there is a passage for the air through the hollow. The idea had occurred to Doctor Franklin a year or two before, but he tried his experiment with a rush, which not succeeding he did not prosecute it. The fact was the rush found too small a cylinder; the one used is of an inch diameter. They make shade candlesticks for studious men, which are excellent for reading; these cost two guineas. I

---

* Charles Thomson (1729-1824) of Pennsylvania was the Secretary of the Continental Congress.

should have sent you a specimen of the phosphoric matches but that I am told Mr. Rittenhouse has had some of them. They are a beautiful discovery and very useful, especially to heads which like yours and mine cannot at all times be got to sleep. The convenience of lighting a candle without getting out of bed, of sealing letters without calling a servant, of kindling a fire without flint, steel, punk, and so forth, are of value.

To James Monroe *

June 17, 1785   *Paris*

I sincerely wish you may find it convenient to come here. The pleasure of the trip will be less than you expect, but the utility greater. It will make you adore your own country, its soil, its climate, its equality, liberty, laws, people, and manners. My God! how little do my countrymen know what precious blessings they are in possession of, and which no other people on earth enjoy. I confess I had no idea of it myself. While we shall see multiplied instances of Europeans going to live in America, I will venture to say no man now living will ever see an instance of an American removing to settle in Europe and continuing there. Come, then, and see the proofs of this, and on your return add your testimony to that of every thinking American, in order to satisfy our countrymen how much it is their interest to preserve, uninfected by contagion, those peculiarities in their government and manners to which they are indebted for these blessings.

---

* Monroe (1758-1831), a lifelong friend and follower of Jefferson, became fifth President of the United States.

To Mrs. Elizabeth Trist *

August 18, 1785   *Paris*

I am much pleased with the people of this country. The roughnesses of the human mind are so thoroughly rubbed off with them, that it seems as if one might glide through a whole life among them without a jostle. Perhaps, too, their manners may be the best calculated for happiness to a people in their situation, but I am convinced they fall far short of effecting a happiness so temperate, so uniform, and so lasting, as is generally enjoyed with us. The domestic bonds here are absolutely done away. And where can their compensation be found? Perhaps they may catch some moments of transport above the level of the ordinary tranquil joy we experience, but they are separated by long intervals, during which all the passions are at sea without rudder or compass. Yet, fallacious as the pursuits of happiness are, they seem on the whole to furnish the most effectual abstraction from a contemplation of the hardness of their government. Indeed, it is difficult to conceive how so good a people, with so good a king, so well-disposed rulers in general, so genial a climate, so fertile a soil, should be rendered so ineffectual for producing human happiness by one single curse— that of a bad form of government. But it is a fact. In spite of the mildness of their governors, the people are ground to powder by the vices of the form of government. Of twenty millions of people supposed to be in France, I am of opinion there are nineteen millions more wretched, more accursed in every circumstance of human existence, than the most conspicuously wretched individual of the whole United States. I beg your pardon for getting into politics. I will add only one senti-

---

* Mrs. Trist was Jefferson's Philadelphia friend with whom he lodged his daughter Patsy.

ment more of that character, that is, nourish peace with their persons, but war against their manners. Every step we take towards the adoption of their manners is a step to perfect misery.

To Peter Carr *

August 19, 1785   *Paris*

Dear Peter, I received, by Mr. Mazzei, your letter of April the 20th. I am much mortified to hear that you have lost so much time; and that, when you arrived in Williamsburg, you were not at all advanced from what you were when you left Monticello. Time now begins to be precious to you. Every day you lose will retard a day your entrance on that public stage whereon you may begin to be useful to yourself. However, the way to repair the loss is to improve the future time. I trust, that with your dispositions, even the acquisition of science is a pleasing employment. I can assure you, that the possession of it is, what (next to an honest heart) will above all things render you dear to your friends, and give you fame and promotion in your own country. When your mind shall be well improved with science, nothing will be necessary to place you in the highest points of view, but to pursue the interests of your country, the interests of your friends, and your own interests also, with the purest integrity, the most chaste honor. The defect of these virtues can never be made up by all the other acquirements of body and mind. Make these then your first object. Give up money, give up fame, give up science, give the earth itself and all it contains, rather than do an immoral act. And never suppose, that in any possible situation, or under any circumstances, that it is best for you to do a dishonorable thing, however slightly so

---

* Carr, Jefferson's nephew, was brought up in his household.

it may appear to you. Whenever you are to do a thing, though it can never be known but to yourself, ask yourself how you would act were all the world looking at you, and act accordingly. Encourage all your virtuous dispositions, and exercise them whenever an opportunity arises; being assured that they will gain strength by exercise, as a limb of the body does, and that exercise will make them habitual. From the practice of the purest virtue, you may be assured you will derive the most sublime comforts in every moment of life, and in the moment of death. If ever you find yourself environed with difficulties and perplexing circumstances, out of which you are at a loss how to extricate yourself, do what is right, and be assured that that will extricate you the best out of the worst situations. Though you cannot see, when you fetch one step, what will be the next, yet follow truth, justice, and plain dealing, and never fear their leading you out of the labyrinth, in the easiest manner possible. The knot which you thought a Gordian one, will untie itself before you. Nothing is so mistaken as the supposition, that a person is to extricate himself from a difficulty by intrigue, by chicanery, by dissimulation, by trimming, by an untruth, by an injustice. This increases the difficulties tenfold; and those who pursue these methods, get themselves so involved at length, that they can turn no way but their infamy becomes more exposed. It is of great importance to set a resolution, not to be shaken, never to tell an untruth. There is no vice so mean, so pitiful, so contemptible; and he who permits himself to tell a lie once, finds it much easier to do it a second and third time, till at length it becomes habitual; he tells lies without attending to it, and truths without the world's believing him. This falsehood of the tongue leads to that of the heart, and in time depraves all its good dispositions.

An honest heart being the first blessing, a knowing head is the second. It is time for you now to begin to be choice in your reading; to begin to pursue a regular course in it; and not to suffer yourself to be turned to the right or left by reading any thing out of that course. I have long ago digested a plan for you, suited to the circumstances in which you will be placed. This I will detail to you, from time to time, as you advance. For the present, I advise you to begin a course of ancient history, reading every thing in the original and not in translations. First read Goldsmith's history of Greece. This will give you a digested view of that field. Then take up ancient history in the detail, reading the following books, in the following order: Herodotus, Thucydides, Xenophontis Hellenica, Xenophontis Anabasis, Arrian, Quintus Curtius, Diodorus Siculus, Justin. This shall form the first stage of your historical reading, and is all I need mention to you now. The next will be of Roman history. From that, we will come down to modern history. In Greek and Latin poetry, you have read or will read at school Virgil, Terence, Horace, Anacreon, Theocritus, Homer, Euripides, Sophocles. Read also Milton's Paradise Lost, Shakespeare, Ossian, Pope's works, Swift's works, in order to form your style in your own language. In morality, read Epictetus, Xenophontis Memorabilia, Plato's Socratic dialogues, Cicero's philosophies, Antoninus, and Seneca. In order to assure a certain progress in this reading, consider what hours you have free from the school and the exercises of the school. Give about two of them, every day, to exercise; for health must not be sacrificed to learning. A strong body makes the mind strong. As to the species of exercise, I advise the gun. While this gives a moderate exercise to the body, it gives boldness, enterprise and independence to the mind. Games played with the ball, and others of that nature, are too violent for the body, and stamp no character on the mind. Let your gun, therefore, be the constant companion of your walks. Never think of taking a book with you. The object of walking is to relax the mind. You should, therefore, not permit yourself even to think while you walk; but divert your attention by the objects surrounding you.

Walking is the best possible exercise. Habituate yourself to walk very far. The Europeans value themselves on having subdued the horse to the uses of man; but I doubt whether we have not lost more than we have gained, by the use of this animal. No one has occasioned so much, the degeneracy of the human body. An Indian goes on foot nearly as far in a day, for a long journey, as an enfeebled white does on his horse; and he will tire the best horses. There is no habit you will value so much as that of walking far without fatigue. I would advise you to take your exercise in the afternoon: not because it is the best time for exercise, for certainly it is not, but because it is the best time to spare from your studies; and habit will soon reconcile it to health, and render it nearly as useful as if you gave to that the more precious hours of the day. A little walk of half an hour in the morning, when you first rise, is advisable also. It shakes off sleep, and produces other good effects in the animal economy. Rise at a fixed and an early hour, and go to bed at a fixed and early hour also. Sitting up late at night is injurious to the health, and not useful to the mind. Having ascribed proper hours to exercise, divide what remain (I mean of your vacant hours) into three portions. Give the principal to history, the other two, which should be shorter, to philosophy and poetry. Write to me once every month or two, and let me know the progress you make. Tell me in what manner you employ every hour in the day. The plan I have proposed for you is adapted to your present situation only. When that is changed, I shall propose a corresponding change of plan. I have ordered the following books to be sent to you from London, to the care of Mr. Madison: Herodotus, Thucydides, Xenophon's Hellenics, Anabasis and Memorabilia, Cicero's works, Baretti's Spanish and English Dictionary, Martin's Philosophical Grammar, and Martin's Philosophia Britannica. I will send you the following from hence: Beyzout's Mathematics, De Lalande's Astronomy, Muschenbroek's Physics, Quintus Curtius, Justin, a Spanish grammar, and some Spanish books. You will observe that Martin, Beyzout, De Lalande, and Muschenbroek, are not in the preceding plan. They are not to be opened till you go to the university. You are now, I expect, learning French. You must push this; because the books which will be put into your hands when you advance into mathematics, natural philosophy, natural history, and so forth, will be mostly French, these sciences being better treated by the French than the English writers. Our future connection with Spain renders that the most necessary of the modern languages, after the French. When you become a public man, you may have occasion for it, and the circumstances of your possessing that language may give you a preference over other candidates. I have nothing further to add for the present, but husband well your time, cherish your instructors, strive to make everybody your friend; and be assured that nothing will be so pleasing as your success to, dear Peter, yours affectionately.

TH: JEFFERSON

To Marquis de Chastellux *

September 2, 1785   *Paris*

Dear Sir, You were so kind as to allow me a fortnight to read your journey through Virginia. But you should have thought of this indulgence while you were writing it, and have rendered it less interesting if you meant that your readers should have been longer engaged with it. In fact I devoured it at a single meal, and a second reading scarce allowed me sang-

---

* François Jean, Marquis de Chastellux (1734-1788), served with the French army in America and kept a journal for the years 1780-82. In his book, *Voyage dans l'Amérique septentrionale* (1786), he describes a visit to Jefferson in Monticello. An English edition appeared in 1827.

froid enough to mark a few errors in the names of persons and
places which I note on a paper herein inclosed, with an inconsiderable error or two in facts which I have also noted because
I supposed you wished to state them correctly. For this general
approbation however you must allow me to except about a
dozen pages in the earlier part of the book which I read with
a continued blush from beginning to end, as it presented me a
lively picture of what I wish to be, but am not. No, my dear
sir, the thousand millionth part of what you there say, is more
than I deserve. It might perhaps have passed in Europe at the
time you wrote it, and the exaggeration might not have been
detected. But consider that the animal is now brought there,
and that everyone will take his dimensions for himself. The
friendly complexion of your mind has betrayed you into a
partiality of which the European spectator will be divested.
Respect to yourself therefore will require indispensably that
you expunge the whole of those pages except your own judicious observations interspersed among them on animal and
physical subjects. With respect to my countrymen there is surely
nothing which can render them uneasy, in the observations
made on them. They know that they are not perfect, and will
be sensible that you have viewed them with a philanthropic
eye. You say much good of them, and less ill than they are
conscious may be said with truth. I have studied their character
with attention. I have thought them, as you found them, aristocratical, pompous, clannish, indolent, hospitable, and I should
have added, disinterested, but you say attached to their interest.
This is the only trait in their character wherein our observations differ. I have always thought them so careless of their
interests, so thoughtless in their expenses and in all their transactions of business that I had placed it among the vices of their
character, as indeed most virtues when carried beyond certain
bounds degenerate into vices. I had even ascribed this to its
cause, to that warmth of their climate which unnerves and

unmans both body and mind. While on this subject I will give
you my idea of the characters of the several states.

In the North they are	In the South they are
cool	fiery
sober	voluptuary
laborious	indolent
persevering	unsteady
independent	independent
jealous of their own liberties, and just to those of others	zealous for their own liberties, but trampling on those of others
interested	generous
chicaning	candid
superstitious and hypocritical in their religion.	without attachment or pretensions to any religion but that of the heart.

These characteristics grow weaker and weaker by gradation
from North to South and South to North, insomuch that an
observing traveller, without the aid of the quadrant may always
know his latitude by the character of the people among whom
he finds himself. It is in Pennsylvania that the two characters
seem to meet and blend, and form a people free from the extremes both of vice and virtue. Peculiar circumstances have
given to New York the character which climate would have
given had she been placed on the south instead of the north
side of Pennsylvania. Perhaps too other circumstances may have
occasioned in Virginia a transplantation of a particular vice
foreign to its climate. You could judge of this with more im-
partiality than I could, and the probability is that your estimate
of them is the most just. I think it for their good that the vices
of their character should be pointed out to them that they may
amend them; for a malady of either body or mind once known
is half cured.

To Maria Jefferson *

September 20, 1785   *Paris*

My dear Polly, I have not received a letter from you since I came to France. If you knew how much I love you and what pleasure the receipt of your letters gave me at Philadelphia, you would have written to me, or at least have told your aunt what to write, and her goodness would have induced her to take the trouble of writing it. I wish so much to see you, that I have desired your uncle and aunt to send you to me. I know, my dear Polly, how sorry you will be, and ought to be, to leave them and your cousins; but your sister and myself cannot live without you, and after a while we will carry you back again to see your friends in Virginia. In the meantime you shall be taught here to play on the harpsichord, to draw, to read and talk French, and such other things as will make you more worthy of the love of your friends; but above all things by our care and love of you, we will teach you to love us more than you will do if you stay so far from us. I had no opportunity since Colonel Le Maire went, to send you anything; but when you come here you shall have as many dolls and playthings as you want for yourself, or to send to your cousins whenever you shall have opportunities. I hope you are a very good girl, that you love your uncle and aunt very much, and are very thankful to them all for their goodness to you; that you never suffer yourself to be angry with anybody, that you give your playthings to those who want them, that you do whatever anybody desires of you that is right, that you never tell stories, never beg for anything, mind your books and your work when your aunt tells you, never play but when she permits you, nor go where she forbids you; remember, too, as a constant charge, not to go out without your bonnet, because it will make you very ugly,

---

* Maria, known as Polly (1778-1804), was Jefferson's second daughter.

and then we shall not love you so much. If you always practice these lessons we shall continue to love you as we do now, and it is impossible to love you any more. We shall hope to have you with us next summer, to find you a very good girl, and to assure you of the truth of our affection for you. Adieu, my dear child. Yours affectionately,

TH: JEFFERSON

To James Currie *

September 27, 1785   *Paris*

Dear Sir, Your favor of August 5th came to hand on the 18th instant, and I mark well what you say, "that my letters shall be punctually answered." This is encouraging, and the more so as it proves to you that in sending your letters in time to arrive at New York the middle of the month, when the French packet sails, they get to hand very speedily. The last was but six weeks from you to me. I thank you again and again for the details it contains, these being precisely of the nature I would wish. Of political correspondents I can find enough, but I can persuade nobody to believe that the small facts which they see passing daily under their eyes are precious to me at this distance; much more interesting to the heart than events of higher rank. Fancy to yourself a being who is withdrawn from his connections of blood, of marriage, of friendship, of acquaintance in all their gradations, who for years should hear nothing of what has passed among them, who returns again to see them and finds the one-half dead. This strikes him like a pestilence sweeping off the half of mankind. Events which had they come to him one by one and in detail he would have weathered as other people do, when presented to his mind all

---

* Currie (1756-1805) was a Virginia physician and trader, who advocated the abolition of the slave trade.

at once are overwhelming. Continue then to give me facts, little facts, such as you think every one imagines beneath notice, and your letters will be the most precious to me. They will place me in imagination in my own country, and they will place me where I am happiest. But what shall I give you in return? Political events are scarcely interesting to a man who looks on them from high ground. There is always war in one place, revolution in another, pestilence in a third, interspersed with spots of quiet. These chequers shift places but they do not vanish, so that to an eye which extends itself over the whole earth there is always uniformity of prospect.

To Carlo Bellini *

September 30, 1785   *Paris*

Behold me at length on the vaunted scene of Europe! It is not necessary for your information, that I should enter into details concerning it. But you are, perhaps, curious to know how this new scene has struck a savage of the mountains of America. Not advantageously, I assure you. I find the general fate of humanity here most deplorable. The truth of Voltaire's observation offers itself perpetually, that very man here must be either the hammer or the anvil. It is a true picture of that country to which they say we shall pass hereafter, and where we are to see God and his angels in splendor, and crowds of the damned trampled under their feet. While the great mass of the people are thus suffering under physical and moral oppression, I have endeavored to examine more nearly the condition of the great, to appreciate the true value of the circumstances in their

---

* Professor of modern languages at William and Mary College. He emigrated from Italy to Virginia in 1774, became a friend of Jefferson and was one of the rare persons to address him as "My dearest Thomas."

situation, which dazzle the bulk of spectators, and, especially, to compare it with that degree of happiness which is enjoyed in America by every class of people. Intrigues of love occupy the younger, and those of ambition, the elder part of the great. Conjugal love having no existence among them, domestic happiness, of which that is the basis, is utterly unknown. In lieu of this are substituted pursuits which nourish and invigorate all our bad passions, and which offer only moments of ecstasy amidst days and months of restlessness and torment. Much, very much, inferior, this, to the tranquil, permanent felicity with which domestic society in America blesses most of its inhabitants; leaving them to follow steadily those pursuits which health and reason approve, and rendering truly delicious the intervals of those pursuits.

In science, the mass of the people is two centuries behind ours; their literati, half a dozen years before us. Books, really good, acquire just reputation in that time, and so become known to us, and communicate to us all their advances in knowledge. Is not this delay compensated by our being placed out of the reach of that swarm of nonsensical publications, which issues daily from a thousand presses, and perishes almost in issuing? With respect to what are termed polite manners, without sacrificing too much the sincerity of language, I would wish my countrymen to adopt just so much of European politeness, as to be ready to make all those little sacrifices of self, which really render European manners amiable, and relieve society from the disagreeable scenes to which rudeness often exposes it. Here, it seems that a man might pass his life without encountering a single rudeness. In the pleasures of the table, they are far before us, because with good taste they unite temperance. They do not terminate the most sociable meals by transforming themselves into brutes. I have never yet seen a man drunk in France, even among the lowest of the people. Were I to proceed to tell you how much I enjoy their architecture, sculpture, painting, music, I should want words. It is in these arts they shine. The last of them, particularly, is an enjoyment, the deprivation of which, with us, cannot be calculated. I am almost ready to say, it is the only thing which from my heart I envy them, and which, in spite of all the authority of the Decalogue, I do covet. But I am running on in an estimate of things infinitely better known to you than to me, and which will only serve to convince you, that I have brought with me all the prejudices of country, habit, and age.

To John Banister *

October 15, 1785   *Paris*

But why send an American youth to Europe for education? What are the objects of an useful American education? Classical knowledge, modern languages, chiefly French, Spanish, and Italian; mathematics, natural philosophy, natural history, civil history, and ethics. In natural philosophy, I mean to include chemistry and agriculture, and in natural history, to include botany, as well as the other branches of those departments. It is true that the habit of speaking the modern languages cannot be so well acquired in America; but every other article can be as well acquired at William and Mary College as at any place in Europe. When college education is done with, and a young man is to prepare himself for public life, he must cast his eyes (for America) either on law or physics. For the former, where can he apply so advantageously as to Mr. Wythe? For the latter, he must come to Europe: the medical class of students, therefore, is the only one which need come to Europe. To enumerate them all would require a volume. I will select a

* Banister (1734-1788) was a member of the Virginia House of Burgesses and of Congress.

few. If he goes to England, he learns drinking, horse racing, and boxing. These are the peculiarities of English education. The following circumstances are common to education in that and the other countries of Europe. He acquires a fondness for European luxury and dissipation, and a contempt for the simplicity of his own country; he is fascinated with the privileges of the European aristocrats, and sees, with abhorrence, the lovely equality which the poor enjoy with the rich in his own country; he contracts a partiality for aristocracy or monarchy; he forms foreign friendships which will never be useful to him, and loses the season of life for forming, in his own country, those friendships which, of all others, are the most faithful and permanent; he is led, by the strongest of all the human passions into a spirit for female intrigue, destructive of his own and others' happiness, or a passion for whores, destructive of his health, and, in both cases, learns to consider fidelity to the marriage bed as an ungentlemanly practice, and inconsistent with happiness; he recollects the voluptuary dress and arts of the European women, and pities and despises the chaste affections and simplicity of those of his own country; he retains, through life, a fond recollection, and a hankering after those places, which were the scenes of his first pleasures and of his first connections; he returns to his own country, a foreigner, unacquainted with the practices of domestic economy, necessary to preserve him from ruin, speaking and writing his native tongue as a foreigner, and therefore unqualified to obtain those distinctions, which eloquence of the pen and tongue ensures in a free country; for I would observe to you, that what is called style in writing or speaking is formed very early in life, while the imagination is warm, and impressions are permanent. I am of opinion, that there never was an instance of a man's writing or speaking his native tongue with elegance, who passed from fifteen to twenty years of age out of the country where it was spoken. Thus, no instance exists of a person's writing two languages perfectly. That will always appear to be his native language, which was most familiar to him in his youth. It appears to me, then, that an American, coming to Europe for education, loses in his knowledge, in his morals, in his health, in his habits, and in his happiness. I had entertained only doubts on this head before I came to Europe: what I see and hear, since I came here, proves more than I had even suspected. Cast your eye over America: who are the men of most learning, of most eloquence, most beloved by their countrymen and most trusted and promoted by them? They are those who have been educated among them, and whose manners, morals, and habits, are perfectly homogeneous with those of the country.

Did you expect by so short a question to draw such a sermon on yourself? I dare say you did not. But the consequences of foreign education are alarming to me, as an American. I sin, therefore, through zeal whenever I enter on the subject.

To James Madison *

October 28, 1785   *Fontainebleau*

Dear Sir, Seven o'clock, and retired to my fireside, I have determined to enter into conversation with you. This is a village of about 15,000 inhabitants when the court is not here, and 20,000 when they are, occupying a valley through which runs a brook and on each side of it a ridge of small mountains, most of which are naked rock. The King comes here, in the fall always, to hunt. His court attend him, as do also the foreign diplomatic corps; but as this is not indispensably required and my finances do not admit the expense of a continued residence

---

* Madison (1749-1812) was Protestant Episcopal Bishop of Virginia, President of William and Mary College, and cousin of his namesake, U. S. President James Madison.

here, I propose to come occasionally to attend the King's levees, returning again to Paris, distant forty miles. This being the first trip, I set out yesterday morning to take a view of the place. For this purpose I shaped my course towards the highest of the mountains in sight, to the top of which was about a league.

As soon as I had got clear of the town I fell in with a poor woman walking at the same rate with myself and going the same course. Wishing to know the condition of the laboring poor I entered into conversation with her, which I began by enquiries for the path which would lead me into the mountain: and thence proceeded to enquiries into her vocation, condition and circumstances. She told me she was a day laborer at 8 sous or 4d. sterling the day: that she had two children to maintain, and to pay a rent of 30 livres for her house (which would consume the hire of 75 days), that often she could get no employment and of course was without bread. As we had walked together near a mile and she had so far served me as a guide, I gave her, on parting, 24 sous. She burst into tears of a gratitude which I could perceive was unfeigned because she was unable to utter a word. She had probably never before received so great an aid. This little *attendrissement,* with the solitude of my walk, led me into a train of reflections on that unequal division of property which occasions the numberless instances of wretchedness which I had observed in this country and is to be observed all over Europe.

The property of this country is absolutely concentrated in a very few hands, having revenues of from half a million of guineas a year downwards. These employ the flower of the country as servants, some of them having as many as 200 domestics, not laboring. They employ also a great number of manufacturers and tradesmen, and lastly the class of laboring husbandmen. But after all these comes the most numerous of all classes, that is, the poor who cannot find work. I asked myself what could be the reason so many should be permitted to beg who are willing to work, in a country where there is a very considerable proportion of uncultivated lands? These lands are undisturbed only for the sake of game. It should seem then that it must be because of the enormous wealth of the proprietors which places them above attention to the increase of their revenues by permitting these lands to be labored. I am conscious that an equal division of property is impracticable, but the consequences of this enormous inequality producing so much misery to the bulk of mankind, legislators cannot invent too many devices for subdividing property, only taking care to let their subdivisions go hand in hand with the natural affections of the human mind. The descent of property of every kind therefore to all the children, or to all the brothers and sisters, or other relations in equal degree, is a politic measure and a practicable one. Another means of silently lessening the inequality of property is to exempt all from taxation below a certain point, and to tax the higher portions or property in geometrical progression as they rise. Whenever there are in any country uncultivated lands and unemployed poor, it is clear that the laws of property have been so far extended as to violate natural right. The earth is given as a common stock for man to labor and live on. If for the encouragement of industry we allow it to be appropriated, we must take care that other employment be provided to those excluded from the appropriation. If we do not, the fundamental right to labor the earth returns to the unemployed. It is too soon yet in our country to say that every man who cannot find employment, but who can find uncultivated land, shall be at liberty to cultivate it, paying a moderate rent. But it is not too soon to provide by every possible means that as few as possible shall be without a little portion of land. The small landholders are the most precious part of a state.

The next object which struck my attention in my walk was the deer with which the wood abounded. They were of the kind called "Cerfs," and are certainly of the same species with ours. They are blackish indeed under the belly, and not white

as ours, and they are more of the chestnut red; but these are
such small differences as would be sure to happen in two races
from the same stock breeding separately a number of ages.
Their hares are totally different from the animals we call by
that name; but their rabbit is almost exactly like him. The only
difference is in their manners; the land on which I walked for
some time being absolutely reduced to a honeycomb by their
burrowing. I think there is no instance of ours burrowing.
After descending the hill again I saw a man cutting fern. I
went to him under pretence of asking the shortest road to
town, and afterwards asked for what use he was cutting fern.
He told me that this part of the country furnished a great deal
of fruit to Paris. That when packed in straw it acquired an ill
taste, but that dry fern preserved it perfectly without communicating any taste at all.

I treasured this observation for the preservation of my apples
on my return to my own country. They have no apples here to
compare with our Newtown pippin. They have nothing which
deserves the name of a peach; there being not sun enough to
ripen the plum-peach and the best of their soft peaches being
like our autumn peaches. Their cherries and strawberries are
fair, but I think less flavored. Their plums I think are better; so
also their gooseberries, and the pears infinitely beyond anything
we possess. They have no grape better than our sweet-water; but
they have a succession of as good from early in the summer till
frost. I am tomorrow to go [to] M. Malesherbes [an uncle of
the Chevalier Luzerne's] about seven leagues from hence, who
is the most curious man in France as to his trees. He is making
for me a collection of the vines from which the Burgundy,
Champagne, Bordeaux, Frontignac, and other of the most valuable wines of this country are made. Another gentleman is col-
lecting for me the best eating grapes, including what we call
the raisin. I propose also to endeavor to colonize their hare,
rabbit, red and grey partridge, pheasants of different kinds, and

some other birds. But I find that I am wandering beyond the limits of my walk and will therefore bid you adieu. Yours affectionately,

TH: JEFFERSON

To Charles Thomson

April 22, 1786 *London*

Dear Sir, In one of your former letters you expressed a wish to have one of the newly invented lamps. I find them made here much better than at Paris, and take the liberty of asking your acceptance of one which will accompany this letter. It is now found that any tolerable oil may be used in them; the spermaceti oil is best of the cheap kinds.

I could write you volumes on the improvements which I find made and making here in the arts. One deserves particular notice, because it is simple, great, and likely to have extensive consequences. It is the application of steam as an agent for working grist mills. I have visited one lately made here. It was at that time turning eight pair of stones. It consumes a hundred bushels of coal a day. It is proposed to put up thirty pair of stones. I do not know whether the quantity of fuel is to be increased. I hear you are applying this same agent in America to navigate boats, and I have little doubt but that it will be applied generally to machines so as to supersede the use of water ponds and of course to lay open all the streams for navigation. We know that steam is one of the most powerful engines we can employ, and in America fuel is abundant. I find no new publication here worth sending to you. I shall set out for Paris within three or four days.

To George Wythe *

August 13, 1786   *Paris*

Our act for freedom of religion is extremely applauded.
The ambassadors and ministers of the several nations of Europe, resident at this court, have asked of me copies of it to
send to their sovereigns, and it is inserted at full length in several books now in the press; among others, in the new Encyclo-
pedie. I think it will produce considerable good even in these
countries, where ignorance, superstition, poverty, and oppression of body and mind, in every form, are so firmly settled on
the mass of the people, that their redemption from them can
never be hoped. If all the sovereigns of Europe were to set
themselves to work, to emancipate the minds of their subjects
from their present ignorance and prejudices, and that as zeal-
ously as they now endeavor the contrary, a thousand years
would not place them on that high ground on which our common people are now setting out. Ours could not have been so
fairly placed under the control of the common sense of the
people, had they not been separated from their parent stock,
and kept from contamination, either from them, or the other
people of the old world, by the intervention of so wide an
ocean. To know the worth of this, one must see the want of it
here.

I think by far the most important bill in our whole code, is
that for the diffusion of knowledge among the people. No other
sure foundation can be devised for the preservation of freedom
and happiness. If anybody thinks that kings, nobles, or priests
are good conservators of the public happiness, send him here.
It is the best school in the universe to cure them of that folly.
They will see here, with their own eyes that these descriptions of
men are an abandoned confederacy against the happiness of the

---

* Wythe (1726-1806) was professor of law at William and Mary College, a
signer of the Declaration of Independence, and one of the most distinguished
jurists in Virginia. Jefferson studied law under him.

mass of the people. The omnipotence of their effect cannot be better proved than in this country particularly, where, notwithstanding the finest soil upon earth, the finest climate under heaven, and a people of the most benevolent, the most gay and amiable character of which the human form is susceptible; where such a people, I say, surrounded by many blessings from nature, are yet loaded with misery by kings, nobles and priests, and by them alone. Preach, my dear sir, a crusade against ignorance; establish and improve the law for educating the common people. Let our countrymen know, that the people alone can protect us against these evils, and that the tax which will be paid for this purpose is not more than the thousandth part of what will be paid to kings, priests and nobles, who will rise up among us if we leave the people in ignorance.

To Charles Thomson

December 17, 1786   *Paris*

Dear Sir, A dislocation of my right wrist has for three months past, disabled me from writing except with my left hand, which was too slow and awkward to be employed often. I begin to have so much use of my wrist as to be able to write, but it is slowly, and in pain. I take the first moment I can, however, to acknowledge the receipt of your letters of April the 6th, July the 8th and 30th. In one of these, you say, you have not been able to learn, whether, in the new mills in London, steam is the immediate mover of the machinery, or raises water to move it? It is the immediate mover. The power of this agent, though long known, is but now beginning to be applied to the various purposes of which it is susceptible. You observe that Whitehurst supposes it to have been the agent, which bursting the earth, threw it up into mountains and valleys. You ask me what I think of his book? I find in it many interesting facts brought together, and many ingenious commentaries on them. But there are great chasms in his facts, and consequently in his reasoning. These he fills up by suppositions, which may be as reasonably denied as granted. A sceptical reader, therefore, like myself, is left in the lurch. I acknowledge, however, he makes more use of fact, than any other writer on a theory of the earth. But I give one answer to all these theorists. That is as follows. They all suppose the earth a created existence. They must suppose a creator then; and that he possessed power and wisdom to a great degree. As he intended the earth for the habitation of animals and vegetables, is it reasonable to suppose, he made two jobs of his creation, that he first made a chaotic lump and set it into rotatory motion, and then waited the millions of ages necessary to form itself? That when it had done this, he stepped in a second time, to create the animals and plants which were to inhabit it? As the hand of a creator is to be called in, it may as well be called in at one stage of the process as another. We may as well suppose he created the earth at once, nearly in the state in which we see it, fit for the preservation of the beings he placed on it. But it is said we have a proof that he did not create it in its present solid form, but in a state of fluidity; because its present shape of an oblate spheroid is precisely that which a fluid mass revolving on its axis would assume.

I suppose that the same equilibrium between gravity and centrifugal force, which would determine a fluid mass into the form of an oblate spheroid, would determine the wise creator of that mass, if he made it in a solid state, to give it the same spheroidical form. A revolving fluid will continue to change its shape, till it attains that in which its principles of contrary motion are balanced. For if you suppose them not balanced, it will change its form. Now, the same balanced form is necessary for the preservation of a revolving solid. The creator, therefore, of a revolving solid, would make it an oblate spheroid, that figure alone admitting a perfect equilibrium. He would make it in that form, for another reason; that is, to prevent a shifting of the axis of rotation. Had he created the earth perfectly spherical its axis might have been perpetually shifting, by the influence of the other bodies of the system; and by placing the inhabitants of the earth successively under its poles, it might have been depopulated; whereas, being spheroidical, it has but one axis on which it can revolve in equilibrio. Suppose the axis of the earth to shift forty-five degrees; then cut it into one hundred and eighty slices, making every section in the plane of a circle of latitude, perpendicular to the axis: every one of these slices, except the equatorial one, would be unbalanced, as there would be more matter on one side of its axis than on the other. There could be but one diameter drawn through such a slice, which would divide it into two equal parts. On every other possible diameter, the parts would hang unequal. This would produce an irregularity in the diurnal rotation. We may, therefore, conclude it impossible for the poles of the earth to shift, if it was made spheroidically; and that it would be made spheroidal, though solid, to obtain this end. I use this reasoning only on the supposition that the earth has had a beginning. I am sure I shall read your conjectures on this subject with great pleasure, though I bespeak, beforehand, a right to indulge my natural incredulity and scepticism. The pain in which I write awakens me here from my reverie, and obliges me to conclude with compliments to Mrs. Thomson, and assurances to yourself of the esteem and affection with which I am sincerely, dear sir, your friend and servant,

Th: Jefferson

P. S. Since writing the preceding, I have had a conversation on the subject of the steam mills, with the famous Boulton, to whom those of London belong, and who is here at this time. He compares the effect of steam with that of horses, in the following manner: Six horses, aided with the most advantageous combination of the mechanical powers hitherto tried, will grind six bushels of flour in an hour; at the end of which time they are all in a foam, and must rest. They can work thus, six hours in the twenty-four, grinding thirty-six bushels of flour, which is six to each horse, for the twenty-four hours. His steam mill in London consumes one hundred and twenty bushels of coal in twenty-four hours, turns ten pair of stones, which grind eight bushels of flour an hour each, which is nineteen hundred and twenty bushels in the twenty-four hours. This makes a peck and a half of coal perform exactly as much as a horse, in one day, can perform.

To Edward Carrington *

January 16, 1787   *Paris*

I am persuaded myself, that the good sense of the people will always be found to be the best army. They may be led astray for a moment, but will soon correct themselves. The people are the only censors of their governors; and even their errors will tend to keep these to the true principles of their institution. To punish these errors too severely, would be to suppress the only safeguard of the public liberty. The way to prevent these irregular interpositions of the people, is to give them full information of their affairs through the channel of the public papers, and to contrive that those papers should penetrate the whole mass of the people. The basis of our government being the opinion of the people, the very first object should be to keep that right; and were it left to me to decide whether we should have a government without newspapers, or newspapers without a government, I should not hesitate a moment to prefer the latter. But I should mean that every man should receive those papers, and be capable of reading them. I am convinced that those societies (as the Indians) which live without government, enjoy in their general mass an infinitely greater degree of happiness, than those who live under the Eu-

---

* Lieutenant Colonel Carrington (1749-1810) was a Revolutionary soldier from Virginia.

ropean governments. Among the former, public opinion is in the place of law, and restrains morals as powerfully as laws ever did anywhere. Among the latter, under pretense of governing, they have divided their nations into two classes, wolves and sheep. I do not exaggerate. This is a true picture of Europe. Cherish, therefore, the spirit of our people, and keep alive their attention. Do not be too severe upon their errors, but reclaim them by enlightening them. If once they become inattentive to the public affairs, you and I, and Congress and assemblies, judges and governors, shall all become wolves. It seems to be the law of our general nature, in spite of individual exceptions, and experience declares that man is the only animal which devours his own kind, for I can apply no milder term to the governments of Europe, and to the general prey of the rich on the poor.

To James Madison *

January 30, 1787   *Paris*

Those characters, wherein fear predominates over hope, may . . . conclude too hastily, that nature has formed man insusceptible of any other government than that of force, a conclusion not founded in truth nor experience. Societies exist under three forms, sufficiently distinguishable. 1. Without government, as among our Indians. 2. Under governments, wherein the will of everyone has a just influence; as is the case in England, in a slight degree, and in our States, in a great one. 3. Under governments of force; as is the case in all other monarchies, and in most of the other republics. To have an idea of the curse of existence under these last, they must be seen. It is a government of wolves over sheep. It is a problem, not clear

---

* Madison (1751-1836), Jefferson's lifelong friend, succeeded him as President in 1809.

in my mind, that the first condition is not the best. But I believe it to be inconsistent with any great degree of population. The second state has a great deal of good in it. The mass of mankind under that, enjoys a precious degree of liberty and happiness. It has its evils, too; the principal of which is the turbulence to which it is subject. But weigh this against the oppressions of monarchy, and it becomes nothing. *Malo periculosam libertatem quam quietam servitutem.* Even this evil is productive of good. It prevents the degeneracy of government, and nourishes a general attention to the public affairs. I hold it, that a little rebellion, now and then, is a good thing, and as necessary in the political world as storms in the physical. Unsuccessful rebellions, indeed, generally establish the encroachments on the rights of the people, which have produced them. An observation of this truth should render honest republican governors so mild in their punishment of rebellions, as not to discourage them too much. It is a medicine necessary for the sound health of government.

To Comtesse de Tessé *

March 20, 1787   *Nismes*

Here I am, Madam, gazing whole hours at the Maison quarrée like a lover at his mistress. The stocking weavers and silk spinners around it consider me a hypochondriac Englishman, about to write with a pistol the last chapter of his history. This is the second time I have been in love since I left Paris. The first was with a Diana at the Chateau de Laye-Epinaye in Beaujolais, a delicious morsel of sculpture by M. A. Slodtz. This, you will say, was in rule, to fall in love with a female

---

* Mme de Tessé, one of Jefferson's circle of friends in Paris, was an aunt of Lafayette's wife.

beauty; but with a house! it is out of all precedent. No, madam, it is not without a precedent in my own history. While at Paris, I was violently smitten with the Hotel de Salm, and used to go to the Tuileries almost daily, to look at it. The *loueuse des chaises,* inattentive to my passion, never had the complaisance to place a chair there, so that, sitting on the parapet, and twisting my neck round to see the object of my admiration, I generally left it with a *torti-collis.*

From Lyons to Nismes I have been nourished with the remains of Roman grandeur. They have always brought you to my mind, because I know your affection for whatever is Roman and noble. At Vienne I thought of you. But I am glad you were not there; for you would have seen me more angry than, I hope, you will ever see me. The Prætorian Palace, as it is called, comparable, for its fine proportions, to the Maison quarrée, defaced by the barbarians who have converted it to its present purpose, its beautiful fluted Corinthian columns cut out, in part, to make space for Gothic windows, and hewed down, in the residue, to the plane of the building, was enough, you must admit, to disturb my composure. At Orange, too, I thought of you. I was sure you had seen with pleasure the sublime triumphal arch of Marius at the entrance of the city. I went then to the Arenæ. Would you believe, madam, that in this eighteenth century, in France, under the reign of Louis XVI., they are at this moment pulling down the circular wall of this superb remain, to pave a road? And that, too, from a hill which is itself an entire mass of stone, just as fit, and more accessible? A former intendant, a M. de Basville, has rendered his memory dear to the traveller and amateur, by the pains he took to preserve and restore these monuments of antiquity. The present one (I do not know who he is) is demolishing the object, to make a good road to it. I thought of you again, and I was then in great good humor, at the Pont du Gard, a sublime antiquity, and well preserved. But most of all here, where Roman taste, genius, and magnificence, excite ideas analogous to yours at every step. I could no longer oppose the inclination to avail myself of your permission to write to you, a permission given with too much complaisance by you, and used by me with too much indiscretion. Madame de Tott did me the same honor. But she, being only the descendant of some of those puny heroes who boiled their own kettles before the walls of Troy, I shall write to her from a Grecian, rather than a Roman canton; when I shall find myself, for example, among her Phocæan relations at Marseilles.

Loving, as you do, madam, the precious remains of antiquity, loving architecture, gardening, a warm sun and a clear sky, I wonder you have never thought of moving Chaville to Nismes. This, as you know, has not always been deemed impracticable; and, therefore, the next time a *Sur-intendant des batiments du roi,* after the example of M. Colbert, sends persons to Nismes to move the Maison quarrée to Paris, that they may not come empty handed, desire them to bring Chaville with them, to replace it. Apropos of Paris. I have now been three weeks from there, without knowing anything of what has passed. I suppose I shall meet it all at Aix, where I have directed my letters to be lodged, *poste restante.* My journey has given me leisure to reflect on this Assemblée des Notables. Under a good and a young King, as the present, I think good may be made of it. I would have the deputies then, by all means, so conduct themselves as to encourage him to repeat the calls of this Assembly. Their first step should be, to get themselves divided into two chambers instead of seven; the noblesse and the commons separately. The second, to persuade the king, instead of choosing the deputies of the commons himself, to summon those chosen by the people for the Provincial administrations. The third, as the noblesse is too numerous to be all of the Assemblée, to obtain permission for that body to choose its own deputies. Two houses, so elected, would contain a mass of wisdom which would make the people happy, and the King great; would place him in history where no other act can possibly place him. They would thus put themselves in the track of the best guide they can follow; they would soon overtake it, become its guide in turn, and lead to the wholesome modifications wanting in that model, and necessary to constitute a rational government. Should they attempt more than the established habits of the people are ripe for, they may lose all, and retard indefinitely the ultimate object of their aim. These, madam, are my opinions; but I wish to know yours, which, I am sure, will be better.

From a correspondent at Nismes, you will not expect news. Were I to attempt to give you news, I should tell you stories one thousand years old. I should detail to you the intrigues of the courts of the Cæsars, how they affect us here, the oppressions of their prætors, and prefects. I am immersed in antiquities from morning to night. For me, the city of Rome is actually existing in all the splendor of its empire. I am filled with alarms for the event of the irruptions daily making on us, by the Goths, the Visigoths, Ostrogoths, and Vandals, lest they should re-conquer us to our original barbarism. If I am sometimes induced to look forward to the eighteenth century, it is only when recalled to it by the recollection of your goodness and friendship, and by those sentiments of sincere esteem and respect with which I have the honor to be, madam, your most obedient, and most humble servant.

TH: JEFFERSON

To Martha Jefferson

April 7, 1787   *Toulon*

My dear Patsy, I received yesterday at Marseilles your letter of March 25th; and I received it with pleasure, because it announced to me that you were well. Experience learns us to be always anxious about the health of those whom we love. I have not been able to write to you as often as I expected, because I am generally on the road; and when I stop anywhere, I am occupied in seeing what is to be seen. It will be some time now, perhaps three weeks, before I shall be able to write you again. But this need not slacken your writing to me, because you have leisure, and your letters come regularly to me. I have received letters which inform me that our dear Polly [the youngest daughter] will certainly come to us this summer. By the time I return, it will be time to expect her. When she arrives, she will become a precious charge on your hands. The difference of your age, and your common loss of a mother, will put that office on you. Teach her, above all things, to be good—because without that, we can neither be valued by others, nor set any value on ourselves. Teach her to be always true; no vice is so mean as the want of truth, and at the same time so useless. Teach her never to be angry: anger only serves to torment ourselves, to divert others, and alienate their esteem. And teach her industry and application to useful pursuits. I will venture to assure you, that if you inculcate this in her mind, you will make her a happy being in herself, a most inestimable friend to you, and precious to all the world. In teaching her these dispositions of mind, you will be more fixed in them yourself, and render yourself dear to all your acquaintances. Practice them, then, my dear, without ceasing. If ever you find yourself in difficulty, and doubt how to extricate yourself, do what is right, and you will find it the easiest way of getting out of the difficulty. Do it for the additional incitement of increasing the happiness of him who loves you infinitely, and who is, my dear Patsy, yours affectionately,

TH: JEFFERSON

To Martha Jefferson

June 14, 1787   *Paris*

I send you, my dear Patsy, the fifteen livres you desired. You propose this to me as an anticipation of five weeks' allowance; but do you not see, my dear, how imprudent it is to lay out in one moment what should accommodate you for five weeks—that this is a departure from that rule which I wish to see you governed by, through your whole life, of never buying anything which you have not money in your pocket to pay for? Be assured that it gives much more pain to the mind to be in debt, than to do without any article whatever which we may seem to want. The purchase you have made is one of those I am always ready to make for you, because it is my wish to see you dressed always cleanly and a little more than decently. But apply to me first for the money before you make a purchase, were it only to avoid breaking .through your rule. Learn yourself the habit of adhering rigorously to the rules you lay down for yourself. I will come for you about eleven o'clock on Saturday. Hurry the making your gown, and also your reding-cote.* You will go with me some day next week to dine at the Marquis Lafayette's. Adieu, my dear daughter, yours affectionately,

TH: JEFFERSON

To Madame de Corny †

June 30, 1787   *Paris*

On my return to Paris, it was among my first intentions to go to the rue Chaussée d'Antin, No. 17, and inquire after my friends whom I had left there. I was told they were in England. And how do you like England, madam? I know your taste for the works of art gives you a little disposition to Anglomania. Their mechanics certainly exceed all others in some lines. But be just to your own nation. They have not patience, it is true, to set rubbing a piece of steel from morning till night, as a lethargic Englishman will do, full charged with porter. But do

---

* Riding coat.

† She belonged to Jefferson's Paris circle of friends and was the wife of Ethis de Corny, a French officer in America during the Revolutionary War.

not their benevolence, their cheerfulness, their amiability, when compared with the growling temper and manners of the people among whom you are, compensate their want of patience? I am in hopes that when the splendor of their shops, which is all that is worth looking at in London, shall have lost their charm of novelty, you will turn a wistful eye to the people of Paris, and find that you cannot be so happy with any others. The Bois de Boulogne invites you earnestly to come and survey its beautiful verdure, to retire to its umbrage from the heats of the season. I was through it today, as I am every day. Every tree charged me with this invitation to you. Passing by la Muette, it wished for you as a mistress. You want a country house. This is for sale; and in the Bois de Boulogne, which I have always insisted to be most worthy of your preference. Come then, and buy it. If I had had confidence in your speedy return, I should have embarrassed you in earnest with my little daughter. But an impatience to have her with me, after her separation from her friends, added to a respect for your ease, has induced me to send a servant for her.

I tell you no news, because you have correspondents infinitely more *au fait* of the details of Paris than I am. And I offer you no services, because I hope you will come as soon as the letter could, which should command them. Be assured, however, that nobody is more disposed to render them, nor entertains for you a more sincere and respectful attachment than him who, after charging you with his compliments to Monsieur de Corny, has the honor of offering you the homage of those sentiments of distinguished esteem and regard, with which he is, dear madam, your most obedient, and most humble servant,

TH: JEFFERSON

To Abbé de Arnal

July 9, 1787   *Paris*

Dear Sir, I had the honor of informing you when at Nismes that we had adopted in America a method of hanging the upper stone of a grist mill which had been found so much more convenient than the ancient as to have brought it into general use. Whether we derive the invention from Europe or have made it ourselves I am unable to say. The difference consists only in the spindle and horns. On the former plan the horns were of a single piece of iron in the form of a cross with a square hole in the middle, which square hole fitted on the upper end of the spindle. The horns were then fixed in cross grooves in the bottom of the upper stone which was to be laid on the spindle so as that the place of its grinding surface would be perfectly perpendicular to the spindles. This was a difficult and tedious operation and was to be repeated every time the stones were dressed. According to our method two distinct pieces of iron are substituted for the horns. The one in this form of such breadth and thickness as to support the whole weight of the stone. Its straight ends are to be firmly fixed in one of the cross grooves of the stone, the circular part should rise through the hole in the center of the stone so as to be near its upper surface; in the middle of this semicircular part and on its under surface—(at *a*)—should be a dimple to which the upper end of the spindle should be adjusted by giving it a convexity fitted to the concavity of the dimple. The other piece of iron is only a straight bar to be firmly fixed in the other of the cross grooves of the stone and to have a square hole in its center, thus: the corresponding part of the spindle must be squared to fit this hole. The office of the first piece of iron is to suspend the stone, that of the last is to give and continue its motion. The stones being dressed and these pieces firmly fixed in it, it is turned over on the spindle so that the point of the spindle may enter the dimple of the semicircular iron, and the stone be suspended on it freely. It will probably not take at first its true position, which is that of the plane of its grinding surface being truly perpendicular to the spindle.

The workman must, therefore, chip it at the top with a chisel till it hangs in that just position. This being once done it is done forever; for whenever they dress the stone afterwards they have only to return the upper one to its point and it will resume its equilibrium. It sometimes happens that one side of the stone being softer than the other wears faster and so the equilibrium is lost in time. Experience has shown that a small departure from the equilibrium will be rectified by the bed stone which serves as a guide to the running stone till it assumes its motion in a true plane which it will afterwards keep. But should a defect of the stone render this departure from the equilibrium too considerable it may be necessary to set it to rights at certain periods by chipping it again on the top. I had promised, when I had the honor of seeing you at Nismes, to send you a model of this manner of fixing the mill-stones, but the expense of sending a model by post, the danger of its being lost or destroyed by the *messagerie,* and the hope that I could render it intelligible by a description and figures, have induced me to prefer the latter method. I shall with great pleasure give any further explanations which may be necessary for your perfect comprehension of it, and the more so as it will furnish me with new occasions of assuring you of those sentiments of respect and esteem with which I have the honor to be, sir, your most obedient and most humble servant,

Th: Jefferson

To Benjamin Hawkins *

August 4, 1787   *Paris*

I am astonished at some people's considering a kingly government as a refuge. Advise such to read the fable of the frogs who solicited Jupiter for a king. If that does not put them to rights, send them to Europe to see something of the trappings of monarchy, and I will undertake that every man shall go back thoroughly cured. If all the evils which can arise among us, from the republican form of our government, from this day to the day of judgment, could be put into a scale against what this country suffers from its monarchical form in a week, or England in a month, the latter would preponderate. Consider the contents of the Red Book in England, or the Almanac Royal in France, and say what a people gain by monarchy. No race of kings has ever presented above one man of common sense in twenty generations. The best they can do is to leave things to their ministers; and what are their ministers but a committee, badly chosen? If the king ever meddles, it is to do harm.

To William S. Smith †

November 13, 1787   *Paris*

The British ministry have so long hired their gazetteers to repeat, and model into every form, lies about our being in anarchy, that the world has at length believed them, the English

---

* Hawkins (1754-1818), Indian agent and a Federalist U. S. Senator from North Carolina (1790-95), has been described as "aristocratic, conservative, proud and wealthy."

† Smith (1755-1816) was the son-in-law of John Adams and member of Congress from 1813 to 1816.

nation has believed them, the ministers themselves have come
to believe them, and what is more wonderful, we have believed
them ourselves. Yet where does this anarchy exist? Where did
it ever exist, except in the single instance of Massachusetts? And
can history produce an instance of rebellion so honorably conducted? I say nothing of its motives. They were founded in
ignorance, not wickedness. God forbid we should ever be
twenty years without such a rebellion. The people cannot be
all, and always, well informed. The part which is wrong will
be discontented, in proportion to the importance of the facts
they misconceive. If they remain quiet under such misconceptions, it is a lethargy, the forerunner of death to the public
liberty. We have had thirteen States independent for eleven
years. There has been one rebellion. That comes to one rebellion in a century and a half, for each State. What country before, ever existed a century and a half without a rebellion? And
what country can preserve its liberties, if its rulers are not
warned from time to time, that their people preserve the spirit
of resistance? Let them take arms. The remedy is to set them
right as to facts, pardon and pacify them. What signify a few
lives lost in a century or two? The tree of liberty must be refreshed from time to time, with the blood of patriots and tyrants. It is its natural manure.

To James Madison

December 20, 1787　　　　　　　　　　　　　　　　　　*Paris*

　　I like much the general idea of framing a government,
which should go on of itself, peaceably, without needing continual recurrence to the State legislatures. I like the organization of the government into legislative, judiciary and executive.
I like the power given the legislature to levy taxes, and for that

reason solely, I approve of the greater House being chosen by the people directly. For though I think a House so chosen, will be very far inferior to the present Congress, will be very illy qualified to legislate for the Union, for foreign nations, and so forth, yet this evil does not weigh against the good, of preserving inviolate the fundamental principle, that the people are not to be taxed but by representatives chosen immediately by themselves. I am captivated by the compromise of the opposite claims of the great and little States, of the latter to equal, and the former to proportional influence. I am much pleased too, with the substitution of the method of voting by person, instead of that of voting by States; and I like the negative given to the Executive, conjointly with a third of either House; though I should have liked it better, had the judiciary been associated for that purpose, or invested separately with a similar power. There are other good things of less moment. I will now tell you what I do not like. First, the omission of a bill of rights, providing clearly, and without the aid of sophism, for freedom of religion, freedom of the press, protection against standing armies, restriction of monopolies, the eternal and unremitting force of the habeas corpus laws, and trials by jury in all matters of fact triable by the laws of the land, and not by the laws of nations. To say, as Mr. Wilson does, that a bill of rights was not necessary, because all is reserved in the case of the general government which is not given, while in the particular ones, all is given which is not reserved, might do for the audience to which it was addressed; but it is surely a *gratis dictum,* the reverse of which might just as well be said; and it is opposed by strong inferences from the body of the instrument, as well as from the omission of the cause of our present Confederation, which had made the reservation in express terms. It was hard to conclude, because there has been a want of uniformity among the States as to the cases triable by jury, because some have been so incautious as to dispense with this mode of trial in certain cases, therefore, the more prudent States shall be reduced to the same level of calamity. It would have been much more just and wise to have concluded the other way, that as most of the States had preserved with jealousy this sacred palladium of liberty, those who had wandered, should be brought back to it; and to have established general right rather than general wrong. For I consider all the ill as established, which may be established. I have a right to nothing, which another has a right to take away; and Congress will have a right to take away trials by jury in all civil cases. Let me add, that a bill of rights is what the people are entitled to against every government on earth, general or particular; and what no just government should refuse, or rest on inference.

The second feature I dislike, and strongly dislike, is the abandonment, in every instance, of the principle of rotation in office, and most particularly in the case of the President. Reason and experience tell us, that the first magistrate will always be re-elected if he may be re-elected. He is then an officer for life. This once observed, it becomes of so much consequence to certain nations, to have a friend or a foe at the head of our affairs, that they will interfere with money and with arms. A Galloman, or an Angloman, will be supported by the nation he befriends. If once elected, and at a second or third election outvoted by one or two votes, he will pretend false votes, foul play, hold possession of the reins of government, be supported by the States voting for him, especially if they be the central ones, lying in a compact body themselves, and separating their opponents; and they will be aided by one nation in Europe, while the majority are aided by another. The election of a President of America, some years hence, will be much more interesting to certain nations of Europe, than ever the election of a King of Poland was. Reflect on all the instances in history, ancient and modern, of elective monarchies, and say if they do not give foundation for my fears; the Roman Emperors, the Popes while they were of any importance, the German Emperors till they became hereditary in practice, the Kings of Poland, the Deys of the Ottoman dependencies. It may be said, that if elections are to be attended with these disorders, the less frequently they are repeated the better. But experience says, that to free them from disorder, they must be rendered less interesting by the necessity of change. No foreign power, nor domestic party, will waste their blood and money to elect a person who must go out at the end of a short period. The power of removing every fourth year by the vote of the people, is a power which they will not exercise, and if they were disposed to exercise it, they would not be permitted. The King of Poland is removable every day by the diet. But they never remove him. Nor would Russia, the Emperor, . . . permit them to do it. Smaller objections are, the appeals on matters of fact as well as laws; and the binding all persons, legislative, executive and judiciary by oath, to maintain that constitution. I do not pretend to decide, what would be the best method of procuring the establishment of the manifold good things in this constitution, and of getting rid of the bad. Whether by adopting it, in hopes of future amendment; or after it shall have been duly weighed and canvassed by the people, after seeing the parts they generally dislike, and those they generally approve, to say to them, "We see now what you wish. You are willing to give to your federal government such and such powers; but you wish, at the same time, to have such and such fundamental rights secured to you, and certain sources of convulsion taken away. Be it so. Send together deputies again. Let them establish your fundamental rights by a sacrosanct declaration, and let them pass the parts of the constitution you have approved. These will give powers to your federal government sufficient for your happiness."

This is what might be said, and would probably produce a speedy, more perfect and more permanent form of government. At all events, I hope you will not be discouraged from making other trials, if the present one should fail. We are never permitted to despair of the commonwealth. I have thus told you freely what I like, and what I dislike, merely as a matter of curiosity; for I know it is not in my power to offer matter of information to your judgment, which has been formed after hearing and weighing everything which the wisdom of man could offer on these subjects. I own, I am not a friend to a very energetic government. It is always oppressive. It places the governors indeed more at their ease, at the expense of the people. The late rebellion in Massachusetts has given more alarm, than I think it should have done. Calculate that one rebellion in thirteen States in the course of eleven years, is but one for each State in a century and a half. No country should be so long without one. Nor will any degree of power in the hands of government, prevent insurrections. In England, where the hand of power is heavier than with us, there are seldom half a dozen years without an insurrection. In France, where it is still heavier, but less despotic, as Montesquieu supposes, than in some other countries, and where there are always two or three hundred thousand men ready to crush insurrections, there have been three in the course of the three years I have been here, in every one of which greater numbers were engaged than in Massachusetts, and a great deal more blood was spilt. In Turkey, where the sole nod of the despot is death, insurrections are the events of every day. Compare again the ferocious depredations of their insurgents, with the order, the moderation and the almost self-extinguishment of ours. And say, finally, whether peace is best preserved by giving energy to the government, or information to the people. This last is the most certain, and the most legitimate engine of government. Educate and inform the whole mass of the people. Enable them to see that it is their interest to preserve peace and order, and they will preserve them. And it requires no very high degree of education to convince them of this. They are the only sure reliance for the preservation of our liberty. After all, it is my principle that the will of the majority should prevail. If they approve the proposed constitution in all its parts, I shall concur in it cheerfully, in hopes they will amend it, whenever they shall find it works wrong. This reliance cannot deceive us, as long as we remain virtuous; and I think we shall be so, as long as agriculture is our principal object, which will be the case, while there remains vacant lands in any part of America. When we get piled upon one another in large cities, as in Europe, we shall become corrupt as in Europe, and go to eating one another as they do there. I have tired you by this time with disquisitions which you have already heard repeated by others, a thousand and a thousand times; and, therefore, shall only add assurances of the esteem and attachment with which I have the honor to be, dear sir, your affectionate friend and servant,

TH: JEFFERSON

To Edward Bancroft *

January 26, 1788   *Paris*

Dear Sir, I have deferred answering your letter on the subject of slaves because you permitted me to do it till a moment of leisure, and that moment rarely comes, and because, too, I could not answer you with such a degree of certainty as to merit any notice. I do not recollect the conversation at Vincennes to which you allude, but can repeat still on the same ground on which I must have done then that as far as I can judge from the experiments which have been made to give liberty to, or rather abandon, persons whose habits have been formed in slavery is like abandoning children. Many Quakers in Virginia seated their slaves on their lands as tenants; they were distant from me, and therefore I cannot be particular in the details because I never had very particular information. I cannot say whether they were to pay a rent in money or a share of the produce, but I remember that the landlord was obliged to plan their crops for them, to direct all their operations during every season and according to the weather; but what is more afflicting, he was obliged to watch them daily and almost constantly to make them work and even to whip them. A man's

---

* Bancroft (1744-1821) was an English writer, inventor and diplomatic spy.

moral sense must be unusually strong if slavery does not make him a thief. He who is permitted by law to have no property of his own can with difficulty conceive that property is founded in anything but force. These slaves chose to steal from their neighbors rather than work; they became public nuisances and in most instances were reduced to slavery again. But I will beg of you to make no use of this imperfect information (unless in common conversation). I shall go to America in the spring and return in the fall. During my stay in Virginia I shall be in the neighborhood where many of these trials were made. I will inform myself very particularly of them and communicate the information to you.

Besides these, there is an instance since I came away of a young man (Mr. Mays) who died and gave freedom to all his slaves, about 200; this is about a year ago. I shall know how they have turned out. Nothwithstanding the discouraging result of these experiments I am decided on my final return to America to try this one. I shall endeavor to import as many Germans as I have grown slaves. I will settle them and my slaves on farms of fifty acres each, intermingled, and place all on the footing of the métayers (medietani) of Europe. Their children shall be brought up as others are in habits of property and foresight, and I have no doubt but that they will be good citizens. Some of their fathers will be so, others I suppose will need government; with these all that can be done is to oblige them to labor as the laboring poor of Europe do, and to apply to their comfortable subsistence the produce of their labor, retaining such a moderate portion of it as may be a just equivalent for the use of the lands they labor and the stocks and other necessary advances.

MINISTER TO FRANCE (1784–1789)

To Angelica Church *

Sunday, February 17, 1788   *Paris*

You speak, madam, in your note of adieu, of civilities which I never rendered you. What you kindly call such were but the gratifications of my own heart; for indeed I was much gratified in seeing and serving you. The morning you left us, all was wrong, even the sunshine was provoking, with which I never quarreled before. I took into my head he shone only to throw light on our loss: to present a cheerfulness not at all in unison with my mind. I mounted my horse earlier than common, and took by instinct the road you had taken. Some spirit whispered this to me: but he whispered by halves only: for, when I turned about at St. Denis, had he told me you were then broke down at Luzarches I should certainly have spurred on to that place, and perhaps not have quitted you till I had seen the carriage perform its office fully by depositing you at Boulogne. I went in the evening to Madam de Corny's, where we talked over our woes, and this morning I found some solace in going for Kitty and the girls. She is now here, just triste enough to show her affection and at the same time her discretion. I think I have discovered a method of preventing this dejection of mind on any future parting. It is this. When you come again, I will employ myself solely in finding or fancying that you have some faults, and I will draw a veil over all your good qualities, if I can find one large enough. I think I shall succeed in this, for, trying myself today, by way of exercise, I recollected immediately one fault in your composition. It is that you give all your attention, Mrs. Church, to your friends, caring nothing about yourself. Now you must agree that I christen this very

* Mrs. Angelica Church, the daughter of Philip Schuyler of New York and sister of Mrs. Alexander Hamilton, was married to an Englishman, John Barker Church, who became a member of Parliament in 1790.

mildly when I call it a folly only, and I dare say I shall find
many like it when I examine you with more sangfroid.

I remember you told me when we parted, you would come
to see me at Monticello. Now though I believe this to be impossible, I have been planning what I would show you: a flower
here, a tree there; yonder a grove, near it a fountain; on this
side a hill, on that a river. Indeed, madam, I know nothing so
charming as our own country. The learned say it is a new
creation; and I believe them; not for their reasons, but because
it is made on an improved plan. Europe is a first idea, a crude
production, before the maker knew his trade, or had made up
his mind as to what he wanted. Let us go back to it together
then. You intend it a visit; so do I. While you are indulging
with your friends on Hudson, I will go to see if Monticello
remains in the same place, or I will attend you to the falls of
Niagara if you will go on with me to the passage of the Potomac, the Natural bridge . . . This done we will come back
together, you for a long, and I for a lesser time. Think of this
plan, and when you come to pay your summer's visit to Kitty
we will talk it over; in the meantime, heaven bless you, madam,
fortify your health, and watch over your happiness, Yours affectionately,

TH: JEFFERSON

To George Washington

May 2, 1788   *Paris*

I had intended to have written a word to your excellency
on the subject of the new constitution, but I have already spun
out my letter to an immoderate length. I will just observe,
therefore, that according to my ideas, there is a great deal of
good in it. There are two things, however, which I dislike
strongly. 1. The want of a declaration of rights. I am in hopes

the opposition of Virginia will remedy this, and produce such a declaration. 2. The perpetual re-eligibility of the President. This, I fear, will make that an office for life, first, and then hereditary. I was much an enemy to monarchies before I came to Europe. I am ten thousand times more so, since I have seen what they are. There is scarcely an evil known in these countries, which may not be traced to their king, as its source, nor a good, which is not derived from the small fibres of republicanism existing among them. I can further say, with safety, there is not a crowned head in Europe, whose talents or merits would entitle him to be elected a vestryman by the people of any parish in America.

To Mrs. William Bingham *

May 11, 1788   *Paris*

Dear Madam, A gentleman going to Philadelphia furnishes me the occasion of sending you some numbers of the Cabinet des Modes and some new theatrical pieces. These last have had great success on the stage, where they have excited perpetual applause. We have now need of something to make us laugh, for the topics of the times are sad and eventful. The gay and thoughtless Paris is now become a furnace of politics. All the world is now politically mad. Men, women, children talk nothing else, and you know that naturally they talk much, loud and warm. Society is spoilt by it, at least for those who, like myself, are but lookers on. . . .

You too have had your political fever. But our good ladies, I trust, have been too wise to wrinkle their foreheads with politics. They are contented to soothe and calm the minds of

* Wife of a Philadelphia banker and Senator whose house was a gathering place of the public figures of the day.

their husbands returning ruffled from political debate. They have the good sense to value domestic happiness above all other, and the art to cultivate it beyond all others. There is no part of the earth where so much of this is enjoyed as in America. You agree with me in this; but you think that the pleasures of Paris more than supply its wants; in other words that a Parisian is happier than an American. You will change your opinion, my dear madam, and come over to mine in the end. Recollect the women of this capital, some on foot, some on horses, and some in carriages hunting pleasure in the streets, in routs and assemblies, and forgetting that they have left it behind them in their nurseries; compare them with our own countrywomen occupied in the tender and tranquil amusements of domestic life, and confess that it is a comparison of Americans and Angels. . . .

You will have known from the public papers that Monsieur de Buffon, the father, is dead and you have known long ago that the son and his wife are separated. They are pursuing pleasure in opposite directions. Madame de Rochambeau is well: so is Madame de Lafayette. I recollect no other nouvelles de societé interesting to you. And as for political news of battles and sieges, Turks and Russians, I will not detail them to you, because you would be less handsome after reading them. I have only to add then, what I take a pleasure in repeating, though it will be the thousandth time that I have the honor to be with sentiments of very sincere respect and attachment, dear madam, your most obedient and most humble servant,

TH: JEFFERSON

To John Jay *

January 11, 1789   *Paris*

As the character of the Prince of Wales is becoming interesting, † I have endeavored to learn what it truly is. This is less difficult in his case, than in that of other persons of his rank, because he has taken no pains to hide himself from the world. The information I most rely on is from a person here with whom I am intimate, who divides his time between Paris and London, an Englishman by birth, of truth, sagacity and science. He is of a circle, when in London, which has had good opportunities of knowing the Prince; but he has also, himself, had special occasions of verifying their information, by his own personal observation. He happened, when last in London, to be invited to a dinner of three persons. The Prince came by chance, and made the fourth. He ate half a leg of mutton; did not taste of small dishes, because small; drank champagne and burgundy, as small beer during dinner, and bordeaux after dinner, as the rest of the company. Upon the whole, he ate as much as the other three, and drank about two bottles of wine without seeming to feel it. My informant sat next him, and being till then unknown to the Prince, personally, (though not by character) and lately from France, the Prince confined his conversation almost entirely to him. Observing to the Prince that he spoke French without the least foreign accent, the Prince told him, that when very young, his father had put only French servants about him, and that it was to that circumstance he owed his pronunciation. He led him from this to give an account of his education, the total of which was the learning a little Latin. He has not a single element of mathematics, of

---

* Jay (1745-1829) was the Secretary for Foreign Affairs of the American Congress and the first Chief Justice of the United States.

† Jefferson referred to the well-known fact that George III was mentally deranged and that, therefore, it was important to know what his successor, the Prince of Wales, the later George IV, was like.

natural or moral philosophy, or of any other science on earth, nor has the society he has kept been such as to supply the void of education. It has been that of the lowest, the most illiterate and profligate persons of the kingdom, without choice of rank or mind, and with whom the subjects of conversation are only horses, drinking-matches, bawdy houses, and in terms the most vulgar. The young nobility, who begin by associating with him, soon leave him, disgusted with the insupportable profligacy of his society; and Mr. Fox, who has been supposed his favorite, and not over-nice in the choice of company, would never keep his company habitually. In fact, he never associated with a man of sense. He has not a single idea of justice, morality, religion, or of the rights of men, or any anxiety for the opinion of the world. He carries that indifference for fame so far, that he would probably not be hurt were he to lose his throne, provided he could be assured of having always meat, drink, horses, and women. In the article of women, nevertheless, he is become more correct, since his connection with Mrs. Fitzherbert, who is an honest and worthy woman: he is even less crapulous than he was. He had a fine person, but it is becoming coarse. He possesses good native common sense; is affable, polite, and very good humored. Saying to my informant, on another occasion, "your friend, such a one, dined with me yesterday, and I made him damned drunk;" he replied, "I am sorry for it; I had heard that your royal highness had left off drinking:" the Prince laughed, tapped him on the shoulder very good naturedly, without saying a word, or ever after showing any displeasure.

To Madame de Bréhan *

March 14, 1789   *Paris*

I have little to communicate to you from this place. It is deserted; everybody being gone into the country to choose or be chosen deputies to the States General. I hope to see that great meeting before my departure. It is to be on the 27th of next month. A great political revolution will take place in your country, and that without bloodshed. A king with two hundred thousand men at his orders, is disarmed by the force of the public opinion and the want of money. Among the economies becoming necessary, perhaps one may be the opera. They say it has cost the public treasury an hundred thousand crowns the last year. A new theatre is established since your departure; that of the Opera Buffons, where Italian operas are given, and good music. It is in the Chateau des Tuilleries. Paris is every day enlarging and beautifying. I do not count among its beauties, however, the wall with which they have enclosed us. They have made some amends for this, by making fine boulevards within and without the walls. These are in considerable forwardness, and will afford beautiful rides round the city, of between fifteen and twenty miles in circuit. We have had such a winter, madam, as makes me shiver yet, whenever I think of it. All communications, almost, were cut off. Dinners and suppers were suppressed, and the money laid out in feeding and warming the poor, whose labors were suspended by the rigor of the season. Loaded carriages passed the Seine on the ice, and it was covered with thousands of people from morning to night, skating and sliding. Such sights were never seen before, and they continued two months. We have nothing new and excellent in your charming art of painting. In fact, I do not feel an interest in any pencil but that of David. But I must not hazard details on a subject wherein I am so ignorant, and you such a con-

---

*She was a painter and member of Jefferson's group of friends in Paris.

noisseur. Adieu, my dear madam; permit me always the honor of esteeming and being esteemed by you, and of tendering you the homage of that respectful attachment with which I am, and shall ever be, dear madam, your most obedient humble servant,

TH: JEFFERSON

To James Madison

March 15, 1789 *Paris*

In the arguments in favor of a declaration of rights, you omit one which has great weight with me; the legal check which it puts into the hands of the judiciary. This is a body, which, if rendered independent and kept strictly to their own department, merits great confidence for their learning and integrity. In fact, what degree of confidence would be too much, for a body composed of such men as Wythe, Blair and Pendleton? On characters like these, the *"civium ardor prava jubentium"* would make no impression. I am happy to find that, on the whole, you are a friend to this amendment.

The declaration of rights is, like all other human blessings, alloyed with some inconveniences, and not accomplishing fully its object. But the good in this instance, vastly overweighs the evil. I cannot refrain from making short answers to the objections which your letter states to have been raised. 1. That the rights in question are reserved, by the manner in which the federal powers are granted. Answer. A constitutive act may, certainly, be so formed, as to need no declaration of rights. The act itself has the force of a declaration, as far as it goes; and if it goes to all material points, nothing more is wanting. In the draft of a constitution which I had once a thought of proposing in Virginia, and printed afterwards, I endeavored to reach all the great objects of public liberty, and did not mean to add a declaration of rights. Probably the object was imperfectly executed; but the deficiencies would have been supplied by others, in the course of discussion. But in a constitutive act which leaves some precious articles unnoticed, and raises implications against others, a declaration of rights becomes necessary, by way of supplement. This is the case of our new federal constitution. This instrument forms us into one State, as to certain objects, and gives us a legislative and executive body for these objects. It should, therefore, guard us against their abuses of power, within the field submitted to them. 2. A positive declaration of some essential rights could not be obtained in the requisite latitude. Answer. Half a loaf is better than no bread. If we cannot secure all our rights, let us secure what we can. 3. The limited powers of the federal government, and jealousy of the subordinate governments, afford a security which exists in no other instance. Answer. The first member of this seems resolvable into the first objection before stated. The jealousy of the subordinate governments is a precious reliance. But observe that those governments are only agents. They must have principles furnished them, whereon to found their opposition. The declaration of rights will be the text, whereby they will try all the acts of the federal government. In this view, it is necessary to the federal government also; as by the same text, they may try the opposition of the subordinate governments. 4. Experience proves the inefficacy of a bill of rights. True. But though it is not absolutely efficacious under all circumstances, it is of great potency always, and rarely inefficacious. A brace the more will often keep up the building which would have fallen, with that brace the less. There is a remarkable difference between the characters of the inconveniences which attend a declaration of rights, and those which attend the want of it. The inconveniences of the declaration are, that it may cramp government in its useful exertions. But the evil of this is short-lived, moderate and reparable. The inconveniences of the want of a declaration are permanent, afflicting and irreparable. They are in constant progression from bad to worse. The executive, in our governments, is not the sole, it is scarcely the principal object of my jealousy. The tyranny of the legislatures is the most formidable dread at present, and will be for many years. That of the executive will come in its turn; but it will be at a remote period. I know there are some among us, who would now establish a monarchy. But they are inconsiderable in number and weight of character. The rising race are all republicans. We were educated in royalism; no wonder, if some of us retain that idolatry still. Our young people are educated in republicanism; an apostasy from that to royalism, is unprecedented and impossible. I am much pleased with the prospect that a declaration of rights will be added; and I hope it will be done in that way, which will not endanger the whole frame of government, or any essential part of it.

To Colonel David Humphreys *

March 18, 1789   *Paris*

Dear Sir, Your favor of November the 29th, 1788, came to hand the last month. How it happened that mine of August, 1787, was fourteen months on its way, is inconceivable. I do not recollect by what conveyance I sent it. I had concluded, however, either that it had miscarried, or that you had become indolent, as most of our countrymen are, in matters of correspondence.

The change in this country since you left it, is such as you can form no idea of. The frivolities of conversation have given way entirely to politics. Men, women and children talk nothing else; and all, you know, talk a great deal. The press groans with daily productions, which, in point of boldness, make an Englishman stare, who hitherto has thought himself the boldest of

---

* Humphreys (1752-1818), an American poet and diplomat, had been General Washington's aide-de-camp, and was secretary to the Jefferson commission in Paris.

men. A complete revolution in this government has, within the space of two years (for it began with the Notables of 1787), been effected merely by the force of public opinion, aided, indeed, by the want of money, which the dissipations of the court had brought on. And this revolution has not cost a single life, unless we charge to it a little riot lately in Bretagne, which began about the price of bread, became afterwards political, and ended in the loss of four or five lives. The assembly of the States General begins the 27th of April. The representation of the people will be perfect. But they will be alloyed by an equal number of nobility and clergy. The first great question they will have to decide will be, whether they shall vote by orders or persons. And I have hopes that the majority of the nobles are already disposed to join the Tiers Etat, in deciding that the vote shall be by persons. This is the opinion *à la mode* at present, and mode has acted a wonderful part in the present instance. All the handsome young women, for example, are for the Tiers Etat, and this is an army more powerful in France, than the two hundred thousand men of the King. Add to this, that the court itself is for the Tiers Etat, as the only agent which can relieve their wants; not by giving money themselves, (they are squeezed to the last drop), but by pressing it from the non-contributing orders. The King stands engaged to pretend no more to the power of laying, continuing or appropriating taxes; to call the States General periodically; to submit *lettres de cachet* to legal restrictions; to consent to freedom of the press; and that all this shall be fixed by a fundamental constitution, which shall bind his successors. He has not offered a participation in the legislature, but it will surely be insisted on. The public mind is so ripened on all these subjects, that there seems to be now but one opinion. The clergy, indeed, think separately, and the old men among the nobles; but their voice is suppressed by the general one of the nation. The writings published on this occasion are, some of them, very valuable; because, unfettered by the prejudices under which the English labor, they give a full scope to reason, and strike out truths, as yet unperceived and unacknowledged on the other side of the channel. An Englishman, dozing under a kind of half reformation, is not excited to think by such gross absurdities as stare a Frenchman in the face, wherever he looks, whether it be towards the throne or the altar. In fine, I believe this nation will, in the course of the present year, have as full a portion of liberty dealt out to them, as the nation can bear at present, considering how uninformed the mass of their people is. This circumstance will prevent the immediate establishment of the trial by jury. The palsied state of the executive in England is a fortunate circumstance for France, as it will give her time to arrange her affairs internally. The consolidation and funding their debts, will give government a credit which will enable them to do what they please. For the present year, the war will be confined to the two empires and Denmark, against Turkey and Sweden. It is not yet evident whether Prussia will be engaged. If the disturbances of Poland break out into overt acts, it will be a power divided in itself, and so of no weight. Perhaps, by the next year, England and France may be ready to take the field. It will depend on the former principally; for the latter, though she may be then able, must wish a little time to see her new arrangements well under way. The English papers and English ministry say the King is well. He is better but not well; no malady requires a longer time to insure against its return than insanity. Time alone can distinguish accidental insanity from habitual lunacy.

The operations which have taken place in America lately, fill me with pleasure. In the first place, they realize the confidence I had, that whenever our affairs go obviously wrong, the good sense of the people will interpose, and set them to rights. The example of changing a constitution, by assembling the wise men of the State, instead of assembling armies, will be worth as much to the world as the former examples we had given them. The Constitution, too, which was the result of our deliberations, is unquestionably the wisest ever yet presented to men, and some of the accommodations of interest which it has

adopted, are greatly pleasing to me, who have before had occasions of seeing how difficult those interests were to accommodate. A general concurrence of opinion seems to authorize us
to say, it has some defects. I am one of those who think it a defect,
that the important rights, not placed in security by the frame of
the Constitution itself, were not explicitly secured by a sup-
plementary declaration. There are rights which it is useless to
surrender to the government, and which governments have yet
always been found to invade. These are the rights of thinking,
and publishing our thoughts by speaking or writing; the right
of free commerce; the right of personal freedom. There are
instruments for administering the government, so peculiarly
trust-worthy, that we should never leave the legislature at liberty to change them. The new Constitution has secured these
in the executive and legislative department; but not in the
judiciary. It should have established trials by the people themselves, that is to say, by jury. There are instruments so dangerous to the rights of the nation, and which place them so totally
at the mercy of their governors, that those governors, whether
legislative or executive, should be restrained from keeping
such instruments on foot, but in well-defined cases. Such an
instrument is a standing army. We are now allowed to say,
such a declaration of rights, as a supplement to the Constitution
where that is silent, is wanting, to secure us in these points. The
general voice has legitimated this objection. It has not, however, authorized me to consider as a real defect, what I thought
and still think one, the perpetual re-eligibility of the President.
But three States out of eleven having declared against this, we
must suppose we are wrong, according to the fundamental law
of every society, the *lex majoris partis,* to which we are bound
to submit. And should the majority change their opinion, and
become sensible that this trait in their Constitution is wrong,
I would wish it to remain uncorrected, as long as we can avail
ourselves of the services of our great leader, whose talents and
whose weight of character, I consider as peculiarly necessary to

get the government so under way, as that it may afterwards be carried on by subordinate characters.

I must give you sincere thanks, for the details of small news contained in your letter. You know how precious that kind of information is to a person absent from his country, and how difficult it is to be procured. I hope to receive soon permission to visit America this summer, and to possess myself anew, by conversation with my countrymen, of their spirit and their ideas. I know only the Americans of the year 1784. They tell me this is to be much a stranger to those of 1789. This renewal of acquaintance is no indifferent matter to one, acting at such a distance, as that instructions cannot be received hot and hot. One of my pleasures, too, will be that of talking over the old and new with you. In the meantime, and at all times, I have the honor to be, with great and sincere esteem, dear sir, your friend and servant,

TH: JEFFERSON

To Lafayette

May 6, 1789   *Paris*

My Dear Friend, As it becomes more and more possible that the noblesse will go wrong, I become uneasy for you. Your principles are decidedly with the Tiers Etat, and your instructions against them. A complaisance to the latter on some occasions, and an adherence to the former on others, may give an appearance of trimming between the two parties, which may lose you both. You will, in the end, go over wholly to the Tiers Etat, because it will be impossible for you to live in a constant sacrifice of your own sentiments to the prejudices of the noblesse. But you would be received by the Tiers Etat at any future day, coldly, and without confidence. This appears to me the moment to take at once that honest and manly stand with them which your own principles dictate. This will win their hearts forever, be approved by the world, which marks and honors you as the man of the people, and will be an eternal consolation to yourself. The noblesse, and especially the noblesse of Auvergne, will always prefer men who will do their dirty work for them. You are not made for that. They will therefore soon drop you, and the people, in that case, will perhaps not take you up. Suppose a scission should take place. The priests and nobles will secede, the nation will remain in place, and, with the King, will do its own business. If violence should be attempted, where will you be? You cannot then take side with the people in opposition to your own vote, that very vote which will have helped to produce the scission. Still less can you array yourself against the people. That is impossible. Your instructions are indeed a difficulty. But to state this at its worst it is only a single difficulty, which a single effort surmounts. Your instructions can never embarrass you a second time, whereas an acquiescence under them will reproduce greater difficulties every day, and without end. Besides, a thousand circumstances offer as many justifications of your departure from your instructions. Will it be impossible to persuade all parties that (as for good legislation two houses are necessary) the placing the privileged classes together in one house, and the unprivileged in another, would be better for both than a scission? I own, I think it would. People can never agree without some sacrifices; and it appears but a moderate sacrifice in each party, to meet on this middle ground. The attempt to bring this about might satisfy your instructions, and a failure in it would justify your siding with the people, even to those who think instructions are laws of conduct. Forgive me, my dear friend, if my anxiety for you makes me talk of things I know nothing about. You must not consider this as advice. I know you and myself too well to presume to offer advice. Receive it merely as the expression of my uneasiness, and the effusion of that sincere friendship with which I am, my dear sir, yours affectionately,

TH: JEFFERSON

To Abbé Arnauld

July 19, 1789   *Paris*

Dear Sir, The annexed is a catalogue of all the books I recollect on the subject of juries. With respect to the value of this institution, I must make a general observation. We think, in America, that it is necessary to introduce the people into every department of government, as far as they are capable of exercising it; and that this is the only way to insure a long-continued and honest administration of its powers.

1. They are not qualified to exercise themselves the executive department, but they are qualified to name the person who shall exercise it. With us, therefore, they choose this officer every four years. 2. They are not qualified to legislate. With us, therefore, they only choose the legislators. 3. They are not qualified to *judge* questions of *law,* but they are very capable of judging questions of *fact.* In the form of juries, therefore, they determine all matters of fact, leaving to the permanent judges, to decide the law resulting from those facts. But we all know that permanent judges acquire an *esprit de corps;* that being known, they are liable to be tempted by bribery; that they are misled by favor, by relationship, by a spirit of party, by a devotion to the executive or legislative power; that it is better to leave a cause to the decision of cross and pile, than to that of a judge biased to one side; and that the opinion of twelve honest jurymen gives still a better hope of right, than cross and pile does. It is in the power, therefore, of the juries, if they think permanent judges are under any bias whatever, in any cause, to take on themselves to judge the law as well as the fact. They never exercise this power but when they suspect partiality in the judges; and by the exercise of this power, they have been the firmest bulwarks of English liberty. Were I called upon to decide, whether the people had best be omitted in the legislative or judiciary department, I would say it is better to leave

them out of the legislative. The execution of the laws is more important than the making them. However, it is best to have the people in all the three departments, where that is possible.

I write in great haste, my dear sir, and have, therefore, only time to add wishes for the happiness of your country, to which a new order of things is opening; and assurances of the sincere esteem with which I have the honor to be, dear sir, your most obedient and humble servant,

TH: JEFFERSON

To James Madison

September 6, 1789   *Paris*

The question, whether one generation of men has a right to bind another, seems never to have been started either on this or our side of the water. Yet it is a question of such consequences as not only to merit decision, but place also among the fundamental principles of every government. The course of reflection in which we are immersed here, on the elementary principles of society, has presented this question to my mind; and that no such obligation can be so transmitted, I think very capable of proof. I set out on this ground, which I suppose to be self-evident, that the *earth belongs in usufruct to the living;* that the dead have neither powers nor rights over it. The portion occupied by any individual ceases to be his when himself ceases to be, and reverts to the society. If the society has formed no rules for the appropriation of its lands in severalty, it will be taken by the first occupants, and these will generally be the wife and children of the decedent. If they have formed rules of appropriation, those rules may give it to the wife and children, or to some one of them, or to the legatee of the deceased. So they may give it to his creditor. But the child, the legatee or creditor, takes it, not by natural right, but by a law of the society of which he is a member, and to which he is subject. Then, no man can, by *natural right,* oblige the lands he occupied, or the persons who succeed him in that occupation, to the payment of debts contracted by him. For if he could, he might during his own life, eat up the usufruct of the lands for several generations to come; and then the lands would belong to the dead, and not to the living, which is the reverse of our principle.

What is true of every member of the society, individually, is true of them all collectively; since the rights of the whole can be no more than the sum of the rights of the individuals. To keep our ideas clear when applying them to a multitude, let us suppose a whole generation of men to be born on the same day, to attain mature age on the same day, and to die on the same day, leaving a succeeding generation in the moment of attaining their mature age, all together. Let the ripe age be supposed of twenty-one years, and their period of life thirty-four years more, that being the average term given by the bills of mortality to persons of twenty-one years of age. Each successive generation would, in this way, come and go off the stage at a fixed moment, as individuals do now. Then I say, the earth belongs to each of these generations during its course, fully and in its own right. The second generation receives it clear of the debts and incumbrances of the first, the third of the second, and so on. For if the first could charge it with a debt, then the earth would belong to the dead and not to the living generation. Then, no generation can contract debts greater than may be paid during the course of its own existence. At twenty-one years of age, they may bind themselves and their lands for thirty-four years to come; at twenty-two, for thirty-three; at twenty-three, for thirty-two; and at fifty-four, for one year only; because these are the terms of life which remain to them at the respective epochs. But a material difference must be noted, between the succession of an individual and that of a whole generation. Individuals are parts only of a society, subject to the laws of the whole. These laws may appropriate the portion of land occupied by a decedent, to his creditor rather than to any other, or to his child, on condition he satisfies the creditor. But when a whole generation, that is, the whole society, dies, as in the case we have supposed, and another generation or society succeeds, this forms a whole, and there is no superior who can give their territory to a third society, who may have lent money to their predecessors, beyond their faculties of paying. . . .

This principle, that the earth belongs to the living and not to the dead, is of very extensive application and consequences in every country, and most especially in France. It enters into the resolution of the questions, whether the nation may change the descent of lands holden in tail; whether they may change the appropriation of lands given anciently to the church, to hospitals, colleges, orders of chivalry, and otherwise in perpetuity; whether they may abolish the charges and privileges attached on lands, including the whole catalogue, ecclesiastical and feudal, it goes to hereditary offices, authorities and jurisdictions, to hereditary orders, distinctions and appellations, to perpetual monopolies in commerce, the arts or sciences, with a long train of *et ceteras;* and it renders the question of reimbursement a question of generosity and not of right. In all these cases, the legislature of the day could authorize such appropriations and establishments for their own time, but no longer; and the present holders, even where they or their ancestors have purchased, are in the case of *bona fide* purchasers of what the seller had no right to convey.

PART FOUR

Secretary of State

(1790–1793)

In THE AUTUMN of *1789*
*President Washington appointed Jefferson Secretary of State.
Jefferson accepted reluctantly and spent the next four years in
New York and Philadelphia, the then capitals of the United
States. This was perhaps the least happy period of his life, for
he was in constant conflict with his colleague in the Cabinet,
Alexander Hamilton. Jefferson became convinced that Secretary
Hamilton and his followers were enemies of the republic and
hostile to democratic ideas. Unable to make headway against
the conservative and powerful Federalist party, Jefferson finally
resigned, despite the urgent appeals of the harassed Washington. The first Secretary of State retired to his family and farms
and swore that he was through with politics for ever.*

To Martha Jefferson Randolph

I am anxious to hear from you of your health, your occupations, where you are. . . . Do not neglect your music. It will be a companion which will sweeten many hours of life to you. I assure you mine here is triste enough. Having had yourself and dear Poll to live with me so long, to exercise my affections and cheer me in the intervals of business, I feel heavily the separation from you. It is a circumstance of consolation to know that you are happier; and to see a prospect of its continuance in the prudence and even temper of Mr. Randolph and yourself. Your new condition* will call for abundance of little sacrifices. But they will be greatly overpaid by the measure of affection they secure to you. The happiness of your life now depends on the continuing to please a single person. To this all other objects must be secondary, even your love for me, were it possible that could ever be an obstacle. But this it never can be. Neither of you can ever have a more faithful friend than myself, nor one on whom you can count for more sacrifices. My own is become a secondary object to the happiness of you both. Cherish, then for me, my dear child, the affection of your husband, and continue to love me as you have done, and to render my life a blessing by the prospect it may hold up to me of seeing you happy.

---

* Her marriage to Thomas Mann Randolph.

To Maria Jefferson *

April 11, 1790   *New York*

Where are you, my dear Maria? How do you do, how are you occupied? Write me a letter by the first post, and answer me all these questions. Tell me whether you see the sun rise every day; how many pages a day you read in Don Quixote; how far you are advanced in him; whether you repeat a grammar lesson every day; what else you read; how many hours a day you sew; whether you have an opportunity of continuing your music; whether you know how to make a pudding yet, to cut out a beefsteak, to sow spinach or to set a hen? Be good, my dear, as I have always found you; never be angry with anybody, nor speak harm of them; try to let everybody's faults be forgotten, as you would wish yours to be; take more pleasure in giving what is best to another than in having it yourself, and then all the world will love you, and I more than all the world. If your sister is with you, kiss her and tell her how much I love her also, and present my affections to Mr. Randolph. Love your aunt and uncle and be dutiful and obliging to them for all their kindness to you. What would you do without them and with such a vagrant for a father? Say to both of them a thousand affectionate things for me; and adieu, my dear Maria,

TH: JEFFERSON

To Martha Jefferson Randolph

May 8, 1791   *Philadelphia*

I thank you for all the small news of your letter, which it is very grateful for me to receive. I am happy to find

---
* She was not yet 12.

you are on good terms with your neighbors. It is almost the most important circumstance in life, since nothing is so corroding as frequently to meet persons with whom one has any difference. The ill-will of a single neighbor is an immense drawback on the happiness of life, and therefore their good-will cannot be bought too dear.

To Martha Jefferson Randolph

May 31, 1791   *Lake Champlain*

My dear Martha, I wrote to Maria yesterday while sailing on Lake George, and the same kind of leisure is afforded me today to write to you. Lake George is, without comparison, the most beautiful water I ever saw; formed by a contour of mountains into a basin thirty-five miles long, and from two to four miles broad, finely interspersed with islands, its water limpid as crystal, and the mountain sides covered with rich groves of thuja, silver fir, white pine, aspen and paper birch down to the water-edge; here and there precipices of rock to checker the scene and save it from monotony. An abundance of speckled trout, salmon trout, bass, and other fish, with which it is stored, have added, to our other amusements, the sport of taking them. Lake Champlain, though much larger, is a far less pleasant water. It is muddy, turbulent, and yields little game. After penetrating into it about twenty-five miles, we have been obliged, by a head wind and high sea, to return, having spent a day and a half in sailing on it. We shall take our route again through Lake George, pass through Vermont, down Connecticut River, and through Long Island to New York and Philadelphia. Our journey has hitherto been prosperous and pleasant, except as to the weather, which has been as sultry and hot through the whole as could be found in Carolina or Georgia. I suspect, indeed, that the heats of northern climates may be more powerful than those of southern ones in proportion as they are shorter. Perhaps vegetation requires this. There is as much fever and ague, too, and other bilious complaints on Lake Champlain as on the swamps of Carolina. Strawberries here are in the blossom or just formed. With you, I suppose, the season is over. On the whole, I find nothing anywhere else, in point of climate, which Virginia need envy to any part of the world. Here they are locked up in ice and snow for six months. Spring and autumn, which make a paradise of our country, are rigorous winter with them. And a tropical summer breaks on them all at once. When we consider how much climate contributes to the happiness of our condition, by the fine sensations it excites, and the productions it is the parent of, we have reason to value highly the accident of birth in such a one as that of Virginia.

From this distance I can have little domestic to write to you about. I must always repeat how much I love you. Kiss the little Anne for me. I hope she grows lustily, enjoys good health, and will make us all, and long, happy as the centre of our common love. Adieu, my dear. Yours affectionately,

TH: JEFFERSON

To Condorcet *

August 30, 1791   *Philadelphia*

Dear Sir, I am to acknowledge the receipt of your favor on the subject of the element of measure adopted by France. Candor obliges me to confess that it is not what I would have approved. It is liable to the inexactitude of mensuration as to

---

* Marie Jean Antoine-Nicolas, Marquis de Condorcet (1743-1794), was the distinguished French philosopher and mathematician who perished on the guillotine.

that part of the quadrant of the earth which is to be measured, that is to say as to one tenth of the quadrant, and as to the remaining nine tenths they are to be calculated on conjectural data, presuming the figure of the earth which has not yet been proved. It is liable too to the objection that no nation but your own can come at it; because yours is the only nation within which a meridian can be found of such extent crossing the 45th degree and terminating at both ends in a level. We may certainly say then that this measure is uncatholic, and I would rather have seen you depart from Catholicism in your religion than in your philosophy.

I am happy to be able to inform you that we have now in the United States a Negro, the son of a black man born in Africa, and of a black woman born in the United States, who is a very respectable mathematician.* I procured him to be employed under one of our chief directors in laying out the new federal city on the Potomac, and in the intervals of his leisure, while on that work, he made an almanac for the next year, which he sent me in his own handwriting,† and which I enclose to you. I have seen very elegant solutions of geometrical problems by

* The reference is to Benjamin Banneker—sometimes spelled Bannaker—(1731-1806), a self-educated Negro freeman, who became a mathematician and astronomer and assisted his patron and neighbor, Major Andrew Ellicott, in the surveying of the District of Columbia. See Saul K. Padover, "Benjamin Banneker: Unschooled Wizard," in *New Republic*, February 2, 1948.

† Upon receipt of Banneker's *Almanac and Ephemeris,* Secretary of State Jefferson, on August 30, 1791, replied:

"Sir, I thank you sincerely for your letter of the 19th instant and for the Almanac it contained. Nobody wishes more than I do to see such proofs as you exhibit, that nature has given to our black brethren, talents equal to those of the other colors of men, and that the appearance of a want of them is owing merely to the degraded condition of their existence, both in Africa and America. I can add with truth, that nobody wishes more ardently to see a good system commenced for raising the condition of both their body and mind to what it ought to be, as fast as the imbecility of their present existence, and other circumstances which cannot be neglected, will admit. I have taken the liberty of sending your Almanac to Monsieur de Condorcet, Secretary of the Academy of Sciences at Paris . . . , because I considered it as a document to which your whole color had a right for their justification against the doubts which have been entertained of them. I am with great esteem, Sir, Your most obedient humble servant." This letter was written on the same day as the one above to Condorcet.

him.* Add to this that he is a very worthy and respectable member of society. He is a free man. I shall be delighted to see these instances of moral eminence so multiplied as to prove that the want of talents observed in them is merely the effect of their degraded condition, and not proceeding from any difference in the structure of the parts on which intellect depends.

I am looking ardently to the completion of the glorious work in which your country is engaged [the French Revolution]. I view the general condition of Europe as hanging on the success or failure of France. Having set such an example of philosophical arrangement within, I hope it will be extended without your limits also, to your dependents and to your friends in every part of the earth.

To Lafayette

June 16, 1792   *Philadelphia*

Behold you, then, my dear friend, at the head of a great army, establishing the liberties of your country against a foreign enemy.† May heaven favor your cause, and make you the channel through which it may pour its favors. While you are exterminating the monster aristocracy, and pulling out the teeth and

---

* Yet years later Jefferson expressed doubts about Banneker's skill and abilities. In a letter to Joel Barlow, written on October 8, 1809, and discussing Bishop Grégoire's friendly book on Negroes, Jefferson wrote:

"His [Grégoire's] credulity has made him gather up every story he could find of men of color . . . , however slight the mention, or light the authority on which they are quoted. The whole do not amount, in point of evidence, to what we know ourselves of Banneker. We know he had spherical trigonometry enough to make almanacs, but not without the suspicion of aid from Ellicott, who was his neighbor and friend, and never missed an opportunity of puffing him. I have a long letter from Banneker, which shows him to have had a mind of very common stature indeed."

See also Jefferson's letter to Grégoire, February 25, 1809.

† Lafayette, Commander-in-Chief of the French National Guard, was placed at the head of a French army on the frontier at the outbreak of the war with Austria in 1792.

fangs of its associate, monarchy, a contrary tendency is discovered in some here. A sect has shown itself among us, who declare they espoused our new Constitution, not as a good and sufficient thing in itself, but only as a step to an English constitution, the only thing good and sufficient in itself, in their eye. It is happy for us that these are preachers without followers, and that our people are firm and constant in their republican purity. You will wonder to be told that it is from the eastward chiefly that these champions for a king, lords and commons come. They get some important associates from New York, and are puffed up by a tribe of agitators which have been hatched in a bed of corruption made up after the model of their beloved England. Too many of these stock-jobbers and king-jobbers have come into our legislature, or rather too many of our legislature have become stock-jobbers and king-jobbers. However, the voice of the people is beginning to make itself heard, and will probably cleanse their seats at the ensuing election.

To Thomas Paine

June 19, 1792   *Philadelphia*

Dear Sir, I received with great pleasure the present of your pamphlets, as well for the thing itself as that it was a testimony of your recollection. Would you believe it possible that in this country there should be high and important characters who need your lessons in republicanism, and who do not heed them? It is but too true that we have a sect preaching up and pouting after an English constitution of king, lords and commons, and whose heads are itching for crowns, coronets and mitres. But our people, my good friend, are firm and unanimous in their principles of republicanism and there is no better proof of it than that they love what you write and read it with delight. The printers season every newspaper with extracts from your last, as they did before from your first part of the Rights of Man. They have both served here to separate the wheat from the chaff, and to prove that though the latter appears on the surface, it is on the surface only. The bulk below is sound and pure. Go on then in doing with your pen what in other times was done with the sword: show that reformation is more practicable by operating on the mind than on the body of man, and be assured that it has not a more sincere votary nor you a more ardent well-wisher than . . .

TH: JEFFERSON

To William Short *

Dear Sir, My last private letter to you was of October 16, since which I have received your Nos. 103, 107, 108, 109, 110, 112, 113 and 114 and yesterday your private one of September 15, came to hand. The tone of your letters had for some time given me pain, on account of the extreme warmth with which they censured the proceedings of the Jacobins of France. I considered that sect as the same with the republican patriots, and the Feuillants as the monarchical patriots, well known in the early part of the Revolution, and but little distant in their views, both having in object the establishment of a free constitution, differing only on the question whether their chief executive should be hereditary or not. The Jacobins (as since called) yielded to the Feuillants, and tried the experiment of retaining their hereditary executive. The experiment failed completely, and would have brought on the re-establishment of despotism had it been pursued. The Jacobins knew this, and

---

* Short (1759-1849) was Jefferson's secretary in Paris and occupied diplomatic posts in Holland and Spain.

that the expunging that office was of absolute necessity. And the
nation was with them in opinion, for however they might have
been formerly for the constitution framed by the first assembly,
they were come over from their hope in it, and were now generally Jacobins. In the struggle which was necessary, many guilty
persons fell without the forms of trial, and with them some
innocent. These I deplore as much as anybody, and shall deplore some of them to the day of my death. But I deplore them
as I should have done had they fallen in battle. It was necessary
to use the arm of the people, a machine not quite so blind as
balls and bombs, but blind to a certain degree. A few of their
cordial friends met at their hands the fate of enemies. But time
and truth will rescue and embalm their memories, while their
posterity will be enjoying that very liberty for which they
would never have hesitated to offer up their lives. The liberty
of the whole earth was depending on the issue of the contest,
and was ever such a prize won with so little innocent blood?
My own affections have been deeply wounded by some of the
martyrs to this cause, but rather than it should have failed I
would have seen half the earth desolated; were there but an
Adam and an Eve left in every country, and left free, it would
be better than as it now is. I have expressed to you my sentiments, because they are really those of ninety-nine in a hundred of our citizens. The universal feasts, and rejoicings which
have lately been had on account of the successes of the French,
showed the genuine effusions of their hearts. You have been
wounded by the sufferings of your friends, and have by this circumstance been hurried into a temper of mind which would
be extremely disrelished if known to your countrymen.

PART FIVE

Farmer

(1794–1796)

JEFFERSON *returned to Monticello and devoted himself to his farms which had become unprofitable during his decade of absence. He owned 10,000 acres of land, but only 2,000 were in use. "I return to farming," he wrote to John Adams, "with an ardor I scarcely knew in my youth." He said that he hated politics and hoped never again to be mixed up in any political movement or office. But the pressure from outside was too great, and in 1796 his friends in the newly founded Republican [now Democratic] party, especially James Madison, nominated him for the Presidency to run against John Adams. Jefferson neither accepted nor rejected the nomination; he did not campaign or orate or make any political move. When the electoral votes were counted, in February 1797, Adams had 71 votes and Jefferson 68. Jefferson thus became Vice-President.*

To Tench Coxe *

Your letters give a comfortable view of French affairs, and later events seem to confirm it. Over the foreign powers I am convinced they will triumph completely, and I cannot but hope that that triumph, and the consequent disgrace of the invading tyrants,† is destined, in the order of events, to kindle the wrath of the people of Europe against those who have dared to embroil them in such wickedness, and to bring at length, kings, nobles, and priests to the scaffolds which they have been so long deluging with human blood. I am still warm whenever I think of these scoundrels, though I do it as seldom as I can, preferring infinitely to contemplate the tranquil growth of my lucerne and potatoes. I have so completely withdrawn myself from these spectacles of usurpation and misrule, that I do not take a single newspaper, nor read one a month; and I feel myself infinitely the happier for it.

To William Branch Giles ‡

December 17, 1794   *Monticello*

The attempt which has been made to restrain the liberty of our citizens meeting together, interchanging sentiments on what subjects they please, and stating their sentiments in the public papers, has come upon us a full century earlier than I expected. To demand the censors of public measures to be

---

* Coxe (1755-1824) was a political economist and attorney-general of Pennsylvania.

† Austria and Prussia, which invaded France to crush the Revolution there.

‡ Giles (1762-1830) was a Republican (Democratic) Congressman from Virginia.

97

given up for punishment is to renew the demand of the wolves in the fable that the sheep should give up their dogs as hostages of the peace and confidence established between them. The tide against our Constitution is unquestionably strong, but it will turn. Everything tells me so, and every day verifies the prediction. Hold on then like a good and faithful seaman till our brother sailors can rouse from their intoxication and right the vessel. Make friends with the trans-Alleghanians. They are gone if you do not. Do not let false pride make a tea-act of your excise-law. Adieu. Yours affectionately,

TH: JEFFERSON

To John Adams

February 28, 1796   *Monticello*

I am to thank you, my dear sir, for forwarding M. D'Ivernois' book on the French Revolution. I receive everything with respect which comes from him. But it is on politics, a subject I never loved and now hate. I will not promise therefore to read it thoroughly. I fear the oligarchical executive of the French will not do. We have always seen a small council get into cabals and quarrels, the more bitter and relentless the fewer they are. We saw this in our committee of the States; and that they were from their bad passions, incapable of doing the business of their country. I think that for the prompt, clear and consistent action so necessary in an executive, unity of person is necessary as with us. . . .

This I hope will be the age of experiments in government, and that their basis will be founded in principles of honesty, not of mere force. We have seen no instance of this since the days of the Roman republic, nor do we read of any before that. Either force or corruption has been the principle of every modern government, unless the Dutch perhaps be excepted, and I am not well enough informed to except them absolutely. If ever the morals of a people could be made the basis of their own government, it is our case; and who could propose to govern such a people by the corruption of a legislature, before he could have one night of quiet sleep must convince himself that the human soul as well as body is mortal. I am glad to see that whatever grounds of apprehension may have appeared of a wish to govern us otherwise than on principles of reason and honesty, we are getting the better of them. I am sure from the honesty of your heart, you join me in detestation of the corruptions of the English government, and that no man on earth is more incapable than yourself of seeing that copied among us, willingly. I have been among those who have feared the design to introduce it here, and it has been a strong reason with me for wishing there was an ocean of fire between that island and us. But away politics.

To Philip Mazzei *

April 24, 1796   *Monticello*

My Dear Friend, The aspect of our politics has wonderfully changed since you left us. In place of that noble love of liberty and republican government which carried us triumphantly through the war, an Anglican monarchical aristocratical party has sprung up, whose avowed object is to draw over us the substance, as they have already done the forms, of the British government. The main body of our citizens, however, remain true to their republican principles; the whole landed interest is republican, and so is a great mass of talents. Against us are the executive, the judiciary, two out of three branches of the legis-

---

* Mazzei (1730-1816) was Jefferson's neighbor in Albemarle County, where he carried on agricultural experiments. During the Revolutionary War he served as Virginia's agent at the court of the Grand Duke of Tuscany.

lature, all the officers of the government, all who want to be
officers, all timid men who prefer the calm of despotism to the
boisterous sea of liberty, British merchants and Americans trad-
ing on British capital, speculators and holders in the banks and
public funds, a contrivance invented for the purposes of corruption, and for assimilating us in all things to the rotten as
well as the sound parts of the British model. It would give you
a fever were I to name to you the apostates who have gone over
to these heresies, men who were Samsons in the field and Solo-
mons in the council, but who have had their heads shorn by
the harlot England. In short, we are likely to preserve the liberty we have obtained only by unremitting labors and perils.
But we shall preserve it; and our mass of weight and wealth
on the good side is so great, as to leave no danger that force will
ever be attempted against us. We have only to awake and snap
the Lilliputian cords with which they have been entangling us
during the first sleep which succeeded our labors.

I will forward the testimonial of the death of Mrs. Mazzei,
which I can do the more incontrovertibly as she is buried in my
grave yard, and I pass her grave daily. The formalities of the
proof you require, will occasion delay. I begin to feel the effects
of age. My health has suddenly broken down, with symptoms
which give me to believe I shall not have much to encounter of the *tedium vitæ*. While it remains, however, my heart will
be warm in its friendships, and among these, will always foster
the affections with which I am, dear sir, your friend and servant,

TH: JEFFERSON

To John Adams

December 28, 1796   *Monticello*

Dear Sir, The public, and the public papers, have been
much occupied lately in placing us in a point of opposition to

each other. I confidently trust we have felt less of it ourselves. In the retired canton where I live, we know little of what is passing. Our last information from Philadelphia is of the 16th instant. At that date the issue of the late election seems not to have been known as a matter of fact. With me, however, its issue was never doubted. I knew the impossibility of your losing a single vote north of the Delaware; and even if you should lose that of Pennsylvania in the mass, you would get enough south of it to make your election sure. I never for a single moment expected any other issue; and though I shall not be believed, yet it is not the less true, that I never wished any other. My neighbors, as my compurgators, could aver this fact, as seeing my occupations and my attachment to them. It is possible, indeed, that even you may be cheated of your succession by a trick worthy the subtlety of your arch friend of New York, who has been able to make of your real friends tools for defeating their and your just wishes. Probably, however, he will be disappointed as to you; and my inclinations put me out of his reach. I leave to others the sublime delights of riding in the storm, better pleased with sound sleep and a warmer berth below it, encircled with the society of my neighbors, friends, and fellow laborers of the earth, rather than with spies and sycophants. Still, I shall value highly the share I may have had in the late vote, as a measure of the share I hold in the esteem of my fellow citizens. In this point of view, a few votes less are but little sensible, while a few more would have been in their effect very sensible and oppressive to me. I have no ambition to govern men. It is a painful and thankless office. And never since the day you signed the treaty of Paris, has our horizon been so overcast. I devoutly wish you may be able to shun for us this war, which will destroy our agriculture, commerce, and credit. If you do, the glory will be all your own. And that your administration may be filled with glory and happiness to yourself, and advantage to us, is the sincere prayer of one, who, though in the course of our voyage, various little incidents have happened or been contrived to separate us, yet retains for you the solid esteem of the times when we were working for our independence, and sentiments of sincere respect and attachment.

To James Madison

January 1, 1797   *Monticello*

Dear Sir, Yours of December the 19th is safely received. I never entertained a doubt of the event of the election.* I knew that the eastern troops were trained in the schools of their town meetings to sacrifice little differences of opinion to the solid advantages of operating in phalanx, and that the more free and moral agency of the other States would fully supply their deficiency. I had no expectation, indeed, that the vote would have approached so near an equality. It is difficult to obtain full credit to declarations of disinclination to honors, and most so with those who still remain in the world. But never was there a more solid unwillingness, founded on rigorous calculation, formed in the mind of any man, short of peremptory refusal. No arguments, therefore, were necessary to reconcile me to a relinquishment of the first office, or acceptance of the second. No motive could have induced me to undertake the first, but that of putting our vessel upon her republican tack, and preventing her being driven too far to leeward of her true principles. And the second is the only office in the world about which I cannot decide in my own mind, whether I had rather have it or not have it. Pride does not enter into the estimate. For I think with the Romans of old, that the general of to-day should be a common soldier to-morrow, if necessary. But as to Mr. Adams, particularly, I could have no feelings which would revolt at being placed in a secondary station to him. I am his

---

* The final result of the Presidential election of 1796 was not officially established until February, when it was found that John Adams had 71 electoral votes and Jefferson 68.

junior in life, I was his junior in Congress, his junior in the
diplomatic line, and lately his junior in our civil government.
I had written him the enclosed letter before the receipt of yours.
I had intended it for some time, but had put it off, from time
to time, from the discouragement of despair to make him believe me sincere. As the information by the last post does
not make it necessary to change anything in the letter, I enclose
it open for your perusal, as well that you may be possessed of
the true state of dispositions between us, as that if there be any
circumstance which might render its delivery ineligible, you
may return it to me. If Mr. Adams could be induced to administer the government on its true principles, quitting his bias for
an English constitution, it would be worthy consideration
whether it would not for the public good, to come to a good
understanding with him as to his future elections. He is the
only sure barrier against Hamilton's getting in. . . .

The Political Progress is a work of value and of a singular
complexion. The author's eye seems to be a natural achromatic,
divesting every object of the glare of color. The former work
of the same title possessed the same kind of merit. They disgust
one, indeed, by opening to his view the ulcerated state of the
human mind. But to cure an ulcer you must go to the bottom
of it, which no author does more radically than this. The reflections into which it leads us are not very flattering to the human
species. In the whole animal kingdom I recollect no family but
man, steadily and systematically employed in the destruction of
itself. Nor does what is called civilization produce any other
effect, than to teach him to pursue the principle of the *bellum
omnium in omnia* on a greater scale, and instead of the little
contest between tribe and tribe, to comprehend all the quarters
of the earth in the same work of destruction. If to this we add,
that as to other animals, the lions and tigers are mere lambs
compared with man as a destroyer, we must conclude that nature has been able to find in man alone a sufficient barrier
against the too great multiplication of other animals and of
man himself, an equilibrating power against the fecundity of

generation. While in making these observations, my situation points my attention to the warfare of man in the physical world, yours may perhaps present him as equally warring in the moral one. Adieu. Yours affectionately,

TH: JEFFERSON

To James Sullivan *

February 9, 1797   *Monticello*

Dear Sir, I have many acknowledgments to make for the friendly anxiety you are pleased to express in your letter of January 12, for my undertaking the office to which I have been elected. The idea that I would accept the office of President, but not that of Vice-President of the United States, had not its origin with me. I never thought of questioning the free exercise of the right of my fellow citizens, to marshal those whom they call into their service according to their fitness, nor ever presumed that they were not the best judges of these. Had I indulged a wish in what manner they should dispose of me, it would precisely have coincided with what they have done. Neither the splendor, nor the power, nor the difficulties, nor the fame or defamation, as may happen, attached to the first magistracy, have any attractions for me. The helm of a free government is always arduous, and never was ours more so, than at a moment when two friendly people are like to be committed in war by the ill temper of their administrations. I am so much attached to my domestic situation, that I would not have wished to leave it at all. However, if I am to be called from it, the shortest absences and most tranquil station suit me best.

---

* Sullivan (1744-1808), a member of Jefferson's party, was an historian and Governor of Massachusetts, 1807-08.

PART SIX

Vice-President

(1797–1801)

DURING THESE *four years, most of them spent in Philadelphia (Washington did not become the capital until the latter part of 1800), Vice-President Jefferson and President Adams were not on harmonious terms. Jefferson resented some of the Adams Administration's oppressive legislation, notably the Alien and Sedition Acts, and secretly encouraged the Republican party's opposition to Adams. When the election year 1800 came around, Jefferson accepted the nomination of the Republicans. The campaign of 1800 was the first great bitter party conflict in American history. Against Jefferson were the powerful conservative interests, especially the moneyed classes and the clergy. It was during this campaign that Jefferson uttered his immortal challenge—"I have sworn upon the altar of God, eternal hostility against every form of tyranny over the mind of man"* —(see his letter to Rush, September 23, 1800). After a good deal of chicanery on the part of his opponents, Jefferson was elected President, an election which he regarded as a veritable "revolution."*

---

* The editor of this volume, together with the late Secretary of the Interior, Harold L. Ickes, was instrumental in having this sentence carved inside the Jefferson Monument in Washington.

To Thomas Pinckney *

May 29, 1797   *Philadelphia*

You have found on your return a higher style of political difference than you had left here. I fear this is inseparable from the different constitutions of the human mind, and that degree of freedom which permits unrestrained expression. Political dissension is doubtless a less evil than the lethargy of despotism, but still it is a great evil, and it would be as worthy the efforts of the patriot as of the philosopher, to exclude its influence, if possible, from social life. The good are rare enough at best. There is no reason to subdivide them by artificial lines. But whether we shall ever be able so far to perfect the principles of society, as that political opinions shall, in its intercourse, be as inoffensive as those of philosophy, mechanics, or any other, may well be doubted.

To Maria Jefferson Eppes †

January 7, 1798   *Philadelphia*

I acknowledged, my dear Maria, the receipt of yours in a letter I wrote to Mr. Eppes. It gave me the welcome news that your sprain was well. But you are not to suppose it entirely so. The joint will remain weak for a considerable time, and give

---

* Pinckney (1750-1828), of South Carolina, was American Minister to Great Britain and Spain.

† Jefferson's youngest daughter Maria married John Wayles Eppes on October 13, 1797.

you occasional pains much longer. The state of things at——
is truly distressing. Mr. ——'s habitual intoxication will destroy himself, his fortune, and family. Of all calamities, this is
the greatest. I wish my sister could bear his misconduct with
more patience. It would lessen his attachment to the bottle, and
at any rate would make her own time more tolerable. When we
see ourselves in a situation which must be endured and gone
through, it is best to make up our minds to it, meet it with
firmness, and accommodate everything to it in the best way
practicable. This lessens the evil, while fretting and fuming
only serves to increase our own torments. The errors and misfortunes of others should be a school for our own instruction.
Harmony in the married state is the very first object to be
aimed at. Nothing can preserve affections uninterrupted but a
firm resolution never to differ in will, and a determination in
each to consider the love of the other as of more value than any
object whatever on which a wish had been fixed. How light, in
fact, is the sacrifice of any other wish, when weighed against
the affections of one with whom we are to pass our whole life.
And though opposition, in a single instance, will hardly of itself
produce alienation, yet every one has their pouch into which all
these little oppositions are put: while that is filling, the alienation is insensibly going on, and when filled it is complete. It
would puzzle either to say why; because no one difference of
opinion has been marked enough to produce a serious effect by
itself. But he finds his affections wearied out by a constant
stream of little checks and obstacles. Other sources of discon-
tent, very common indeed, are the little cross purposes of husband and wife, in common conversation, a disposition in either
to criticize and question whatever the other says, a desire always
to demonstrate and make him feel himself in the wrong, and
especially in company. Nothing is so goading. Much better,
therefore, if our companion views a thing in a light different
from what we do, to leave him in quiet possession of his view.
What is the use of rectifying him, if the thing be unimportant;
and if important, let it pass for the present, and wait a softer

moment and more conciliatory occasion of revising the subject together. It is wonderful how many persons are rendered unhappy by inattention to these little rules of prudence. I have been insensibly led, by the particular case you mention, to sermonize you on the subject generally; however, if it be the means of saving you from a single heartache, it will have contributed a great deal to my happiness—but before I finish the sermon, I must add a word on economy. The unprofitable condition of Virginia estates in general, leaves it now next to impossible for the holder of one to avoid ruin. And this condition will continue until some change takes place in the mode of working them. In the meantime, nothing can save us and our children from beggary, but a determination to get a year beforehand, and restrain ourselves vigorously this year to the clear profits of the last. If a debt is once contracted by a farmer, it is never paid but by a sale. The article of dress is perhaps that in which economy is the least to be recommended. It is so important to each to continue to please the other, that the happiness of both requires the most pointed attention to whatever may contribute to it—and the more as time makes greater inroads on our person. Yet, generally, we become slovenly in proportion as personal decay requires the contrary. I have great comfort in believing that your understanding and dispositions will engage your attention to these considerations; and that you are connected with a person and family who, of all within the circle of my acquaintance, are most in the dispositions which will make you happy. Cultivate their affections, my dear, with assiduity. Think every sacrifice a gain, which shall tend to attach them to you. My only object in life is to see yourself and your sister, and those deservedly dear to you, not only happy, but in no danger of becoming unhappy.

To Martha Jefferson Randolph

February 8, 1798   *Philadelphia*

I ought oftener, my dear Martha, to receive your letters, for the very great pleasure they give me, and especially when they express your affections for me; for, though I cannot doubt them, yet they are among those truths which, though not doubted, we love to hear repeated. Here, too, they serve, like gleams of light, to cheer a dreary scene; where envy, hatred, malice, revenge, and all the worst passions of men, are marshalled, to make one another as miserable as possible. I turn from this with pleasure, to contrast it with your fireside, where the single evening I passed at it was worth more than ages here. Indeed, I find myself detaching very fast, perhaps too fast, from everything but yourself, your sister, and those who are identified with you. These form the last hold the world will have on me, the cords which will be cut only when I am loosened from this state of being.

To Martha Jefferson Randolph

May 17, 1798   *Philadelphia*

Having nothing of business to write on to Mr. Randolph this week, I with pleasure take up my pen to express all my love to you, and my wishes once more to find myself in the only scene where, for me, the sweeter affections of life have any exercise. . . . For you to feel all the happiness of your quiet situation, you should know the rancorous passions which tear every breast here, even of the sex which should be a stranger to them. Politics and party hatreds destroy the happiness of every being here. They seem, like salamanders, to consider fire as their element. The children, I am afraid, will have forgotten me. However, my memory may perhaps be hung on the Game of the Goose which I am to carry them. Kiss them for me, . . . And to yourself, my tenderest love, and adieu,

TH: JEFFERSON

To Elbridge Gerry *

January 26, 1799   *Philadelphia*

I had myself, during the whole of your absence, as well as since your return, been a constant butt for every shaft of calumny which malice and falsehood could form, and the presses, public speakers, or private letters disseminate. . . . In confutation of these and all future calumnies, by way of antic-ipation, I shall make to you a profession of my political faith; in confidence that you will consider every future imputation on me of a contrary complexion, as bearing on its front the mark of falsehood and calumny.

I do then, with sincere zeal, wish an inviolable preservation of our present Federal Constitution, according to the true sense in which it was adopted by the States, that in which it was ad-vocated by its friends, and not that which its enemies appre-hended, who therefore became its enemies; and I am opposed to the monarchizing its features by the forms of its administra-tion, with a view to conciliate a first transition to a President and Senate for life, and from that to an hereditary tenure of these offices, and thus to worm out the elective principle. I am for preserving to the States the powers not yielded by them to the Union, and to the legislature of the Union its constitu-

---

* Gerry (1744-1814) was a signer of the Declaration of Independence, Gov-ernor of Massachusetts, and Vice-President of the United States (elected in 1812); Jefferson had won him over from the Federalists to his own Republican (Demo-cratic) party.

tional share in the division of powers; and I am not for trans-
ferring all the powers of the States to the general government,
and all those of that government to the executive branch. I am
for a government rigorously frugal and simple, applying all the
possible savings of the public revenue to the discharge of the
national debt; and not for a multiplication of officers and salaries merely to make partisans, and for increasing, by every
device, the public debt, on the principle of its being a public
blessing. I am for relying, for internal defense, on our militia
solely, till actual invasion, and for such a naval force only as
may protect our coasts and harbors from such depredations as
we have experienced; and not for a standing army in time of
peace, which may overawe the public sentiment; nor for a navy,
which, by its own expenses and the eternal wars in which it will
implicate us, will grind us with public burthens, and sink us
under them. I am for free commerce with all nations; political
connection with none; and little or no diplomatic establishment. And I am not for linking ourselves by new treaties with
the quarrels of Europe; entering that field of slaughter to preserve their balance, or joining in the confederacy of kings to
war against the principles of liberty. I am for freedom of religion, and against all maneuvers to bring about a legal ascend-
ancy of one sect over another: for freedom of the press, and
against all violations of the Constitution to silence by force and
not by reason the complaints or criticisms, just or unjust, of our
citizens against the conduct of their agents. And I am for encouraging the progress of science in all its branches; and not
for raising a hue and cry against the sacred name of philosophy;
for awing the human mind by stories of raw head and bloody
bones to a distrust of its own vision, and to repose implicitly
on that of others; to go backwards instead of forwards to look
for improvement; to believe that government, religion, morality, and every other science were in the highest perfection in
ages of the darkest ignorance, and that nothing can ever be
devised more perfect than what was established by our fore-
fathers. To these I will add, that I was a sincere well-wisher to

the success of the French Revolution, and still wish it may end in the establishment of a free and well-ordered republic; but I have not been insensible under the atrocious depredations they have committed on our commerce.

The first object of my heart is my own country. In that is embarked my family, my fortune, and my own existence. I have not one farthing of interest, nor one fibre of attachment out of it, nor a single motive of preference of any one nation to another, but in proportion as they are more or less friendly to us. . . .

These, my friend, are my principles; they are unquestionably the principles of the great body of our fellow citizens, and I know there is not one of them which is not yours also.

To Robert R. Livingston *

February 23, 1799   *Philadelphia*

Dear Sir, I have received with great pleasure your favor on the subject of the steam engine. Though deterred by the complexity of that hitherto known, from making myself minutely acquainted with it, yet I am sufficiently acquainted with it to be sensible of the superior simplicity of yours, and its superior economy. I particularly thank you for the permission to communicate it to the Philosophical Society; and though there will not be another session before I leave town, yet I have taken care, by putting it into the hands of one of the Vice-Presidents to-day, to have it presented at the next meeting. I lament the not receiving it a fortnight sooner, that it might have been inserted in a volume now closed, and to be published

---

* Livingston (1746-1813) helped to draw up the Declaration of Independence, was American Ambassador to Paris, 1801-05, and negotiated the Louisiana Purchase.

in a few days, before it would be possible for this engraving to be ready. There is one object to which I have often wished a steam engine could be adopted. You know how desirable it is both in town and country to be able to have large reservoirs of water on the top of our houses, not only for use (by pipes) in the apartments, but as a resource against fire. This last is most especially a desideratum in the country. We might indeed have water carried from time to time in buckets to cisterns on the top of the house, but this is troublesome, and therefore we never do it—consequently are without resource when a fire happens. Could any agent be employed which would be little or no additional expense or trouble except the first purchase, it would be done. Every family has such an agent, its kitchen fire. It is small indeed, but if its small but constant action could be accumulated so as to give a stroke from time to time which might throw ever so small a quantity of water from the bottom of a well to the top of the house (say one hundred feet), it would furnish more than would waste by evaporation, or be used by the family. I know nobody who must better know the value of such a machine than yourself, nor more equal to the invention of it, and especially with your familiarity with the subject. I have imagined that the iron back of the chimney might be a cistern for holding the water, which should supply steam and would be constantly kept in a boiling state by the ordinary fire. I wish the subject may appear as interesting to you as it does to me, it would then engage your attention, and we might hope this desideratum would be supplied.

To Joseph Priestley *

January 27, 1800   *Philadelphia*

Dear Sir, In my last letter of the 18th, I omitted to say anything of the languages as part of our proposed university. It was not that I think, as some do, that they are useless. I am of a very different opinion. I do not think them essential to the obtaining eminent degrees of science; but I think them very useful towards it. I suppose there is a portion of life during which our faculties are ripe enough for this, and for nothing more useful. I think the Greeks and Romans have left us the present models which exist of fine composition, whether we examine them as works of reason, or of style and fancy; and to them we probably owe these characteristics of modern composition. I know of no composition of any other ancient people, which merits the least regard as a model for its matter or style. To all this I add, that to read the Latin and Greek authors in their original, is a sublime luxury; and I deem luxury in science to be at least as justifiable as in architecture, painting, gardening, or the other arts. I enjoy Homer in his own language infinitely beyond Pope's translation of him, and both beyond the dull narrative of the same events by Dares Phrygius; and it is an innocent enjoyment. I thank on my knees, him who directed my early education, for having put into my possession this rich source of delight; and I would not exchange it for anything which I could then have acquired, and have not since acquired.

---

* Priestley (1733-1804), the famous English scientist who discovered oxygen, was also a Unitarian minister whose ideas on religion influenced those of Jefferson.

To Samuel Adams

February 26, 1800   *Philadelphia*

Dear Sir, Mr. Erving delivered me your favor of January 31st, and I thank you for making me acquainted with him. You will always do me a favor in giving me an opportunity of knowing gentlemen as estimable in their principles and talents as I find Mr. Erving to be. I have not yet seen Mr. Winthrop. A letter from you, my respectable friend, after three and twenty years of separation, has given me a pleasure I cannot express. It recalls to my mind the anxious days we then passed in struggling for the cause of mankind. Your principles have been tested in the crucible of time, and have come out pure. You have proved that it was monarchy, and not merely British monarchy, you opposed. A government by representatives, elected by the people at *short* periods, was our object; and our maxim at that day was, "where annual election ends, tyranny begins;" nor have our departures from it been sanctioned by the happiness of their effects. A debt of a hundred millions growing by usurious interest, and an artificial paper phalanx overruling the agricultural mass of our country, with other *et ceteras,* have a portentous aspect.

I fear our friends on the other side of the water, laboring in the same cause, have yet a great deal of crime and misery to wade through. My confidence has been placed in the head, not in the heart of Bonaparte. I hoped he would calculate truly the difference between the fame of a Washington and a Cromwell. Whatever his views may be, he has at least transferred the destinies of the republic from the civil to the military arm. Some will use this as a lesson against the practicability of republican government. I read it as a lesson against the danger of standing armies.

Adieu, my ever respected and venerable friend. May that kind overruling providence which has so long spared you to our country, still foster your remaining years with whatever may make them comfortable to yourself and soothing to your friends. Accept the cordial salutations of your affectionate friend,

TH: JEFFERSON

To Uriah McGregory

August 13, 1800   *Monticello*

Sir, Your favor of July the 19th has been received, and received with the tribute of respect due to a person, who, unurged by motives of personal friendship or acquaintance, and unaided by particular information, will so far exercise his justice as to advert to the proofs of approbation given a public character by his own State and by the United States, and weigh them in the scale against the fatherless calumnies he hears uttered against him. These public acts are known even to those who know nothing of my private life, and surely are better evidence to a mind disposed to truth, than slanders which no man will affirm on his own knowledge, or ever saw one who would. From the moment that a portion of my fellow citizens looked towards me with a view to one of their highest offices, the floodgates of calumny have been opened upon me; not where I am personally known, where their slanders would be instantly judged and suppressed, from a general sense of their falsehood; but in the remote parts of the union, where the means of detection are not at hand, and the trouble of an inquiry is greater than would suit the hearers to undertake. I know that I might have filled the courts of the United States with actions for these slanders, and have ruined perhaps many persons who are not innocent. But this would be no equivalent to the loss of character. I leave them, therefore, to the reproof of their own consciences. If these do not condemn them, there will yet come a day when the false witness will meet a judge who has not slept over his slanders. If the Reverend Cotton Mather Smith of Shena believed this as firmly as I do, he would surely never have affirmed that "I had obtained my property by fraud and robbery; that in one instance, I had defrauded and robbed a widow and fatherless children of an estate to which I was executor, of ten thousand pounds sterling, by keeping the property and paying them in money at the nominal rate, when it was worth no more than forty for one; and that all this could be proved." Every tittle of it is fable; there not having existed a single circumstance of my life to which any part of it can hang. I never was executor but in two instances, both of which having taken place about the beginning of the Revolution, which withdrew me immediately from all private pursuits, I never meddled in either executorship. In one of the cases only, were there a widow and children. She was my sister. She retained and managed the estate in her own hands, and no part of it was ever in mine. In the other, I was a copartner, and only received on a division the equal portion allotted me. To neither of these executorships, therefore, could Mr. Smith refer. Again, my property is all patrimonial, except about seven or eight hundred pounds' worth of lands, purchased by myself and paid for, not to widows and orphans, but to the very gentleman from whom I purchased. If Mr. Smith, therefore, thinks the precepts of the gospel intended for those who preach them as well as for others, he will doubtless some day feel the duties of repentance, and of acknowledgment in such forms as to correct the wrong he has done. Perhaps he will have to wait till the passions of the moment have passed away. All this is left to his own conscience.

These, sir, are facts, well known to every person in this quarter, which I have committed to paper for your own satisfaction, and that of those to whom you may choose to mention them. I only pray that my letter may not go out of your own hands, lest it should get into the newspapers, a bear-garden

scene into which I have made it a point to enter on no provo-
cation.

I am, sir, your most obedient humble servant,

TH: JEFFERSON

To Benjamin Rush *

September 23, 1800   *Monticello*

Dear Sir, I have to acknowledge the receipt of your favor
of August the 22d, and to congratulate you on the healthiness
of your city. Still Baltimore, Norfolk and Providence admonish
us that we are not clear of our new scourge. When great evils
happen, I am in the habit of looking out for what good may
arise from them as consolations to us, and Providence has in
fact so established the order of things, as that most evils are the
means of producing some good. The yellow fever will discourage the growth of great cities in our nation, and I view great
cities as pestilential to the morals, the health and the liberties
of man. True, they nourish some of the elegant arts, but the
useful ones can thrive elsewhere, and less perfection in the
others, with more health, virtue and freedom, would be my
choice.

I agree with you entirely, in condemning the mania of giving
names to objects of any kind after persons still living. Death
alone can seal the title of any man to this honor, by putting it
out of his power to forfeit it. There is one other mode of re-
cording merit, which I have often thought might be introduced,
so as to gratify the living by praising the dead. In giving, for
instance, a commission of Chief Justice to Bushrod Washington, it should be in consideration of his integrity, and science
in the laws, and of the services rendered to our country by his

* Rush (1745-1813) was a distinguished physician, signer of the Declaration of
Independence, Surgeon-General of the Continental Army, and professor of medicine at the University of Pennsylvania.

illustrious relation. . . . A commission to a descendant of Dr. Franklin, besides being in consideration of the proper qualifications of the person, should add that of the great services rendered by his illustrious ancestor, Benjamin Franklin, by the advancement of science, by inventions useful to man. . . . I am not sure that we ought to change all our names. And during the regal government, sometimes, indeed, they were given through adulation; but often also as the reward of the merit of the times, sometimes for services rendered the colony. Perhaps, too, a name when given, should be deemed a sacred property.

I promised you a letter on Christianity, which I have not forgotten. On the contrary, it is because I have reflected on it, that I find much more time necessary for it than I can at present dispose of. I have a view of the subject which ought to displease neither the rational Christian nor Deists, and would reconcile many to a character they have too hastily rejected. I do not know that it would reconcile the *genus irritabile vatum* who are all in arms against me. Their hostility is on too interesting ground to be softened. The delusion into which the X. Y. Z. plot showed it possible to push the people; the successful experiment made under the prevalence of that delusion on the clause of the Constitution, which, while it secured the freedom of the press, covered also the freedom of religion, had given to the clergy a very favorite hope of obtaining an establishment of a particular form of Christianity through the United States; and as every sect believes its own form the true one, every one perhaps hoped for his own, but especially the Episcopalians and Congregationalists. The returning good sense of our country threatens abortion to their hopes, and they believe that any portion of power confided to me, will be exerted in opposition to their schemes. And they believe rightly: for *I have sworn upon the altar of God, eternal hostility against every form of tyranny over the mind of man.** But this is all they have to fear from me: and enough too in their opinion. And this is the cause

---

* My italics: SKP. These words are now inscribed inside the Jefferson monument in Washington, D.C.

of their printing lying pamphlets against me, forging conversations for me with Mazzei, Bishop Madison . . . which are absolute falsehoods without a circumstance of truth to rest on;
falsehoods, too, of which I acquit Mazzei and Bishop Madison,
for they are men of truth.

To Hugh Williamson *

January 10, 1801   *Washington*

I suppose the opinion to be universal that the turkey is
a native of America. Nobody, as far as I know, has ever con-
tradicted it but Daines Barrington; and the arguments he produces are such as none but a head, entangled and kinked as his
is, would ever have urged. Before the discovery of America, no
such bird is mentioned in a single author, all those quoted by
Barrington, by description referring to the crane, hen, pheasant
or peacock; but the book of every traveller, who came to America soon after its discovery, is full of accounts of the turkey and
its abundance; and immediately after that discovery we find
the turkey served up at the feasts of Europe, as their most extraordinary rarity. Mr. William Strickland, the eldest son of
St. George Strickland, of York, in England, told me the anec-
dote. Some ancestor of his commanded a vessel in the naviga-
tions of Cabot. Having occasion to consult the Herald's office
concerning his family, he found a petition from that ancestor
to the crown, stating that Cabot's circumstances being slender,
he had been rewarded by the bounties he needed from the
crown; that as to himself, he asked nothing in that way, but that
as a consideration for his services in the same way, he might be
permitted to assume for the crest of his family arms, the turkey,

* Williamson (1735-1819) was a writer, doctor and politician; he represented
North Carolina in Congress.

an American bird; and Mr. Strickland observed that their crest is actually a turkey. You ask whether we may be quoted. In the first place, I now state the thing from memory, and may be inexact in some small circumstances. Mr. Strickland, too, stated it to me in a conversation, and not considering it of importance, might be inexact too. We should both dislike to be questioned before the public for any little inaccuracy of style or recollection. I think if you were to say that the Herald's office may be referred to in proof of the fact, it would be authority sufficient, without naming us.

To William Dunbar *

January 12, 1801   *Washington*

Dear Sir, Your favor of July 14th, with the papers accompanying it, came safely to hand about the last of October. That containing remarks on the line of demarcation I perused according to your permission, and with great satisfaction, and then enclosed to a friend in Philadelphia, to be forwarded to its address. The papers addressed to me, I took the liberty of communicating to the Philosophical Society. That on the language by signs is quite new. Soon after receiving your meteorological diary, I received one of Quebec; and was struck with the comparison between—32 and 19¾ the lowest depression of the thermometer at Quebec and the Natchez. I have often wondered that any human being should live in a cold country who can find room in a warm one. I have no doubt but that cold is the source of more sufferance to all animal nature than hunger, thirst, sickness, and all the other pains of life and of death itself put together. I live in a temperate climate, and under circumstances which do not expose me often to cold. Yet when I recollect on one hand all the sufferings I have had from cold, and

* Dunbar (1749-1810) was a Mississippi planter and scientist.

on the other all my other pains, the former preponderate greatly. What then must be the sum of that evil if we take in the vast proportion of men who are obliged to be out in all weather, by land and by sea, all the families of beasts, birds, reptiles, and even the vegetable kingdom! for that too has life, and where there is life there may be sensation. I remark a rainbow of a great portion of the circle observed by you when on the line of demarcation. I live in a situation which has given me an opportunity of seeing more than the semicircle often. I am on a hill five hundred feet perpendicularly high. On the west side it breaks down abruptly to the base, where a river passes through. A rainbow, therefore, about sunset, plunges one of its legs down to the river, five hundred feet below the level of the eye on the top of the hill. I have twice seen bows formed by the moon. They were of the color of the common circle round the moon, and were very near, being within a few paces of me in both instances. I thank you for the little vocabularies of Bedais, Tankawis and Teghas. I have it much at heart to make as extensive a collection as possible of the Indian tongues. I have at present about thirty tolerably full, among which the number radically different, is truly wonderful. It is curious to consider how such handfuls of men, came by different languages, and how they have preserved them so distinct. I at first thought of reducing them all to one orthography, but I soon become sensible that this would occasion two sources of error instead of one. I therefore think it best to keep them in the form of orthography in which they were taken, only noting whether that were English, French, German, or what. I have never been a very punctual correspondent, and it is possible that new duties may make me less so. I hope I shall not on that account lose the benefit of your communications. Philosophical vedette at the distance of one thousand miles, and on the verge of the terra incognita of our continent, is precious to us here. I pray you to accept assurances of my high consideration and esteem, and friendly salutations,

TH: JEFFERSON

PART SEVEN

President

(1801–1809)

JEFFERSON entered the *White House, which he helped to design,* at the age of nearly fifty-eight and he remained in office for eight years. His first Administration was so prosperous and popular that he was re-elected almost unanimously in 1804. He made the Republican (Democratic) party a national power, democratized political institutions, reduced taxes, and doubled the territory of the United States by his purchase of the Louisiana Territory from Napoleon. His second Administration was troubled by international violence. To steer a neutral course in the global conflict between Napoleon and the British Empire, both of which violated American rights, the President ran into insoluble difficulties. He managed to keep America out of the war but brought much criticism upon himself. At the age of sixty-six he left the White House and retired permanently from politics. His intimate friend and protégé James Madison succeeded him as President.*

---

* See Saul K. Padover, *Thomas Jefferson and the National Capital* (Government Printing Office: Washington, 1946).

To Joseph Priestley

Dear Sir, I learned some time ago that you were in Philadelphia, but that it was only for a fortnight; and I supposed you
were gone. It was not till yesterday I received information that
you were still there, had been very ill, but were on the recovery.
I sincerely rejoice that you are so. Yours is one of the few lives
precious to mankind, and for the continuance of which every
thinking man is solicitous. Bigots may be an exception. What
an effort, my dear sir, of bigotry in politics and religion have we
gone through! The barbarians really flattered themselves they
should be able to bring back the times of vandalism, when ignorance put everything into the hands of power and priestcraft.
All advances in science were proscribed as innovations. They
pretended to praise and encourage education, but it was to be
the education of our ancestors. We were to look backwards, not
forwards, for improvement; the President himself declaring, in
one of his answers to addresses, that we were never to expect to
go beyond them in real science. This was the real ground of all
the attacks on you. Those who live by mystery and *charlatan-
erie,* fearing you would render them useless by simplifying the
Christian philosophy—the most sublime and benevolent, but
most perverted system that ever shone on man—endeavored to
crush your well-earned and well-deserved fame. But it was the
Lilliputians upon Gulliver. Our countrymen have recovered
from the alarm into which art and industry had thrown them;
science and honesty are replaced on their high ground; and you,
my dear sir, as their great apostle, are on its pinnacle. It is with
heartfelt satisfaction that, in the first moments of my public
action, I can hail you with welcome to our land, tender to you
the homage of its respect and esteem, cover you under the protection of those laws which were made for the wise and good

like you, and disdain the legitimacy of that libel on legislation, which, under the form of a law, was for some time placed among them.*

As the storm is now subsiding, and the horizon becoming serene, it is pleasant to consider the phenomenon with attention. We can no longer say there is nothing new under the sun. For this whole chapter in the history of man is new. The great extent of our republic is new. Its sparse habitation is new. The mighty wave of public opinion which has rolled over it is new. But the most pleasing novelty is, its so quietly subsiding over such an extent of surface to its true level again. The order and good sense displayed in this recovery from delusion, and in the momentous crisis which lately arose, really bespeak a strength of character in our nation which augurs well for the duration of our republic; and I am much better satisfied now of its stability than I was before it was tried. I have been, above all things, solaced by the prospect which opened on us, in the event of a non-election of a President; in which case, the Federal government would have been in the situation of a clock or watch run down. There was no idea of force, nor of any occasion for it. A convention, invited by the republican members of Congress, with the virtual President and Vice-President, would have been on the ground in eight weeks, would have repaired the Constitution where it was defective, and wound it up again.

To George Jefferson

March 27, 1801   *Washington*

Dear Sir, I have to acknowledge the receipt of yours of March 4th, and to express to you the delight with which I found the just, disinterested, and honorable point of view in

---

* In the margin Jefferson wrote, "Alien law."

which you saw the proposition it covered. The resolution you so properly approved had long been formed in my mind. The public will never be made to believe that an appointment of a relative is made on the ground of merit alone, uninfluenced by family views; nor can they ever see with approbation offices, the disposal of which they entrust to their Presidents for public purposes, divided out as family property. Mr. Adams degraded himself infinitely by his conduct on this subject, as General Washington had done himself the greatest honor. With two such examples to proceed by, I should be doubly inexcusable to err. It is true that this places the relations of the President in a worse situation than if he were a stranger, but the public good, which cannot be affected if its confidence be lost, requires this sacrifice. Perhaps, too, it is compensated by sharing in the public esteem. I could not be satisfied till I assured you of the increased esteem with which this transaction fills me for you. Accept my affectionate expressions of it,

TH: JEFFERSON

To Samuel Adams

March 29, 1801 *Washington*

I addressed a letter to you, my very dear and ancient friend, on the 4th of March: not indeed to you by name, but through the medium of some of my fellow citizens, whom occasion called on me to address. In meditating the matter of that address, I often asked myself, is this exactly in the spirit of the patriarch, Samuel Adams? Is it as he would express it? Will he approve of it? I have felt a great deal for our country in the times we have seen. But individually for no one so much as yourself. When I have been told that you were avoided, insulted, frowned on, I could but ejaculate, "Father, forgive them, for they know not what they do." I confess I felt an indignation for you, which for myself I have been able, under every trial, to keep entirely passive. However, the storm is over, and we are in port. The ship was not rigged for the service she was put on. We will show the smoothness of her motions on her republican tack. I hope we shall once more see harmony restored among our citizens, and an entire oblivion of past feuds. Some of the leaders who have most committed themselves cannot come into this. But I hope the great body of our fellow citizens will do it. I will sacrifice everything but principle to procure it. A few examples of justice on officers who have perverted their functions to the oppression of their fellow citizens, must, in justice to those citizens, be made. But opinion, and the just maintenance of it, shall never be a crime in my view: nor bring injury on the individual. Those whose misconduct in office ought to have produced their removal even by my predecessor, must not be protected by the delicacy due only to honest men. How much I lament that time has deprived me of your aid. It would have been a day of glory which should have called you to the first office of the administration. But give us your counsel, my friend, and give us your blessing; and be assured that there exists not in the heart of man a more faithful esteem than mine to you, and that I shall ever bear you the most affectionate veneration and respect,

TH: JEFFERSON

To Elbridge Gerry

March 29, 1801   *Washington*

Officers who have been guilty of gross abuses of office, such as marshals packing juries . . . I shall now remove, as my predecessor ought in justice to have done. The instances will be few, and governed by strict rule, and not party passion. The right of opinion shall suffer no invasion from me. Those who

have acted well have nothing to fear, however they have differed from me in opinion: those who have done ill, however,
have nothing to hope; nor shall I fail to do justice lest it should
be ascribed to that difference of opinion.

A coalition of sentiments is not for the interest of the printers. They, like the clergy, live by the zeal they can kindle, and
the schisms they can create. It is contest of opinion in politics
as well as religion which makes us take great interest in them,
and bestow our money liberally on those who furnish food to
our appetite. The mild and simple principles of the Christian
philosophy would produce too much calm, too much regularity
of good, to extract from its disciples a support from a numerous
priesthood, were they not to sophisticate it, ramify it, split it
into hairs, and twist its texts till they cover the divine morality
of its author with mysteries, and require a priesthood to explain
them. The Quakers seem to have discovered this. They have no
priests, therefore no schisms. They judge of the text by the dictates of common sense and common morality. So the printers
can never leave us in a state of perfect rest and union of opinion. They would be no longer useful, and would have to go to
the plough.

In the first moments of quietude which have succeeded the
election, they seem to have aroused their lying faculties beyond
their ordinary state, to re-agitate the public mind. What appointments to office have they detailed which had never been
thought of, merely to found a text for their calumniating commentaries. However, the steady character of our countrymen is
a rock to which we may safely moor; and notwithstanding the
efforts of the papers to disseminate early discontents, I expect
that a just, dispassionate and steady conduct, will at length rally
to a proper system the great body of our country. Unequivocal
in principle, reasonable in manner, we shall be able I hope to
do a great deal of good to the cause of freedom and harmony.

To Isaac Story *

December 5, 1801   *Washington*

Sir, Your favor of October 27 was received some time since and read with pleasure. It is not for me to pronounce on the hypothesis you present of a transmigration of souls from one body to another in certain cases. The laws of nature have withheld from us the means of physical knowledge of the country of spirits, and revelation has, for reasons unknown to us, chosen to leave us in the dark as we were. When I was young I was fond of the speculations which seemed to promise some insight into that hidden country, but observing at length that they left me in the same ignorance in which they had found me, I have for very many years ceased to read or to think concerning them, and have reposed my head on that pillow of ignorance which a benevolent Creator has made so soft for us, knowing how much we should be forced to use it. I have thought it better, by nourishing the good passions and controlling the bad, to merit an inheritance in a state of being of which I can know so little, and to trust for the future to Him who has been so good for the past. I perceive too that these speculations have with you been only the amusement of leisure hours; while your labors have been devoted to the education of your children, making them good members of society, to the instructing men in their duties, and performing the other offices of a large parish.

---

* Story (1749-1816), a minister in Marblehead, Mass., from 1771 to 1800, was the father of the poet Isaac Story and cousin of the famous U. S. Supreme Court Justice and jurist, Joseph Story.

To Levi Lincoln *

January 1, 1802   *Washington*

Averse to receive addresses, yet unable to prevent them, I have generally endeavored to turn them to some account, by making them the occasion, by way of answer, of sowing useful truths and principles among the people, which might germinate and become rooted among their political tenets. The Baptist address, now enclosed, admits of a condemnation of the alliance between church and state, under the authority of the Constitution. It furnishes an occasion, too, which I have long wished to find, of saying why I do not proclaim fastings and thanksgivings, as my predecessors did. The address, to be sure, does not point at this, and its introduction is awkward. But I foresee no opportunity of doing it more pertinently. I know it will give great offense to the New England clergy; but the advocate of religious freedom is to expect neither peace nor forgiveness from them. Will you be so good as to examine the answer, and suggest any alterations which might prevent an ill effect, or promote a good one, among the people? You understand the temper of those in the North, and can weaken it, therefore, to their stomachs: it is at present seasoned to the Southern taste only. I would ask the favor of you to return it, with the address, in the course of the day or evening. Health and affection,

TH: JEFFERSON

---

* Lincoln (1749-1820) was Jefferson's Attorney-General from 1801 to 1805 and Acting Governor of Massachusetts in 1808-09.

To Dupont de Nemours *

January 18, 1802   *Washington*

Dear Sir, It is rare I can indulge myself in the luxury of philosophy. Your letters give me a few of these delicious moments. Placed as you are in a great commercial town, with little opportunity of discovering the dispositions of the country portions of our citizens, I do not wonder at your doubts whether they will generally and sincerely concur in the sentiment and measures developed in my message of the 7th of January. But from forty-one years of intimate connection with the agricultural inhabitants of my country, I can pronounce them as different from those of the cities, as those of any two nations known. The sentiments of the former can in no degree be inferred from those of the latter. You have spoken a profound truth in these words *"il y a dans les États-Unis un bon sens silencieux, un esprit de justice froide, qui, lorsqu'il est question d'émettre un vote, couvre tous les bavardages de ceux qui font les habiles."* A plain country farmer has written recently a pamphlet on our public affairs. His testimony of the sense of the country is the best which can be produced of the justness of your observation. His words are the tongue of man if not his whole body, so in this case the noisy part of the community was not all the body politic. During the career of fury and contention (in 1800) the sedate, grave part of the people were still, hearing all, and judging for themselves what method to take, when the constitutional time of action should come, the exercise of the right of suffrage. The majority of the present legislature are in unison with the agricultural part of our citizens and you will see that there is nothing in the message, to which they do not accord. Something may perhaps be left undone from motives of compromise for a time, and not to claim by too

---

* Pierre Samuel Dupont de Nemours (1739-1817), the French economist, settled in the United States in 1799.

sudden a reformation; but with a view to be resumed at another time. I am perfectly satisfied the effect of the proceedings of this session of Congress will be to consolidate the present body of well meaning citizens together, whether Federal or Republican, heretofore called. I do not mean to include royalists or priests, their opposition is unmovable, but they will be *vox et preterea nihil,* leaders without followers. I am satisfied that within one year from this time were an election to take place between two candidates, merely Republican and Federal, where no personal opposition existed against either, the Federal candidate would not get the vote of a single elector in the United States.

It was my destiny to come to the government when it had for several years been committed to a particular political sect, to the absolute and entire exclusion of those who were in sentiment with the body of the nation. I found the country entirely in the enemy's hands. It was necessary to dislodge some of them, out of the thousands of officers in the United States. Nine only have been removed for political principle and eighteen for delinquencies chiefly pecuniary. The whole herd have squealed out as if all their throats were cut. These acts of justice, few as they have been, have raised great personal objections to me, of which a new character would be [unclear]. When this government was first established, it was possible to have set it going on two principles, but the contracted-English half-lettered ideas of Hamilton destroyed that hope in the bud. We can pay off his debt in fifteen years but we can never get rid of his financial system. It mortifies me to be strengthened by principles which I deem radically vicious, but this vice is entailed on us by a just error. In other parts of our government I hope we shall be able by degrees to introduce sound principles and make them habitual. What is practicable must often control what is pure theory, and the habits of the governed determine in a great degree what is practicable. Hence the same original principles, modified in practice according to the different habits of different nations, present governments of very different aspects. The same principles reduced to forms of practice accommodated to our habits, and put into forms accommodated to the habits of the French nation would present governments very unlike each other. I have no doubt that a great man, thoroughly knowing the habits of France, might so accommodate to them the principles of free governments, as to enable them to live free. But in the hands of those who have not this *coup d'oeil* many unsuccessful experiments I fear are yet to be tried before they will settle down in freedom and tranquillity. I applaud therefore your determination to remain here, where, though for yourself and the adults of your family the dissimilitude of our manners and the difference of tongue will be sources of real unhappiness, yet lesser than the horrors and dangers which France would present to you; and as to those of your family still in infancy, they will be formed to the circumstances of the country, and will, I doubt not, be happier here than they could have been in Europe, under any circumstances.

To Maria Jefferson Eppes

March 3, 1802   *Washington*

I think I discover in you a willingness to withdraw from society more than is prudent. I am convinced our own happiness requires that we should continue to mix with the world, and to keep pace with it as it goes; and that every person who retires from free communication with it is severely punished afterwards by the state of mind into which he gets, and which can only be prevented from feeding our sociable principles. I can speak from experience on this subject. From 1793 to 1797 I remained closely at home, saw none but those who came there, and at length became very sensible of the ill effect it had upon my own mind, and of its direct and irresistible tendency to render me unfit for society and uneasy when necessarily engaged in it. I felt enough of the effect of withdrawing from the world then, to see that it led to an anti-social and misanthropic state of mind, which severely punishes him who gives in to it; and it will be a lesson I shall never forget.

To Joseph Priestley

April 9, 1803 *Washington*

Dear Sir, While on a short visit lately to Monticello, I received from you a copy of your comparative view of Socrates and Jesus, and I avail myself of the first moment of leisure after my return to acknowledge the pleasure I had in the perusal of it, and the desire it excited to see you take up the subject on a more extended scale. In consequence of some conversation with Dr. Rush, in the year 1798-99, I had promised some day to write him a letter giving him my view of the Christian system. I have reflected often on it since, and even sketched the outlines in my own mind. I should first take a general view of the moral doctrines of the most remarkable of the ancient philosophers, of whose ethics we have sufficient information to make an estimate, say Pythagoras, Epicurus, Epictetus, Socrates, Cicero, Seneca, Antoninus. I should do justice to the branches of morality they have treated well; but point out the importance of those in which they are deficient. I should then take a view of the deism and ethics of the Jews, and show in what a degraded state they were, and the necessity they presented of a reformation. I should proceed to a view of the life, character, and doctrines of Jesus, who sensible of incorrectness of their ideas of the Deity, and of morality, endeavored to bring them to the principles of a pure deism, and juster notions of the attributes of God, to reform their moral doctrines to the standard of reason, justice and philanthropy, and to inculcate the belief of a future state. This view would purposely omit the question of his divinity, and even his inspiration. To do him justice, it would be necessary to remark the disadvantages his doctrines had to encounter, not having been committed to writing by himself, but by the most unlettered of men, by memory, long after they had heard them from him; when much was forgotten, much misunderstood, and presented in every paradoxical shape. Yet such are the fragments remaining as to show a master workman, and that his system of morality was the most benevolent and sublime probably that has been ever taught, and consequently more perfect than those of any of the ancient philosophers. His character and doctrines have received still greater injury from those who pretend to be his special disciples, and who have disfigured and sophisticated his actions and precepts, from views of personal interest, so as to induce the unthinking part of mankind to throw off the whole system in disgust, and to pass sentence as an impostor on the most innocent, the most benevolent, the most eloquent and sublime character that ever has been exhibited to man. This is the outline; but I have not the time, and still less the information which the subject needs. It will therefore rest with me in contemplation only. You are the person of all others would do it best, and most promptly. You have all the materials at hand, and you put together with ease. I wish you could be induced to extend your late work to the whole subject. I have not heard particularly what is the state of your health; but as it has been equal to the journey to Philadelphia, perhaps it might encourage the curiosity you must feel to see for once this place, which nature has formed on a beautiful scale, and circumstances destine for a great one. As yet we are but a cluster of villages; we cannot offer you the learned society of Philadelphia; but you will have that of a few characters whom you esteem, and a bed and hearty welcome with one who will rejoice in every opportunity of testifying to you his high veneration and affectionate attachment.

To Edward Dowse

April 19, 1803   *Washington*

Dear Sir, I now return the sermon you were so kind as to enclose me, having perused it with attention. The reprinting it by me, as you have proposed, would very readily be ascribed to hypocritical affectation, by those who, when they cannot blame our acts, have recourse to the expedient of imputing them to bad motives. This is a resource which can never fail them, because there is no act, however virtuous, for which ingenuity may not find some bad motive. I must also add that though I concur with the author in considering the moral precepts of Jesus as more pure, correct, and sublime than those of the ancient philosophers, yet I do not concur with him in the mode of proving it. He thinks it necessary to libel and decry the doctrines of the philosophers; but a man must be blinded indeed by prejudice, who can deny them a great degree of merit. I give them their just due, and yet maintain that the morality of Jesus, as taught by himself, and freed from the corruptions of latter times, is far superior. Their philosophy went chiefly to the government of our passions, so far as respected ourselves, and the procuring our own tranquillity. In our duties to others they were short and deficient. They extended their cares scarcely beyond our kindred and friends individually, and our country in the abstract. Jesus embraced with charity and philanthropy our neighbors, our countrymen, and the whole family of mankind. They confined themselves to actions; he pressed his sentiments into the region of our thoughts, and called for purity at the fountain head. In a pamphlet lately published in Philadelphia by Dr. Priestley,* he has treated, with more justice and skill than Mr. Bennet, a small portion of this subject. His is a comparative view of Socrates only with Jesus. I have urged him to take up the subject on a broader scale.

---

* See Jefferson's letter to Rush, April 21, 1803.

Every word which goes from me, whether verbally or in writing, becomes the subject of so much malignant distortion, and perverted construction, that I am obliged to caution my friends against admitting the possibility of my letters getting into the public papers, or a copy of them to be taken under any degree of confidence. The present one is perhaps of a tenor to silence some calumniators, but I never will, by any word or act, bow to the shrine of intolerance, or admit a right of inquiry into the religious opinions of others. On the contrary, we are bound, you, I, and everyone, to make common cause, even with error itself, to maintain the common right of freedom of conscience. We ought with one heart and one hand to hew down the daring and dangerous efforts of those who would seduce the public opinion to substitute itself into that tyranny over religious faith which the laws have so justly abdicated. For this reason, were my opinions up to the standard of those who arrogate the right of questioning them, I would not countenance that arrogance by descending to an explanation. Accept my friendly salutations and high esteem,

TH: JEFFERSON

To Benjamin Rush

April 21, 1803   *Washington*

Dear Sir, In some of the delightful conversations with you, in the evenings of 1798-99, and which served as an anodyne to the afflictions of the crisis through which our country was then laboring, the Christian religion was sometimes our topic; and I then promised you, that one day or other, I would give you my views of it. They are the result of a life of inquiry and reflection, and very different from that anti-Christian system imputed to me by those who know nothing of my opinions. To the corruptions of Christianity I am indeed opposed; but not to the genuine precepts of Jesus himself. I am a Christian, in the only sense in which he wished any one to be; sincerely attached to his doctrines, in preference to all others; ascribing to himself every *human* excellence; and believing he never claimed any other. At the short intervals since these conversations, when I could justifiably abstract my mind from public affairs, the subject has been under my contemplation. But the more I considered it, the more it expanded beyond the measure of either my time or information. In the moment of my late departure from Monticello, I received from Doctor Priestley, his little treatise of "Socrates and Jesus compared." This being a section of the general view I had taken of the field, it became a subject of reflection while on the road, and unoccupied otherwise. The result was, to arrange in my mind a syllabus, or outline of such an estimate of the comparative merits of Christianity, as I wished to see executed by some one of more leisure and information for the task, than myself. This I now send you, as the only discharge of my promise I can probably ever execute. And in confiding it to you, I know it will not be exposed to the malignant perversions of those who make every word from me a text for new misrepresentations and calumnies. I am, moreover, averse to the communication of my religious tenets to the public; because it would countenance the presumption of those who have endeavored to draw them before that tribunal, and to seduce public opinion to erect itself into that inquisition over the rights of conscience, which the laws have so justly proscribed. It behooves every man who values liberty of conscience for himself, to resist invasions of it in the case of others; or their case may, by change of circumstances, become his own. It behooves him, too, in his own case, to give no example of concession, betraying the common right of independent opinion, by answering questions of faith, which the laws have left between God and himself. Accept my affectionate salutations,

TH: JEFFERSON

To Benjamin Rush

October 4, 1803   *Washington*

Dear Sir, No one would more willingly than myself pay the just tribute due to the services of Captain Barry,* by writing a letter of condolence to his widow, as you suggest. But when one undertakes to administer justice, it must be with an even hand, and by rule; what is done for one, must be done for every one in equal degree. To what a train of attentions would this draw a President? How difficult would it be to draw the line between that degree of merit entitled to such a testimonial of it, and that not so entitled? If drawn in a particular case differently from what the friends of the deceased would judge right, what offense would it give, and of the most tender kind? How much offense would be given by accidental inattentions, or want of information? The first step into such an undertaking ought to be well weighed. On the death of Doctor Franklin, the King and Convention of France went into mourning. So did the House of Representatives of the United States: the Senate refused. I proposed to General Washington that the executive department should wear mourning; he declined it, because he said he should not know where to draw the line, if he once began that ceremony. Mr. Adams was then Vice-President, and I thought General Washington had his eye on him, whom he certainly did not love. I told him the world had drawn so broad a line between himself and Doctor Franklin, on the one side, and the residue of mankind, on the other, that we might wear mourning for them, and the question still remain new and undecided as to all others. He thought it best, however, to avoid it. On these considerations alone, however well affected to the merit of Commodore Barry, I think it prudent not to engage myself in a practice which may become embarrassing.

* John Barry (1745-1803), an American naval officer, distinguished himself during the Revolutionary War.

Tremendous times in Europe! How mighty this battle of lions and tigers! With what sensations should the common herd of cattle look on it? With no partialities, certainly. If they can so far worry one another as to destroy their power of tyrannizing, the one over the earth, the other the waters, the world may perhaps enjoy peace, till they recruit again.

Affectionate and respectful salutations,

TH: JEFFERSON

To Maria Jefferson Eppes

December 26, 1803   *Washington*

Not knowing the time destined for your expected indisposition, I am anxious on your account. You are prepared to meet it with courage, I hope. Some female friend of your mama's (I forget who) used to say it was no more than a jog of the elbow. The material thing is to have scientific aid in readiness, that if anything uncommon takes place it may be redressed on the spot, and not be made serious by delay. It is a case which least of all will wait for doctors to be sent for, therefore with this single precaution nothing is ever to be feared.

To Abigail Adams *

June 13, 1804   *Washington*

Dear Madam, The affectionate sentiments which you have had the goodness to express in your letter of May the 20th, towards my dear departed daughter, † have awakened in me

---

* Abigail Adams (1744-1818) married John Adams in 1764.

† His daughter Maria (Eppes) died on April 17, 1804, at the age of 26.

sensibilities natural to the occasion, and recalled your kind-
nesses to her, which I shall ever remember with gratitude and
friendship. I can assure you with truth, they had made an in-
delible impression on her mind, and that to the last, on our
meetings after long separations, whether I had heard lately of
you, and how you did, were among the earliest of her inquiries.
In giving you this assurance I perform a sacred duty for her,
and, at the same time, am thankful for the occasion furnished
me, of expressing my regret that circumstances should have
arisen, which have seemed to draw a line of separation between
us. The friendship with which you honored me has ever been
valued, and fully reciprocated; and although events have been
passing which might be trying to some minds, I never believed
yours to be of that kind, nor felt that my own was. Neither my
estimate of your character, nor the esteem founded in that, has
ever been lessened for a single moment, although doubts
whether it would be acceptable may have forbidden manifestations of it.

Mr. Adams' friendship and mine began at an earlier date. It
accompanied us through long and important scenes. The different conclusions we had drawn from our political reading and
reflections, were not permitted to lessen personal esteem; each
party being conscious they were the result of an honest conviction in the other. Like differences of opinion existing among
our fellow citizens, attached them to one or the other of us, and
produced a rivalship in their minds which did not exist in ours.
We never stood in one another's way; for if either had been
withdrawn at any time, his favorers would not have gone over
to the other, but would have sought for some one of homogeneous opinions. This consideration was sufficient to keep
down all jealousy between us, and to guard our friendship from
any disturbance by sentiments of rivalship; and I can say with
truth, that one act of Mr. Adams' life, and one only, ever gave
me a moment's personal displeasure. I did consider his last appointments to office as personally unkind. They were from
among my most ardent political enemies, from whom no faith-

ful co-operation could ever be expected; and laid me under the embarrassment of acting through men whose views were to defeat mine, or to encounter the odium of putting others in their places. It seems but common justice to leave a successor free to act by instruments of his own choice. If my respect for him did not permit me to ascribe the whole blame to the influence of others, it left something for friendship to forgive, and after brooding over it for some little time, and not always resisting the expression of it, I forgave it cordially, and returned to the same state of esteem and respect for him which had so long subsisted. Having come into life a little later than Mr. Adams, his career has preceded mine, as mine is followed by some other; and it will probably be closed at the same distance after him which time originally placed between us. I maintain for him, and shall carry into private life, an uniform and high measure of respect and good will, and for yourself a sincere attachment.*

I have thus, my dear madam, opened myself to you without reserve, which I have long wished an opportunity of doing; and without knowing how it will be received, I feel relief from being unbosomed. And I have now only to entreat your forgiveness for this transition from a subject of domestic affliction, to one which seems of a different aspect. But though connected with political events, it has been viewed by me most strongly in its unfortunate bearings on my private friendships. The injury these have sustained has been a heavy price for what has never given me equal pleasure. That you may both be favored with health, tranquillity and long life, is the prayer of one who tenders you the assurance of his highest consideration and esteem,

TH: JEFFERSON

---

* The estrangement between Jefferson and Adams, however, continued until 1812, when the two men began their brilliant correspondence. See Jefferson's letter to Rush, January 16, 1811, and the one to Adams, January 21, 1812.

To Alexander I, Czar of Russia *

June 15, 1804   *Washington*

Great and Good Friend, Your friendly interposition for
the relief of the crew of an American frigate stranded on the
coast of Tripoli has been recently made known to me. For this
act of benevolence and proof of your disposition to befriend our
young republic, its Secretary of State conveys the official expression of its sensibility. But I should illy satisfy my own feelings
did I not add my individual acknowledgments for a favor directly tending to facilitate the administration of affairs of my
country with which I am personally charged. †

To the barbarians whose habitual violations of the laws of
nature have produced the occasion of this friendly office, we
have sent expressions of very different feelings by the squadron
which has just left our ports destined for theirs. Should the
Commodore find that in consequence of your Imperial Majesty's interposition, they shall already have done us voluntary
justice, he will let them owe to your favor his abstinence from

---

* Czar Alexander I (1777-1825) and Jefferson maintained very friendly relations, particularly during the Napoleonic period when the President of the
United States courted the powerful influence of Russia's ruler in the defense of
American neutrality. On April 19, 1806, President Jefferson again wrote to the
Czar: "The northern nations of Europe, at the head of which your Majesty is
distinguished, are habitually peaceable. The United States of America, like them,
are attached to peace. We have then with them a common interest in the
neutral rights. . . . Two personages in Europe, of which your Majesty is one,
have it in their power, at the approaching pacification, to render eminent
service to nations in general, by incorporating . . . a correct definition of the
rights of neutrals on the high seas. . . . By monuments of such good offices, may
your life become an epoch in the history of the condition of man; and may He
who called it into being, for the good of the human family, give it length of
days and success, and have it always in His holy keeping."

† Jefferson always felt that Czar Alexander was a friend of the United States.
On November 13, 1810, he wrote to William Duane: "Of Alexander's sense of
the merits of our form of government . . . and of the interest he takes in the
success of our experiment, we possess the most unquestionable proofs. . . . I
thought it a salutary measure to engage the powerful patronage of Alexander
at conferences for peace, at a time when Bonaparte was courting him; . . . it is
prudent for us to cherish his good dispositions."

every act of force. Otherwise he will endeavor, by the means he is furnished with, to convince them it will be their interest to injure us no more.

I see with great pleasure the rising commerce between our two countries. We have not gone into the policy which the European nations have so long tried and to so little effect of multiplying commercial treaties. In national as in individual dealings, more liberality will, perhaps, be found in voluntary regulations than in those which are measured out by the strict letter of a treaty, which, whenever it becomes onerous, is made by forced construction to mean anything or nothing, engenders disputes and brings on war. But your flag will find in our harbors hospitality, freedom and protection and your subjects enjoy all the privileges of the most favored nation. The favorable reception of our consul at St. Petersburg, and the friendly sentiments conveyed through your Minister of Foreign Affairs, is an earnest that our merchants also will meet due favor in your ports.

I avail myself of this occasion of expressing the exalted pleasure I have felt in observing the various acts of your administration during the short time you have yet been on the throne of your country, and seeing in them manifestations of the virtue and wisdom from which they flow. What has not your country to hope from a career which has begun from such auspicious developments! Sound principles, pursued with a steady step, dealing out good progressively as your people are prepared to receive and to hold it fast, cannot fail to carry them and yourself far in the improvement of their condition during the course of your life.

I pray to God that it may long continue for their happiness and your glory, and that too He may always have you in His safe and holy keeping!

TH: JEFFERSON

To John Page

June 25, 1804   *Washington*

Your letter, my dear friend, of the 25th, is a new proof of the goodness of your heart, and the part you take in my loss marks an affectionate concern for the greatness of it. It is great indeed. Others may lose of their abundance, but I, of my want, have lost even the half of all I had.* My evening prospects now hang on the slender thread of a single life. Perhaps I may be destined to see even this last cord of parental affection broken! The hope with which I had looked forward to the moment, when, resigning public cares to younger hands, I was to retire to that domestic comfort from which the last great step is to be taken, is fearfully blighted. When you and I look back on the country over which we have passed, what a field of slaughter does it exhibit! Where are all the friends who entered it with us, under all the inspiring energies of health and hope? As if pursued by the havoc of war, they are strewed by the way, some earlier, some later, and scarce a few stragglers remain to count the numbers fallen, and to mark yet, by their own fall, the last footsteps of their party. Is it a desirable thing to bear up through the heat of the action, to witness the death of all our companions, and merely be the last victim? I doubt it. We have, however, the traveller's consolation. Every step shortens the distance we have to go; the end of our journey is in sight, the bed wherein we are to rest, and to rise in the midst of the friends we have lost. "We sorrow not then as others who have no hope;" but look forward to the day which "joins us to the great majority." But whatever is to be our destiny, wisdom, as well as duty, dictates that we should acquiesce in the will of Him whose it is to give and take away, and be contented in the enjoyment of those who are still permitted to be with us. Of those connected

---

* The death of Maria in April, 1804, left Jefferson with only one daughter, Martha.

by blood, the number does not depend on us. But friends we have, if we have merited them. Those of our earliest years stand nearest in our affections. But in this too, you and I have been unlucky. Of our college friends (and they are the dearest), how few have stood with us in the great political questions which have agitated our country; and these were of a nature to justify agitation. I did not believe the Lilliputian fetters of that day strong enough to have bound so many. Will not Mrs. Page, yourself and family, think it prudent to seek a healthier region for the months of August and September? And may we not flatter ourselves that you will cast your eye on Monticello? We have not many summers to live. While fortune places us then within striking distance, let us avail ourselves of it, to meet and talk over the tales of other times.

Present me respectfully to Mrs. Page, and accept yourself my friendly salutations, and assurances of constant affection,

TH: JEFFERSON

To John Tyler *

June 28, 1804   *Washington*

Dear Sir, Your favor of the 10th has been duly received. Amidst the direct falsehoods, the misrepresentations of truth, the calumnies and the insults resorted to by a faction to mislead the public mind, and to overwhelm those entrusted with its interests, our support is to be found in the approving voice of our conscience and country, in the testimony of our fellow citizens, that their confidence is not shaken by these artifices. When to the plaudits of the honest multitude, the sober approbation of the sage in his closet is added, it becomes a gratification of an higher order. It is the sanction of wisdom superadded to the

---

* Judge Tyler (1747-1813), the father of President Tyler, and Governor of Virginia from 1808 to 1811, was a friend of Jefferson's.

voice of affection. The terms, therefore, in which you are so good as to express your satisfaction with the course of the present administration cannot but give me great pleasure. I may err in my measures, but never shall deflect from the intention to fortify the public liberty by every possible means, and to put it out of the power of the few to riot on the labors of the many.

No experiment can be more interesting than that we are now trying, and which we trust will end in establishing the fact, that man may be governed by reason and truth. Our first object should therefore be, to leave open to him all the avenues to truth. The most effectual hitherto found, is the freedom of the press. It is, therefore, the first shut up by those who fear the investigation of their actions. The firmness with which the people have withstood the late abuses of the press, the discernment they have manifested between truth and falsehood, show that they may safely be trusted to hear everything true and false, and to form a correct judgment between them. As little is it necessary to impose on their senses, or dazzle their minds by pomp, splendor, or forms. Instead of this artificial, how much surer is that real respect, which results from the use of their reason, and the habit of bringing everything to the test of common sense.

I hold it, therefore, certain, that to open the doors of truth, and to fortify the habit of testing everything by reason, are the most effectual manacles we can rivet on the hands of our successors to prevent their manacling the people with their own consent. The panic into which they were artfully thrown in 1798, the frenzy which was excited in them by their enemies against their apparent readiness to abandon all the principles established for their own protection, seemed for awhile to countenance the opinions of those who say they cannot be trusted with their own government. But I never doubted their rallying; and they did rally much sooner than I expected. On the whole, that experiment on their credulity has confirmed my confidence in their ultimate good sense and virtue.

To Philip Mazzei

July 18, 1804   *Washington*

My dear Sir, It is very long, I know, since I wrote you. So constant is the pressure of business that there is never a moment, scarcely, that something of public importance is not waiting for me. I have, therefore, on a principle of conscience, thought it my duty to withdraw almost entirely from all private correspondence, and chiefly the trans-Atlantic; I scarcely write a letter a year to any friend beyond sea. Another consideration has led to this, which is the liability of my letters to miscarry, be opened, and made ill use of. Although the great body of our country are perfectly returned to their ancient principles, yet there remains a phalanx of old tories and monarchists, more envenomed, as all their hopes become more desperate. Every word of mine which they can get hold of, however innocent, however orthodox even, is twisted, tormented, perverted, and, like the words of holy writ, are made to mean everything but what they were intended to mean. I trust little, therefore, unnecessarily in their way, and especially on political subjects.

To Abigail Adams

July 22, 1804   *Washington*

Dear Madam, Your favor of the 1st was duly received, and I would not have again intruded on you, but to rectify certain facts which seem not to have been presented to you under their true aspect. My charities to Callender are considered as rewards for his calumnies.* As early, I think, as 1796, I was told

---

* During the Presidential campaign of 1800, Jefferson gave $50 to the writer, James T. Callender, who was a victim of the infamous Sedition Act which was passed under the Adams Administration.

in Philadelphia that Callender, the author of the Political
Progress of Britain, was in that city, a fugitive from persecution
for having written that book, and in distress. I had read and approved the book; I considered him as a man of genius, unjustly
persecuted. I knew nothing of his private character, and immediately expressed my readiness to contribute to his relief, and to
serve him. It was a considerable time after, that, on application
from a person who thought of him as I did, I contributed to his relief, and afterwards repeated the contribution. Himself I did
not see till long after, nor ever more than two or three times.
When he first began to write, he told some useful truths in his
coarse way; but nobody sooner disapproved of his writing than
I did, or wished more that he would be silent. My charities to
him were no more meant as encouragements to his scurrilities,
than those I give to the beggar at my door are meant as rewards
for the vices of his life, and to make them chargeable to myself.
In truth, they would have been greater to him, had he never
written a word after the work for which he fled from Britain.
With respect to the calumnies and falsehoods which writers and
printers at large published against Mr. Adams, I was as far from
stooping to any concern or approbation of them, as Mr. Adams
was respecting those of Porcupine, Fenno, or Russel, who published volumes against me for every sentence vended by their
opponents against Mr. Adams. But I never supposed Mr. Adams
had any participation in the atrocities of these editors, or their
writers. I knew myself incapable of that base warfare, and believed him to be so. On the contrary, whatever I may have
thought of the acts of the Administration of that day, I have ever
borne testimony to Mr. Adams' personal worth; nor was it ever
impeached in my presence, without a just vindication of it on
my part. I never supposed that any person who knew either of
us, could believe that either of us meddled in that dirty work.
But another fact is, that I "liberated a wretch who was suffering
for a libel against Mr. Adams." I do not know who was the
particular wretch alluded to; but I discharged every person
under punishment or prosecution under the Sedition Law, be-

cause I considered, and now consider, that law to be a nullity, as absolute and as palpable as if Congress had ordered us to fall down and worship a golden image; and that it was as much my duty to arrest its execution in every stage, as it would have been to have rescued from the fiery furnace those who should have been cast into it for refusing to worship the image. It was accordingly done in every instance, without asking what the offenders had done, or against whom they had offended, but whether the pains they were suffering were inflicted under the pretended Sedition Law. It was certainly possible that my motives for contributing to the relief of Callender, and liberating sufferers under the Sedition Law, might have been to protect, encourage, and reward slander; but they may also have been those which inspire ordinary charities to objects of distress, meritorious or not, or the obligation of an oath to protect the Constitution, violated by an unauthorized act of Congress. Which of these were my motives, must be decided by a regard to the general tenor of my life. On this I am not afraid to appeal to the nation at large, to posterity, and still less to that Being who sees himself our motives, who will judge us from his own knowledge of them, and not on the testimony of Porcupine or Fenno.

You observe, there has been one other act of my Administration personally unkind, and suppose it will readily suggest itself to me. I declare on my honor, madam, I have not the least conception what act was alluded to. I never did a single one with an unkind intention. My sole object in this letter being to place before your attention, that the acts imputed to me are either such as are falsely imputed, or as might flow from good as well as bad motives, I shall make no other addition, than the assurances of my continued wishes for the health and happiness of yourself and Mr. Adams.

TH: JEFFERSON

To Abigail Adams

September 11, 1804   *Monticello*

You seem to think it devolved on the judges to decide on the validity of the Sedition Law. But nothing in the Constitution has given them a right to decide for the executive, more than to the executive to decide for them. Both magistrates are equally independent in the sphere of action assigned to them. The judges, believing the law constitutional, had a right to pass a sentence of fine and imprisonment; because the power was placed in their hands by the Constitution. But the executive, believing the law to be unconstitutional, were bound to remit the execution of it; because that power has been confided to them by the Constitution. That instrument meant that its co-ordinate branches should be checks on each other. But the opinion which gives to the judges the right to decide what laws are constitutional, and what not, not only for themselves in their own sphere of action, but for the legislature and executive also, in their spheres, would make the judiciary a despotic branch. Nor does the opinion of the unconstitutionality, and consequent nullity of that law, remove all restraint from the overwhelming torrent of slander, which is confounding all vice and virtue, all truth and falsehood, in the United States. The power to do that is fully possessed by the several State legislatures. It was reserved to them, and was denied to the general government, by the Constitution, according to our construction of it. While we deny that Congress has a right to control the freedom of the press, we have ever asserted the right of the States, and their exclusive right, to do so. They have accordingly, all of them, made provisions for punishing slander, which those who have time and inclination, resort to for the vindication of their characters. In general, the State laws appear to have made the presses responsible for slander as far as is consistent with its useful freedom. In those States where they do not admit even the truth of allegations to protect the printer, they have gone too far.

The candor manifested in your letter, and which I ever believed you to possess, has alone inspired the desire of calling your attention, once more, to those circumstances of fact and motive by which I claim to be judged. I hope you will see these intrusions on your time to be, what they really are, proofs of my great respect for you. I tolerate with the utmost latitude the right of others to differ from me in opinion without imputing to them criminality. I know too well the weakness and uncertainty of human reason to wonder at its different results. Both of our political parties, at least the honest part of them, agree conscientiously in the same object—the public good; but they differ essentially in what they deem the means of promoting that good. One side believes it best done by one composition of the governing powers; the other, by a different one. One fears most the ignorance of the people; the other, the selfishness of rulers independent of them. Which is right, time and experience will prove. We think that one side of this experiment has been long enough tried, and proved not to promote the good of the many; and that the other has not been fairly and sufficiently tried. Our opponents think the reverse. With whichever opinion the body of the nation concurs, that must prevail. My anxieties on this subject will never carry me beyond the use of fair and honorable means, of truth and reason; nor have they ever lessened my esteem for moral worth, nor alienated my affections from a single friend, who did not first withdraw himself. Whenever this has happened, I confess I have not been insensible to it; yet have ever kept myself open to a return of their justice. I conclude with sincere prayers for your health and happiness, that yourself and Mr. Adams may long enjoy the tranquillity you desire and merit, and see in the prosperity of your family what is the consummation of the last and warmest of human wishes.

TH: JEFFERSON

To John Taylor *

January 6, 1805   *Washington*

Dear Sir, Your favor of December 26th has been duly received, as a proof of your friendly partialities to me, of which I have so often had reason to be sensible. My opinion originally was that the President of the United States should have been elected for seven years, and forever ineligible afterwards. I have since become sensible that seven years is too long to be irremovable, and that there should be a peaceable way of withdrawing a man in midway who is doing wrong. The service for eight years, with a power to remove at the end of the first four, comes nearly to my principle as corrected by experience; and it is in adherence to that, that I determine to withdraw at the end of my second term. The danger is that the indulgence and attachments of the people will keep a man in the chair after he becomes a dotard, that re-election through life shall become habitual, and election for life follow that. General Washington set the example of voluntary retirement after eight years. I shall follow it. And a few more precedents will oppose the obstacle of habit to any one after awhile who shall endeavor to extend his term. Perhaps it may beget a disposition to establish it by an amendment of the Constitution. I believe I am doing right, therefore, in pursuing my principle. I have determined to declare my intention, but I have consented to be silent on the opinion of friends, who think it best not to put a continuance out of my power in defiance of all circumstances. There is, however, but one circumstance which could engage my acquiescence in another election; to wit, such a division about a successor, as might bring in a monarchist. But that circumstance is impossible. While, therefore, I shall make no formal declaration to the public of my purpose, I have freely let it be understood in

---

* John Taylor "of Caroline" (1753-1824), a supporter of Jefferson, was a famous political writer and three times U. S. Senator from Virginia.

private conversation. In this I am persuaded yourself and my friends generally will approve of my views. And should I, at the end of a second term, carry into retirement all the favor which the first has acquired, I shall feel the consolation of having done all the good in my power, and expect with more than composure the termination of a life no longer valuable to others or of importance to myself. Accept my affectionate salutations and assurances of great esteem and respect.

TH: JEFFERSON

To Benjamin Henry Latrobe *

April 22, 1807   *Monticello*

Dear Sir, The idea of spending 1000 D. for the temporary purpose of covering the panel lights over the Representatives chamber, merely that the room may be plastered before the roof is closed, is totally inadmissible. But I do not see why that particular part of the plastering should not be postponed until the panel lights are glazed. I hope there is no danger but that the glazing may be ready so as to leave time enough to so much of the plastering as would be injured by the want of it. It is with real pain I oppose myself to your passion for the lantern, and that in a matter of taste, I differ from a professor in his own art. But the object of the artist is lost if he fails to please the general eye. You know my reverence for the Grecian and Roman style of architecture. I do not recollect ever to have seen in their buildings a single instance of a lantern, cupola, or belfry. I have ever supposed the cupola an Italian invention, produced by the introduction of bells in the churches, and one

* From the MS Jefferson Papers in Library of Congress; reproduced in Saul K. Padover, *Thomas Jefferson and the National Capital*. Latrobe (1764-1820) was the architect of the Capitol whom President Jefferson appointed surveyor of the public buildings in 1803.

of the degeneracies of modern architecture. I confess they are most offensive to my eye, and a particular observation has strengthened my disgust at them. In the project for the central part of the Capitol which you were so kind as to give me, there is something of this kind on the crown of the dome. The drawing was exhibited for the view of the members, in the President's house, and the disapprobation of that feature in the drawing was very general. On the whole, I cannot be afraid of having our dome like that of the Pantheon, on which had a lantern been placed it would never have obtained that degree of admiration in which it is now held by the world. I shall be with you in three weeks: in the meantime I salute you with esteem and respect.

TH: JEFFERSON

To John Norvell *

June 11, 1807   *Washington*

I think there does not exist a good elementary work on the organization of society into civil government: I mean a work which presents in one full and comprehensive view the system of principles on which such an organization should be founded, according to the rights of nature. For want of a single work of that character, I should recommend Locke on Government, Sidney, Priestley's Essay on the first Principles of Government, Chipman's Principles of Government, and the Federalist. Adding, perhaps, Beccaria on crimes and punishments, because of the demonstrative manner in which he has treated that branch of the subject. If your views of political inquiry go further, to the subjects of money and commerce, Smith's Wealth of Nations is the best book to be read, unless Say's Political Econ-

* Norvell (1790-1850) was a Philadelphia printer who moved to Michigan and became a U. S. Senator.

omy can be had, which treats the same subjects on the same principles, but in a shorter compass and more lucid manner. But I believe this work has not been translated into our language.

History, in general, only informs us what bad government is. But as we have employed some of the best materials of the British constitution in the construction of our own government, a knowledge of British history becomes useful to the American politician. There is, however, no general history of that country which can be recommended. The elegant one of Hume seems intended to disguise and discredit the good principles of the government, and is so plausible and pleasing in its style and manner, as to instil its errors and heresies insensibly into the minds of unwary readers. Baxter has performed a good operation on it. He has taken the text of Hume as his ground work, abridging it by the omission of some details of little interest, and wherever he has found him endeavoring to mislead, by either the suppression of a truth or by giving it a false coloring, he has changed the text to what it should be, so that we may properly called it Hume's history republicanized. He has moreover continued the history (but indifferently) from where Hume left it, to the year 1800. The work is not popular in England, because it is republican; and but a few copies have ever reached America. It is a single quarto volume. Adding to this Ludlow's Memoirs, Mrs. McCauley's and Belknap's histories, a sufficient view will be presented of the free principles of the English constitution.

To your request of my opinion of the manner in which a newspaper should be conducted, so as to be most useful, I should answer, "by restraining it to true facts and sound principles only." Yet I fear such a paper would find few subscribers. It is a melancholy truth, that a suppression of the press could not more completely deprive the nation of its benefits, than is done by its abandoned prostitution to falsehood. Nothing can now be believed which is seen in a newspaper. Truth itself becomes suspicious by being put into that polluted vehicle. The real extent of this state of misinformation is known only to those who are in situations to confront facts within their knowledge with the lies of the day. I really look with commiseration over the great body of my fellow citizens, who, reading newspapers, live and die in the belief, that they have known something of what has been passing in the world in their time; whereas the accounts they have read in newspapers are just as true a history of any other period of the world as of the present, except that the real names of the day are affixed to their fables. General facts may indeed be collected from them, such as that Europe is now at war, that Bonaparte has been a successful warrior, that he has subjected a great portion of Europe to his will . . . ; but no details can be relied on. I will add, that the man who never looks into a newspaper is better informed than he who reads them; inasmuch as he who knows nothing is nearer to truth than he whose mind is filled with falsehoods and errors. He who reads nothing will still learn the great facts, and the details are all false.

Perhaps an editor might begin a reformation in some such way as this. Divide his paper into four chapters, heading the 1st, Truths. 2d, Probabilities. 3d, Possibilities. 4th, Lies. The first chapter would be very short, as it would contain little more than authentic papers, and information from such sources, as the editor would be willing to risk his own reputation for their truth. The second would contain what, from a mature consideration of all circumstances, his judgment should conclude to be probably true. This, however, should rather contain too little than too much. The third and fourth should be professedly for those readers who would rather have lies for their money than the blank paper they would occupy.

Such an editor, too, would have to set his face against the demoralizing practice of feeding the public mind habitually on slander, and the depravity of taste which this nauseous ailment induces. Defamation is becoming a necessary of life; insomuch, that a dish of tea in the morning or evening cannot be digested without this stimulant. Even those who do not believe these

abominations, still read them with complaisance to their audi-
tors, and instead of the abhorrence and indignation which
should fill a virtuous mind, betray a secret pleasure in the possibility that some may believe them, though they do not themselves. It seems to escape them, that it is not he who prints, but
he who pays for printing a slander, who is its real author.

These thoughts on the subjects of your letter are hazarded at
your request. Repeated instances of the publication of what has
not been intended for the public eye, and the malignity with
which political enemies torture every sentence from me into
meanings imagined by their own wickedness only, justify my
expressing a solicitude, that this hasty communication may in
nowise be permitted to find its way into the public papers. Not
fearing these political bull-dogs, I yet avoid putting myself in
the way of being baited by them, and do not wish to volunteer
away that portion of tranquillity, which a firm execution of my
duties will permit me to enjoy.

I tender you my salutations, and best wishes for your success.

TH: JEFFERSON

To Caspar Wistar *

June 21, 1807   *Washington*

I have a grandson, the son of Mr. Randolph, now about
fifteen years of age, in whose education I take a lively interest. . . .

I am not a friend to placing young men in populous cities,
because they acquire there habits and partialities which do not
contribute to the happiness of their after life. But there are particular branches of science, which are not so advantageously
taught anywhere else in the United States as in Philadelphia.

* Wistar (1761-1818) was a Philadelphia physician and professor of anatomy
at the University of Pennsylvania.

The garden at the Woodlands for botany, Mr. Peale's museum for natural history, your medical school for anatomy, and the able professors in all of them, give advantages not to be found elsewhere. We propose, therefore, to send him to Philadelphia to attend the schools of botany, natural history, anatomy, and perhaps surgery; but not of medicine. And why not of medicine, you will ask? Being led to the subject, I will avail myself of the occasion to express my opinions on that science, and the extent of my medical creed. But, to finish first with respect to my grandson, I will state the favor I ask of you, and which is the object of this letter. . . .

This subject dismissed, I may now take up that which it led to, and further tax your patience with unlearned views of medicine; which, as in most cases, are, perhaps, the more confident in proportion as they are less enlightened.

We know, from what we see and feel, that the animal body is in its organs and functions subject to derangement, inducing pain, and tending to its destruction. In this disordered state, we observe nature providing for the re-establishment of order, by exciting some salutary evacuation of the morbific matter, or by some other operation which escapes our imperfect senses and researches. She brings on a crisis, by stools, vomiting, sweat, urine, expectoration, bleeding . . . which, for the most part, ends in the restoration of healthy action. Experience has taught us, also, that there are certain substances, by which, applied to the living body, internally or externally, we can at will produce these same evacuations, and thus do, in a short time, what nature would do but slowly, and do effectually, what perhaps she would not have strength to accomplish. Where, then, we have seen a disease, characterized by specific signs or phenomena, and relieved by a certain natural evacuation or process, whenever that disease recurs under the same appearances, we may reasonably count on producing a solution of it, by the use of such substances as we have found produce the same evacuation or movement. Thus, fullness of the stomach we can relieve by emetics; diseases of the bowels, by purgatives; inflammatory cases, by bleeding; intermittents, by the Peruvian bark; syphilis, by mercury; watchfulness, by opium. So far, I bow to the utility of medicine. It goes to the well-defined forms of disease, and happily, to those the most frequent. But the disorders of the animal body, and the symptoms indicating them, are as various as the elements of which the body is composed. The combinations, too, of these symptoms are so infinitely diversified, that many associations of them appear too rarely to establish a definite disease; and to an unknown disease, there cannot be a known remedy. Here then, the judicious, the moral, the humane physician should stop. Having been so often a witness to the salutary efforts which nature makes to re-establish the disordered functions, he should rather trust to their action, than hazard the interruption of that, and a greater derangement of the system, by conjectural experiments on a machine so complicated and so unknown as the human body, and a subject so sacred as human life. Or, if the appearance of doing something be necessary to keep alive the hope and spirits of the patient, it should be of the most innocent character. One of the most successful physicians I have ever known, has assured me, that he used more bread pills, drops of colored water, and powders of hickory ashes, than of all other medicines put together. It was certainly a pious fraud. But the adventurous physician goes on, and substitutes presumption for knowledge. From the scanty field of what is known, he launches into the boundless region of what is unknown. He establishes for his guide some fanciful theory of corpuscular attraction, of chemical agency, of mechanical powers, of stimuli, of irritability accumulated or exhausted, of depletion by the lancet and repletion by mercury, or some other ingenious dream, which lets him into all nature's secrets at short hand. On the principle which he thus assumes, he forms his table of nosology, arrays his diseases into families, and extends his curative treatment, by analogy, to all the cases he has thus arbitrarily marshalled together. I have lived myself to see the disciples of Hoffmann, Boerhaave, Stahl, Cullen, Brown, succeed one another like the shifting figures of a magic lantern, and their fancies, like the dresses of the annual doll-babies from Paris, becoming, from their novelty, the vogue of the day, and yielding to the next novelty their ephemeral favor. The patient, treated on the fashionable theory, sometimes gets well in spite of the medicine. The medicine, therefore, restored him, and the young doctor receives new courage to proceed in his bold experiments on the lives of his fellow creatures. I believe we may safely affirm, that the inexperienced and pre-sumptuous band of medical tyros let loose upon the world, de-stroys more of human life in one year, than all the Robin Hoods, Cartouches, and MacHeaths do in a century. It is in this part of medicine that I wish to see a reform, an abandonment of hypothesis for sober facts, the first degree of value set on clin-ical observation, and the lowest on visionary theories. I would wish the young practitioner, especially, to have deeply im-pressed on his mind, the real limits of his art, and that when the state of his patient gets beyond these, his office is to be a watchful, but quiet spectator of the operations of nature, giving them fair play by a well-regulated regimen, and by all the aid they can derive from the excitement of good spirits and hope in the patient. I have no doubt, that some diseases not yet under-stood may in time be transferred to the table of those known. But, were I a physician, I would rather leave the transfer to the slow hand of accident, than hasten it by guilty experiments on those who put their lives into my hands. The only sure founda-tions of medicine are, an intimate knowledge of the human body, and observation on the effects of medicinal substances on that. The anatomical and clinical schools, therefore, are those in which the young physician should be formed. If he enters with innocence that of the theory of medicine, it is scarcely pos-sible he should come out untainted with error. His mind must be strong indeed, if, rising above juvenile credulity, it can maintain a wise infidelity against the authority of his instruc-tors, and the bewitching delusions of their theories. You see that I estimate justly that portion of instruction which our medical students derive from your labors; and, associating with it one of the chairs which my old and able friend, Doctor Rush, so honorably fills, I consider them as the two fundamental pillars of the edifice. Indeed, I have such an opinion of the talents of the professors in the other branches which constitute the school of medicine with you, as to hope and believe, that it is from this side of the Atlantic, that Europe, which has taught us so many other things, will at length be led into sound principles in this branch of science, the most important of all others, being that to which we commit the care of health and life.

I dare say, that by this time, you are sufficiently sensible that old heads as well as young, may sometimes be charged with ignorance and presumption. The natural course of the human mind is certainly from credulity to scepticism; and this is perhaps the most favorable apology I can make for venturing so far out of my depth, and to one too, to whom the strong as well as the weak points of this science are so familiar. But having stumbled on the subject in my way, I wished to give a confession of my faith to a friend; and the rather, as I had perhaps, at times, to him as well as others, expressed my scepticism in medicine, without defining its extent or foundation. At any rate, it has permitted me, for a moment, to abstract myself from the dry and dreary waste of politics, into which I have been impressed by the times on which I happened, and to indulge in the rich fields of nature, where alone I should have served as a volunteer, if left to my natural inclinations and partialities.

I salute you at all times with affection and respect,

TH: JEFFERSON

To Robert Fulton *

August 16, 1807   *Monticello*

I consider your torpedoes † as very valuable means of the defense of harbors, and have no doubt that we should adopt them to a considerable degree. Not that I go the whole length (as I believe you do) of considering them as solely to be relied on. Neither a nation nor those entrusted with its affairs, could be justifiable, however sanguine their expectations, in trusting solely to an engine not yet sufficiently tried, under all the circumstances which may occur, and against which we know not as yet what means of parrying may be devised. If, indeed, the mode of attaching them to the cable of a ship be the only one proposed, modes of prevention cannot be difficult. But I have ever looked to the submarine boat as most to be depended on for attaching them, and though I see no mention of it in your letter, or your publications, I am in hopes it is not abandoned as impracticable. I should wish to see a corps of young men trained to this service. It would belong to the engineers if at land, but being nautical, I suppose we must have a corps of naval engineers, to practice and use them. I do not know whether we have authority to put any part of our existing naval establishment in a course of training, but it shall be the subject of a consultation with the Secretary of the Navy.‡

---

* Fulton (1765-1815), the inventor, operated the first steamboat on the Hudson.

† Jefferson was deeply impressed with the efficacy of torpedoes. On March 17, 1810, he wrote again to Fulton: "Your torpedoes will be to cities what vaccination has been to mankind. It extinguishes their greatest danger. But there will still be navies."

‡ In August, 1808, Jefferson asked his Secretary of the Navy, Robert Smith, to assign to Fulton two specialists (at a cost of $130) to make a torpedo experiment at Washington.

To Benjamin Rush

January 3, 1808   *Washington*

Dear Sir, Doctor Waterhouse has been appointed to the Marine Hospital of Boston, as you wished. It was a just though small return for his merit, in introducing the vaccination earlier than we should have had it. His appointment there makes some noise there and here, being unacceptable to some; but I believe that schismatic divisions in the medical fraternity are at the bottom of it. My usage is to make the best appointment my information and judgment enable me to do, and then fold myself up in the mantle of conscience, and abide unmoved the peltings of the storm. And oh! for the day when I shall be withdrawn from it; when I shall have leisure to enjoy my family, my friends, my farm and books.

In the ensuing autumn, I shall be sending on to Philadelphia a grandson of about fifteen years of age,* to whom I shall ask your friendly attentions. Without that bright fancy which captivates, I am in hopes he possesses sound judgment and much observation; and, what I value more than all things, good humor. For thus I estimate the qualities of the mind: 1, good humor; 2, integrity; 3, industry; 4, science. The preference of the first to the second quality may not at first be acquiesced in; but certainly we had all rather associate with a good-humored, light-principled man, than with an ill-tempered rigorist in morality.

---

* Thomas Jefferson Randolph, the son of Jefferson's daughter, Martha.

To William Wirt *

January 10, 1808   *Washington*

Dear Sir, I pray you that this letter may be sacredly secret, because it meddles in a line wherein I should myself think it wrong to intermeddle, were it not that it looks to a period when I shall be out of office, but others might think it wrong notwithstanding that circumstance. I suspected, from your desire to go into the army, that you disliked your profession, notwithstanding that your prospects in it were inferior to none in the State. Still I know that no profession is open to stronger antipathies than that of the law. The object of this letter, then, is to propose to you to come into Congress. That is the great commanding theatre of this nation, and the threshold to whatever department of office a man is qualified to enter. With your reputation, talents, and correct views, used with the necessary prudence, you will at once be placed at the head of the Republican body in the House of Representatives; and after obtaining the standing which a little time will ensure you, you may look, at your own will, into the military, the judiciary, diplomatic, or other civil departments, with a certainty of being in either whatever you please. And in the present state of what may be called the eminent talents of our country, you may be assured of being engaged through life in the most honorable employments. If you come in at the next election, you will begin your course with a new Administration. That Administration will be opposed by a faction, small in numbers, but governed by no principle but the most envenomed malignity. They will endeavor to batter down the executive before it will have time, by its purity and correctness, to build up a confidence with the people, founded on experiment. By supporting them you will lay for yourself a broad foundation in the public confidence, and indeed

---

* Wirt (1772-1834), a Virginia lawyer, was U. S. Attorney-General under Presidents Monroe and John Quincy Adams.

you will become the Colossus of the republican government of your country. I will not say that public life is the line for making a fortune. But it furnishes a decent and honorable support, and places one's children on good grounds for public favor. The family of a beloved father will stand with the public on the most favorable ground of competition. Had General Washington left children, what would have been denied to them?

Perhaps I ought to apologize for the frankness of this communication. It proceeds from an ardent zeal to see this government (the idol of my soul) continue in good hands, and from a sincere desire to see you whatever you wish to be. To this apology I shall only add my friendly salutations, and assurances of sincere esteem and respect,

TH: JEFFERSON

To Samuel Miller

January 23, 1808   *Washington*

I consider the government of the United States as interdicted by the Constitution from intermeddling with religious institutions, their doctrines, discipline, or exercises. This results not only from the provision that no law shall be made respecting the establishment or free exercise of religion, but from that also which reserves to the States the powers not delegated to the United States. Certainly, no power to prescribe any religious exercise, or to assume authority in religious discipline, has been delegated to the general government. It must then rest with the States, as far as it can be in any human authority. But it is only proposed that I should *recommend,* not prescribe a day of fasting and prayer. That is, that I should *indirectly* assume to the United States an authority over religious exercises, which the Constitution has directly precluded them from. It must be meant, too, that this recommendation is to carry some authority, and to be sanctioned by some penalty on those who disregard it; not indeed of fine and imprisonment, but of some degree of proscription, perhaps in public opinion. And does the change in the nature of the penalty make the recommendation less a *law* of conduct for those to whom it is directed? I do not believe it is for the interest of religion to invite the civil magistrate to direct its exercises, its discipline, or its doctrines; nor of the religious societies, that the general government should be invested with the power of effecting any uniformity of time or matter among them. Fasting and prayer are religious exercises; the enjoining them an act of discipline. Every religious society has a right to determine for itself the times for these exercises, and the objects proper for them, according to their own particular tenets; and this right can never be safer than in their own hands, where the Constitution has deposited it.

I am aware that the practice of my predecessors may be quoted. But I have ever believed, that the example of State executives led to the assumption of that authority by the general government, without due examination, which would have discovered that what might be a right in a State government, was a violation of that right when assumed by another. Be this as it may, every one must act according to the dictates of his own reason, and mine tells me that civil powers alone have been given to the President of the United States, and no authority to direct the religious exercises of his constituents.

I again express my satisfaction that you have been so good as to give me an opportunity of explaining myself in a private letter, in which I could give my reasons more in detail than might have been done in a public answer; and I pray you to accept the assurances of my high esteem and respect,

TH: JEFFERSON

To James Monroe

I see with infinite grief a contest arising between yourself and another,* who have been very dear to each other, and equally so to me. I sincerely pray that these dispositions may not be affected between you; with me I confidently trust they will not. For independently of the dictates of public duty, which prescribes neutrality to me, my sincere friendship for you both will ensure its sacred observance. I suffer no one to converse with me on the subject. I already perceive my old friend Clinton, estranging himself from me. No doubt lies are carried to him, as they will be to the other two candidates, under forms which, however false, he can scarcely question. Yet I have been equally careful as to him also, never to say a word on this subject. The object of the contest is a fair and honorable one, equally open to you all; and I have no doubt the personal conduct of all will be so chaste, as to offer no ground of dissatisfaction with each other. But your friends will not be as delicate. I know too well from experience the progress of political controversy, and the exacerbation of spirit into which it degenerates, not to fear for the continuance of your mutual esteem. One piquing thing said draws on another, that a third, and always with increasing acrimony, until all restraint is thrown off, and it becomes difficult for yourselves to keep clear of the toils in which your friends will endeavor to interlace you, and to avoid the participation in their passions which they will endeavor to produce. A candid recollection of what you know of each other will be the true corrective. With respect to myself, I hope they will spare me. My longings for retirement are so strong, that I with difficulty encounter the daily drudgeries of my duty. But my wish for retirement itself is not stronger than

---

* James Madison. Monroe and Madison were rivals in the candidacy for the Presidency to succeed Jefferson.

that of carrying into it the affections of all my friends. I have
ever viewed Mr. Madison and yourself as two principal pillars
of my happiness. Were either to be withdrawn, I should consider it as among the greatest calamities which could assail my
future peace of mind. I have great confidence that the candor
and high understanding of both will guard me against this
misfortune, the bare possibility of which has so far weighed on
my mind, that I could not be easy without unburdening it.

Accept my respectful salutations for yourself and Mrs. Monroe, and be assured of my constant and sincere friendship,

TH: JEFFERSON

To Cornelia Randolph *

April 3, 1808   *Washington*

My dear Cornelia, I have owed you a letter two months,
but have had nothing to write about, till last night I found in
a newspaper the four lines which I now enclose you: and as you
are learning to write, they will be a good lesson to convince you
of the importance of minding your stops in writing. I allow
you a day to find out yourself how to read these lines, so as to
make them true. If you cannot do it in that time, you may call
in assistance. At the same time, I will give you four other lines,
which I learnt when I was but a little older than you, and I
still remember.

I've seen the sea all in a blaze of fire
I've seen a house high as the moon and higher
I've seen the sun at twelve o'clock at night
I've seen the man who saw this wondrous sight.

All this is true, whatever you may think of it at first reading.
I mentioned in my letter of last week to Ellen, that I was under

---

* Jefferson's granddaughter, who was born in 1799 and died in 1871.

an attack of periodical headache. This is the tenth day. It has been very moderate, and yesterday did not last more than three hours. Tell your mamma that I fear I shall not get away as soon as I expected. Congress has spent the last five days without employing a single hour in the business necessary to be finished. Kiss her for me, and all the sisterhood. To Jefferson I give my hand, to your papa my affectionate salutations. You have always my love,

TH: JEFFERSON

To Meriwether Lewis *

August 21, 1808   *Monticello*

With the Sacs and Foxes I hope you will be able to settle amicably, as nothing ought more to be avoided than the embarking ourselves in a system of military coercion on the Indians. If we do this, we shall have general and perpetual war. When a murder has been committed on one of our stragglers, the murderer should be demanded. If not delivered, give time, and still press the demand. We find it difficult, with our regular government, to take and punish a murderer of an Indian. Indeed, I believe we have never been able to do it in a single instance. They have their difficulties also, and require time. In fact, it is a case where indulgence on both sides is just and necessary, to prevent the two nations from being perpetually committed in war, by the acts of the most vagabond and ungovernable of their members. When the refusal to deliver the murderer is permanent, and proceeds from the want of will, and not of ability, we should then interdict all trade and intercourse with them till they give us complete satisfaction. Commerce is the great engine by which we are to coerce them, and not war.

---

* Lewis (1774-1809), Governor of Louisiana Territory, was the famous leader of the Lewis and Clark Expedition.

To Thomas Jefferson Randolph *

November 24, 1808   *Washington*

My dear Jefferson, Your situation, thrown at such a distance from us, and alone, cannot but give us all great anxieties for you. As much has been secured for you, by your particular position and the acquaintance to which you have been recommended, as could be done towards shielding you from the dangers which surround you. But thrown on a wide world, among entire strangers, without a friend or guardian to advise, so young too, and with so little experience of mankind, your dangers are great, and still your safety must rest on yourself. A determination never to do what is wrong, prudence and good humor, will go far towards securing to you the estimation of the world. When I recollect that at fourteen years of age, the whole care and direction of myself was thrown on myself entirely, without a relation or friend qualified to advise or guide me, and recollect the various sorts of bad company with which I associated from time to time, I am astonished I did not turn off with some of them, and become as worthless to society as they were. I had the good fortune to become acquainted very early with some characters of very high standing, and to feel the incessant wish that I could ever become what they were. Under temptations and difficulties, I would ask myself what would Dr. Small, Mr. Wythe, Peyton Randolph do in this situation? What course in it will insure me their approbation? I am certain that this mode of deciding on my conduct, tended more to correctness than any reasoning powers I possessed. Knowing the even and dignified line they pursued, I could never doubt for a moment which of two courses would be in character for them. Whereas, seeking the same object through a process of moral reasoning, and with the jaundiced eye of youth, I should

---

* Jefferson's grandson, who was sent to school in Philadelphia at the age of 15. He was born in 1792 and died in 1875.

often have erred. From the circumstances of my position, I was often thrown into the society of horse racers, card players, fox hunters, scientific and professional men, and of dignified men; and many a time have I asked myself, in the enthusiastic moment of the death of a fox, the victory of a favorite horse, the issue of a question eloquently argued at the bar, or in the great council of the nation, well, which of these kinds of reputation should I prefer? That of a horse jockey, a fox hunter, an orator, or the honest advocate of my country's rights? Be assured, my dear Jefferson, that these little returns into ourselves, this self-catechising habit, is not trifling nor useless, but leads to the prudent selection and steady pursuit of what is right.

I have mentioned good humor as one of the preservatives of our peace and tranquillity. It is among the most effectual, and its effect is so well imitated and aided, artificially, by politeness, that this also becomes an acquisition of first rate value. In truth, politeness is artificial good humor, it covers the natural want of it, and ends by rendering habitual a substitute nearly equivalent to the real virtue. It is the practice of sacrificing to those whom we meet in society, all the little conveniences and preferences which will gratify them, and deprive us of nothing worth a moment's consideration; it is the giving a pleasing and flattering turn to our expressions, which will conciliate others, and make them pleased with us as well as themselves. How cheap a price for the good will of another! When this is in return for a rude thing said by another, it brings him to his senses, it mortifies and corrects him in the most salutary way, and places him at the feet of your good nature, in the eyes of the company. But in stating prudential rules for our government in society, I must not omit the important one of never entering into dispute or argument with another. I never saw an instance of one of two disputants convincing the other by argument. I have seen many, on their getting warm, becoming rude, and shooting one another. Conviction is the effect of our own dispassionate reasoning, either in solitude, or weighing within ourselves, dispassionately, what we hear from others,

standing uncommitted in argument ourselves. It was one of the
rules which, above all others, made Doctor Franklin the most
amiable of men in society, "never to contradict anybody." If he
was urged to announce an opinion, he did it rather by asking
questions, as if for information, or by suggesting doubts. When
I hear another express an opinion which is not mine, I say to
myself, he has a right to his opinion, as I to mine; why should
I question it? His error does me no injury, and shall I become
a Don Quixote, to bring all men by force of argument to one
opinion? If a fact be misstated, it is probable he is gratified by
a belief of it, and I have no right to deprive him of the gratification. If he wants information, he will ask it, and then I will
give it in measured terms; but if he still believes his own story,
and shows a desire to dispute the fact with me, I hear him and
say nothing. It is his affair, not mine, if he prefers error. There
are two classes of disputants most frequently to be met with
among us. The first is of young students, just entered the threshold of science, with a first view of its outlines, not yet filled
up with the details and modifications which a further progress
would bring to their knowledge. The other consists of the ill-
tempered and rude men in society, who have taken up a passion
for politics. (Good humor and politeness never introduce into
mixed society a question on which they foresee there will be a
difference of opinion.) From both of those classes of disputants,
my dear Jefferson, keep aloof, as you would from the infected
subjects of yellow fever or pestilence. Consider yourself, when
with them, as among the patients of Bedlam, needing medical
more than moral counsel. Be a listener only, keep within yourself, and endeavor to establish with yourself the habit of silence,
especially on politics. In the fevered state of our country, no
good can ever result from any attempt to set one of these fiery
zealots to rights, either in fact or principle. They are determined as to the facts they will believe, and the opinions on
which they will act. Get by them, therefore, as you would by an
angry bull; it is not for a man of sense to dispute the road with
such an animal. You will be more exposed than others to have

these animals shaking their horns at you, because of the relation in which you stand with me. Full of political venom, and will-ing to see me and to hate me as a chief in the antagonist party, your presence will be to them what the vomit grass is to the sick dog, a nostrum for producing ejaculation. Look upon them ex-actly with that eye, and pity them as objects to whom you can administer only occasional ease. My character is not within their power. It is in the hands of my fellow citizens at large, and will be consigned to honor or infamy by the verdict of the re-publican mass of our country, according to what themselves will have seen, not what their enemies and mine shall have said. Never, therefore, consider these puppies in politics as requiring any notice from you, and always show that you are not afraid to leave my character to the umpirage of public opinion. Look steadily to the pursuits which have carried you to Philadelphia, be very select in the society you attach yourself to, avoid tav-erns, drinkers, smokers, idlers, and dissipated persons generally; for it is with such that broils and contentions arise; and you will find your path more easy and tranquil. The limits of my paper warn me that it is time for me to close with my affectionate adieu,

TH: JEFFERSON

P.S. Present me affectionately to Mr. Ogilvie, and, in doing the same to Mr. Peale, tell him I am writing with his polygraph, and shall send him mine the first moment I have leisure enough to pack it.

To Cornelia Randolph

December 26, 1808   *Washington*

I congratulate you, my dear Cornelia, on having ac-quired the valuable art of writing. How delightful to be en-abled by it to converse with an absent friend, as if present! To this we are indebted for all our reading; because it must be written before we can read it. To this we are indebted for the Iliad, the Aeneid, the Columbiad, Henriad, Dunciad, and now, for the most glorious poem of all, the Terrapiniad, which I now enclose you. This sublime poem consigns to everlasting fame the greatest achievement in war ever known to ancient or modern times: in the battle of David and Goliath, the disparity between the combatants was nothing in comparison to our case. I rejoice that you have learnt to write, for another reason; for as that is done with a goose-quill, you now know the value of a goose, and of course you will assist Ellen in taking care of the half-dozen very fine grey geese which I shall send by Davy. But as to this, I must refer to your mamma to decide whether they will be safest at Edgehill or at Monticello till I return home, and to give orders accordingly.

To Henri Grégoire *

February 25, 1809   *Washington*

Sir, I have received the favor of your letter of August 17th, and with it the volume you were so kind as to send me on the "Literature of Negroes." Be assured that no person living wishes more sincerely than I do, to see a complete refutation of the doubts I have myself entertained and expressed on the grade of understanding allotted to them by nature, and to find that in this respect they are on a par with ourselves. My doubts were the result of personal observation on the limited sphere of my own State, where the opportunities for the development of their genius were not favorable, and those of exercising it still less so. I expressed them therefore with great hesitation; but

---

* Grégoire (1750-1831) was a French Revolutionist, liberal Catholic bishop, and political writer.

whatever be their degree of talent, it is no measure of their rights.* Because Sir Isaac Newton was superior to others in understanding, he was not therefore lord of the person or property of others. On this subject they are gaining daily in the opinions of nations, and hopeful advances are making towards their re-establishment on an equal footing with the other colors of the human family. I pray you, therefore, to accept my thanks for the many instances you have enabled me to observe of respectable intelligence in that race of men, which cannot fail to have effect in hastening the day of their relief.

To Dupont de Nemours †

March 2, 1809   *Washington*

Within a few days ‡ I retire to my family, my books and farms; and having gained the harbor myself, I shall look on my friends still buffeting the storm with anxiety indeed, but not with envy. Never did a prisoner, released from his chains, feel such relief as I shall on shaking off the shackles of power. Nature intended me for the tranquil pursuits of science, by rendering them my supreme delight. But the enormities of the times in which I have lived, have forced me to take a part in resisting them, and to commit myself on the boisterous ocean of political passions. I thank God for the opportunity of retiring from them without censure, and carrying with me the most consoling proofs of public approbation. I leave everything in the hands of men so able to take care of them, that if we are destined to meet

---

* See also the footnotes to Jefferson's letter to Condorcet, August 30, 1791.

† Pierre Samuel Dupont de Nemours (1739-1817) was a French economist who came to the U. S. in 1799 and was employed by Jefferson on a diplomatic mission to France.

‡ Jefferson's term of office expired on March 4, two days after this letter was written.

misfortunes, it will be because no human wisdom could avert them. Should you return to the United States, perhaps your curiosity may lead you to visit the hermit of Monticello. He will receive you with affection and delight; hailing you in the meantime with his affectionate salutations and assurances of constant esteem and respect,

TH: JEFFERSON

P.S. If you return to us, bring a couple of pair of true-bred shepherd's dogs. You will add a valuable possession to a country now beginning to pay great attention to the raising of sheep.

To the Citizens of Washington *

March 4, 1809   *Washington*

I received with peculiar gratification the affectionate address of the citizens of Washington and in the patriotic sentiments it expresses, I see the true character of the national metropolis.

The station we occupy among the nations of the earth is honorable, but awful. Trusted with the destinies of this solitary republic of the world, the only monument of human rights, and the sole repository of the sacred fire of freedom and self-government, from hence it is to be lighted up in other regions of the earth, if other regions of the earth ever become susceptible of its genial influence. All mankind ought, then, with us, to rejoice in its prosperous, and sympathize in its adverse fortunes, as involving everything dear to man. And to what sacrifices of interest or convenience, ought not these considerations to animate us! To what compromises of opinion and inclination, to

---

* This is Jefferson's reply to a committee of Washington citizens who, on the day of his retirement from the Presidency, came to bid him a "respectful and affectionate farewell."

maintain harmony and union among ourselves, and to preserve from all danger this hallowed ark of human hope and happiness! That differences of opinion should arise among men, on politics, on religion, and on every topic of human inquiry, and that these should be freely expressed in a country where all our facilities are free, is to be expected. But these valuable privileges are much perverted when permitted to disturb the harmony of social intercourse, and to lessen the tolerance of opinion. To the honor of society here, it has been characterized by a just and generous liberality, and an indulgence of those affections which, without regard to political creeds, constitute the happiness of life. That the improvements of this city must proceed with sure and steady steps, follows from its many obvious advantages, and from the enterprising spirit of its inhabitants, which promises to render it the fairest seat of wealth and science.

It is very gratifying to me that the general course of my administration is approved by fellow-citizens, and particularly that the motives of my retirement are satisfactory. I part with the powers entrusted to me by my country, as with a burden of heavy bearing; but it is with sincere regret that I part with the society in which I have lived here. It has been the source of much happiness to me during my residence at the seat of government, and I owe it much for its kind dispositions. I shall ever feel a high interest in the prosperity of the city, and an affectionate attachment to its inhabitants.

PART EIGHT

Last Years

(1809–1826)

THE REMAINING *seventeen years of his life Jefferson spent on his estate. Completely withdrawn from public life, the Sage of Monticello nevertheless enjoyed a universal reputation and corresponded with thousands of people in the United States and in Europe. To this period belongs Jefferson's resumed correspondence with his old and for a time estranged friend, John Adams, one of the most brilliant epistolary exchanges in history. Jefferson's first letter to Adams, here given, was dated January 21, 1812; the last, in this collection, was September 24, 1823, although the two continued to exchange letters to the very end. His mind remained active and lively until the end. His last great achievement, which absorbed his final years, was the University of Virginia at Charlottesville, near Monticello. Jefferson conceived, planned, designed, built, and organized the University. Even at the age of 82 he rode frequently to Charlottesville to see how the University was coming along.*

At the age of 83, on July 4, 1826, he died. It was exactly fifty years after he wrote the Declaration of Independence.

The last letter in this collection, written three weeks before his death, contains a ringing affirmation:

*"All eyes are opened, or opening, to the rights of man. . . .
The mass of mankind has not been born with saddles on their
backs, nor a favored few booted and spurred, ready to ride
them."*

To James Madison

I had a very fatiguing journey, having found the roads excessively bad, although I have seen them worse. The last three days I found it better to be on horseback, and travelled eight hours through as disagreeable a snow storm as I was ever in. Feeling no inconvenience from the expedition but fatigue, I have more confidence in my *vis vitae* than I had before entertained. The spring is remarkably backward. No oats sown, not much tobacco seed, and little done in the gardens. Wheat has suffered considerably. No vegetation visible yet but the red maple, weeping willow and lilac. Flour is said to be at eight dollars at Richmond, and all produce is hurrying down.

I feel great anxiety for the occurrences of the ensuing four or five months. If peace can be preserved, I hope and trust you will have a smooth Administration. I know no government which would be so embarrassing in war as ours. This would proceed very much from the lying and licentious character of our papers; but much, also, from the wonderful credulity of the members of Congress in the floating lies of the day. And in this no experience seems to correct them. I have never seen a Congress during the last eight years, a great majority of which I would not implicitly have relied on in any question, could their minds have been purged of all errors of fact. The evil, too, increases greatly with the protraction of the session, and I apprehend, in case of war, their session would have a tendency to become permanent. It is much, therefore, to be desired that war may be avoided, if circumstances will admit. Nor in the present maniac state of Europe, should I estimate the point of honor by the ordinary scale. I believe we shall, on the contrary, have credit with the world, for having made the avoidance of being engaged in the present unexampled war, our first object. War, however, may become a less losing business than unresisted depredation. With every wish that events may be propitious to your Administration, I salute you with sincere affection and every sympathy of the heart,

TH: JEFFERSON

To Isham Lewis

May 1, 1809   *Monticello*

Dear Sir, It is with real concern that I learn the disagreeable situation in which you are for want of employment, and the more so as I do not see any way in which I can propose to you any certain relief. As to offices under the government, they are few, are always full, and twenty applicants for one vacancy when it happens. They are miserable also, giving a bare subsistence without the least chance of doing anything for the future. The army is full and, in consequence of the late pacification, will probably be reduced, so that from the government nothing seems attainable and besides in that way I could not be useful to you, as I stand solemnly engaged never to solicit it for any person. The public lands in the Orleans and Mississippi territories are now under a course of survey, and offer, I think the best chance of employment. I am acquainted with the surveyor general, Mr. Pease, and could give you a letter to him which might probably induce him to employ you as a surveyor, if there be any room: and this would give chances of doing something for yourself. Mr. Gideon Fitch, whom you know, is in that department. If you have never learnt to survey, and will come and stay here some time, I will teach it to you. It is not the affair of more than a week or a fortnight, if you already understand common arithmetic, say multiplication and division. If you will do us the favor to come and see us, perhaps in this or some other way, something may, on consultation, be thought of. I salute you with affectionate esteem,

TH: JEFFERSON

To Benjamin Rush

September 22, 1809   *Monticello*

Dear Doctor, I am become sensible of a great advantage your profession has over most others, that, to the close of your life, you can be always doing good to mankind: whereas a retired politician is like a broken down courser, unfit for the turf, and good for little else. I am endeavoring to recover the little I once knew of farming, gardening, . . . and would gladly now exchange any branch of science I possess for the knowledge of a common farmer. Too old to learn I must be contented with the occupation and amusement of the art. Already it keeps me so much without doors that I have little time to read, and still less to write. This must be my apology for the tardiness of the present letter.

I find I am losing sight of the progress of the world of letters. Here we talk but of rains and droughts, of blights and frosts, of our ploughs and cattle; and if the topic changes to politics I meddle little with them. In truth, I never had a cordial relish for them, and abhor the contentions and strife they generate. You know what were the times which forced us both from our first loves, the natural sciences. The interest I have taken in the success of the experiment, whether a government can be contrived which shall secure man in his rightful liberties and acquirements, has engaged a longer portion of my life than I had ever proposed: and certainly the experiment could never have fallen into more inauspicious times, when nations have openly renounced all obligations of morality, and shamelessly assume the character of robbers and pirates. In any other time our experiment would have been more easy; and if it can pass safely through the ordeal of the present trial, we may hope we have set an example which will not be without consequences favorable to human happiness. May we not hope that when the robbers of Copenhagen [the British], and the ravagers of Spain [the French] shall be arrested in their course by those means which Providence has always in reserve for the restoration of order among his works, the pendulum will vibrate the more strongly in the opposite direction, and that nations will return to the reestablishment of moral law with an enthusiasm which shall more solidly confirm its future empire. So be it, and God bless you,

TH: JEFFERSON

To Samuel Kercheval *

January 19, 1810　　　　　　　　　　　　　　　*Monticello*

Sir, Yours of the 7th has been duly received, with the pamphlet enclosed, for which I return you my thanks. Nothing can be more exactly and seriously true than what is there stated: that but a short time elapsed after the death of the great reformer of the Jewish religion, before his principles were departed from by those who professed to be his special servants, and perverted into an engine for enslaving mankind, and aggrandizing their oppressors in church and state: that the purest system of morals ever before preached to man has been adulterated and sophisticated by artificial constructions, into

---

* Kercheval (1786-1845?), a writer from the western part of Virginia, published *A History of the Valley of Virginia* in 1833.

a mere contrivance to filch wealth and power to themselves: *
that rational men, not being able to swallow their impious
heresies, in order to force them down their throats, they raise
the hue and cry of infidelity, while themselves are the greatest
obstacles to the advancement of the real doctrines of Jesus,
and do, in fact, constitute the real Anti-Christ.

You expect that your book will have some effect on the
prejudices which the Society of Friends entertain against the
present and late Administrations. In this I think you will be
disappointed. The Friends are men formed with the same
passions, and swayed by the same natural principles and prejudices as others.† In cases where the passions are neutral, men
will display their respect for the religious *professions* of their
sect. But where their passions are enlisted, these *professions*
are no obstacle. You observe very truly, that both the late and
present Administration conducted the government on principles
professed by the Friends. Our efforts to preserve peace, our
measures as to the Indians, as to slavery, as to religious freedom,
were all in consequence with their *profession*. Yet I never
expected we should get a vote from them, and in this I was
neither deceived nor disappointed. There is no riddle in this
to those who do not suffer themselves to be duped by the
professions of religious sectaries. The theory of American
Quakerism is a very obvious one. The mother society is in
England. Its members are English by birth and residence,
devoted to their own country as good citizens ought to be.
The Quakers of these States are colonies or filiations from the
mother society, to whom that society sends its yearly lessons.
On these, the filiated societies model their opinions, their conduct, their passions and attachments. A Quaker is essentially
an Englishman, in whatever part of the earth he is born or
lives. The outrages of Great Britain on our navigation and

---

* See also Jefferson's letters to John Adams, October 13, 1813; to Charles Clay,
January 29, 1815; to Charles Thomson, January 9, 1816; to William Short,
October 31, 1819, and April 13, 1820; to Benjamin Waterhouse, June 26, 1822.

† For additional comments on the Quakers, see also Jefferson's letter to Elbridge Gerry, March 29, 1801.

commerce, have kept us in perpetual bickerings with her. The Quakers here have taken side against their own government, not on their *profession* of peace, for they saw that peace was our object also; but from devotion to the views of the mother society. In 1797—8, when an Administration sought war with France, the Quakers were the most clamorous for war. Their principle of peace, as a secondary one, yielded to the primary one of adherence to the Friends in England, and what was patriotism in the original, became treason in the copy. On that occasion, they obliged their good old leader, Mr. Pemberton, to erase his name from a petition to Congress against war, which had been delivered to a Representative of Pennsylvania, a member of the late and present Administration; he accordingly permitted the old gentleman to erase his name. You must not therefore expect that your book will have any more effect on the Society of Friends here, than on the English merchants settled among us. I apply this to the Friends in general, not universally. I know individuals among them as good patriots as we have.

I thank you for the kind wishes and sentiments towards myself, expressed in your letter, and sincerely wish to yourself the blessings of heaven and happiness,

TH: JEFFERSON

To John Langdon *

March 5, 1810   *Monticello*

Your letter, my dear friend, of the 18th, comes like the refreshing dews of the evening on a thirsty soil. It recalls ancient as well as recent recollections, very dear to my heart. For five and thirty years we have walked together through a

---

* Langdon (1741-1819), a Jeffersonian politician, and U. S. Senator from 1789 to 1801, was elected Governor of New Hampshire in 1805.

land of tribulations. Yet these have passed away, and so, I trust, will those of the present day. The Toryism with which we struggled in '77, differed but in name from the Federalism of '99, with which we struggled also; and the Anglicism of 1808, against which we are now struggling, is but the same thing still in another form. It is a longing for a king, and an English king rather than any other. This is the true source of their sorrows and wailings.

The fear that Bonaparte will come over to us and conquer us also, is too chimerical to be genuine. Supposing him to have finished Spain and Portugal, he has yet England and Russia to subdue. The maxim of war was never sounder than in this case, not to leave an enemy in the rear; and especially where an insurrectionary flame is known to be under the embers, merely smothered, and ready to burst at every point. These two subdued (and surely the Anglomen will not think the conquest of England alone a short work), ancient Greece and Macedonia, the cradle of Alexander, his prototype, and Constantinople, the seat of empire for the world, would glitter more in his eye than our bleak mountains and rugged forests. Egypt, too, and the golden apples of Mauritania, have for more than half a century fixed the longing eyes of France; and with Syria, you know, he has an old affront to wipe out. Then come "Pontus and Galatia, Cappadocia, Asia and Bithynia," the fine countries of the Euphrates and Tigris, the Oxus and Indus, and all beyond the Hyphasis, which bounded the glories of his Macedonian rival; with the invitations of his new British subjects on the banks of the Ganges, whom, after receiving under his protection the mother country, he cannot refuse to visit. When all this is done and settled, and nothing of the old world remains unsubdued, he may turn to the new one. But will he attack us first, from whom he will get but hard knocks and no money? Or will he first lay hold of the gold and silver of Mexico and Peru, and the diamonds of Brazil? A *republican* emperor, from his affection to republics, independent of motives of expediency, must grant to ours the Cyclops' boon of being the last devoured.

While all this is doing, we are to suppose the chapter of accidents read out, and that nothing can happen to cut short or to disturb his enterprises.

But the Anglomen, it seems, have found out a much safer dependence than all these chances of death or disappointment. That is, that we should first let England plunder us, as she has been doing for years, for fear Bonaparte should do it; and then ally ourselves with her, and enter into the war. A conqueror, whose career England could not arrest when aided by Russia, Austria, Prussia, Sweden, Spain and Portugal, she is now to destroy, with all these on his side, by the aid of the United States alone. This, indeed, is making us a mighty people. And what is to be our security, that when embarked for her in the war, she will not make a separate peace and leave us in the lurch? Her good faith! The faith of a nation of merchants! The *Punica fides* of modern Carthage! Of the friend and protectress of Copenhagen! Of the nation who never admitted a chapter of morality into her political code! And is now boldly avowing that whatever power can make hers, is hers of right. Money, and not morality, is the principle of commerce and commercial nations. But, in addition to this, the nature of the English government forbids, of itself, reliance on her engagements; and it is well known she has been the least faithful to her alliances of any nation of Europe, since the period of her history wherein she has been distinguished for her commerce and corruption, that is to say, under the houses of Stuart and Brunswick. To Portugal alone she has steadily adhered, because, by her Methuen treaty, she had made it a colony, and one of the most valuable to her. It may be asked, what, in the nature of her government, unfits England for the observation of moral duties? In the first place, her King is a cipher, his only function being to name the oligarchy which is to govern her. The parliament is, by corruption, the mere instrument of the will of the administration. The real power and property in the government is in the great aristocratical families of the nation. The nest of office being too small for all of them to cuddle into at once, the contest is eternal, which shall crowd the other out. For this purpose, they are divided into two parties, the Ins and the Outs, so equal in weight that a small matter turns the balance. To keep themselves in, when they are in, every stratagem must be practiced, every artifice used which may flatter the pride, the passions or power of the nation. Justice, honor, faith must yield to the necessity of keeping themselves in place. The question whether a measure is moral, is never asked; but whether it will nourish the avarice of their merchants, or the piratical spirit of their navy, or produce any other effect which may strengthen them in their places. As to engagements, however positive, entered into by the predecessors of the Ins, why, they were their enemies; they did everything which was wrong; and to reverse everything which they did, must, therefore, be right. This is the true character of the English government in practice, however different its theory; and it presents the singular phenomenon of a nation, the individuals of which are as faithful to their private engagements and duties, as honorable, as worthy, as those of any nation on earth, and whose government is yet the most unprincipled at this day known. In an absolute government there can be no such equiponderant parties. The despot is the government. His power suppressing all opposition, maintains his ministers firm in their places. What he has contracted, therefore, through them, he has the power to observe with good faith; and he identifies his own honor and faith with that of his nation.

When I observed, however, that the King of England was a cipher, I did not mean to confine the observation to the mere individual now on that throne. The practice of kings marrying only in the families of kings has been that of Europe for some centuries. Now, take any race of animals, confine them in idleness and inaction, whether in a sty, a stable or a state-room, pamper them with high diet, gratify all their sexual appetites, immerse them in sensualities, nourish their passions, let everything bend before them, and banish whatever might lead them to think, and in a few generations they become all body and no mind; and this, too, by a law of nature, by that very law by which we are in the constant practice of changing the characters and propensities of the animals we raise for our own purposes. Such is the regimen in raising kings, and in this way they have gone on for centuries. While in Europe, I often amused myself with contemplating the characters of the then reigning sovereigns of Europe. Louis the XVI was a fool, of my own knowledge, and in despite of the answers made for him at his trial.* The King of Spain was a fool, and of Naples the same. They passed their lives in hunting, and dispatched two couriers a week, one thousand miles, to let each other know what game they had killed the preceding days. The King of Sardinia was a fool. All these were Bourbons. The Queen of Portugal, a Braganza, was an idiot by nature. And so was the King of Denmark. Their sons, as regents, exercised the powers of government. The King of Prussia, successor to the great Frederick, was a mere hog in body as well as in mind. Gustavus of Sweden and Joseph of Austria † were really crazy, and George of England, you know, was in a strait waistcoat. There remained, then, none but old Catherine, who had been too lately picked up to have lost her common sense. In this state Bonaparte found Europe; and it was this state of its rulers which lost it with scarce a struggle. These animals had become without mind and powerless; and so will every hereditary monarch be after a few generations. Alexander, the grandson of Catherine, is as yet an exception. He is able to hold his own. But he is only of the third generation. His race is not yet worn out. And so endeth the book of kings, from all of whom the Lord deliver us, and have you, my friend, and all such good men and true, in his holy keeping,

TH: JEFFERSON

---

* See Saul K. Padover, *The Life and Death of Louis XVI* (1939).
† See Saul K. Padover, *The Revolutionary Emperor: Joseph II* (1934).

To Benjamin Rush

January 16, 1811   *Monticello*

Dear Sir, I receive with sensibility your observations on the discontinuance of friendly correspondence between Mr. Adams and myself, and the concern you take in its restoration. This discontinuance has not proceeded from me, nor from the want of sincere desire and of effort on my part, to renew our intercourse. You know the perfect coincidence of principle and of action, in the early part of the Revolution, which produced a high degree of mutual respect and esteem between Mr. Adams and myself. Certainly no man was ever truer than he was, in that day, to those principles of rational republicanism which, after the necessity of throwing off our monarchy, dictated all our efforts in the establishment of a new government. And although he swerved, afterwards, towards the principles of the English constitution, our friendship did not abate on that account. While he was Vice-President, and I Secretary of State, I received a letter from President Washington, then at Mount Vernon, desiring me to call together the heads of departments, and to invite Mr. Adams to join us (which, by-the-bye, was the only instance of that being done) in order to determine on some measure which required dispatch; and he desired me to act on it, as decided, without again recurring to him. I invited them to dine with me, and after dinner, sitting at our wine, having settled our question, other conversation came on, in which a collision of opinion arose between Mr. Adams and Colonel Hamilton, on the merits of the British constitution, Mr. Adams giving it as his opinion, that, if some of its defects and abuses were corrected, it would be the most perfect constitution of government ever devised by man. Hamilton, on the contrary, asserted, that with its existing vices, it was the most perfect model of government that could be formed; and that the correction of its vices would render it an impracticable govern-

ment. And this you may be assured was the real line of difference between the political principles of these two gentlemen.
Another incident took place on the same occasion, which will
further delineate Mr. Hamilton's political principles. The room
being hung around with a collection of the portraits of remarkable men, among them were those of Bacon, Newton and Locke,
Hamilton asked me who they were. I told him they were my
trinity of the three greatest men the world had ever produced,
naming them. He paused for some time: "The greatest man,"
said he, "that ever lived, was Julius Cæsar." Mr. Adams was
honest as a politician, as well as a man; Hamilton honest as a
man, but, as a politician, believing in the necessity of either
force or corruption to govern men.

You remember the machinery which the Federalists played
off, about that time, to beat down the friends to the real principles of our Constitution, to silence by terror every expression in
their favor, to bring us into war with France and alliance with
England, and finally to homologize our Constitution with that
of England. Mr. Adams, you know, was overwhelmed with
feverish addresses, dictated by the fear, and often by the pen,
of the *bloody buoy,* and was seduced by them into some open
indications of his new principles of government, and in fact
was so elated as to mix with his kindness a little superciliousness
towards me. Even Mrs. Adams, with all her good sense and prudence, was sensibly flushed. And you recollect the short suspension of our intercourse, and the circumstance which gave rise to
it, which you were so good as to bring to an early explanation,
and have set to rights, to the cordial satisfaction of us all. The
nation at length passed condemnation on the political principles of the Federalists, by refusing to continue Mr. Adams in the
Presidency. On the day on which we learned in Philadelphia
the vote of the city of New York, which it was well known
would decide the vote of the State, and that, again, the vote of
the union, I called on Mr. Adams on some official business. He
was very sensibly affected, and accosted me with these words:
"Well, I understand that you are to beat me in this contest, and

I will only say that I will be as faithful a subject as any you will have." "Mr. Adams," said I, "this is no personal contest between you and me. Two systems of principles on the subject of government divide our fellow citizens into two parties. With one of these you concur, and I with the other. As we have been longer on the public stage than most of those now living, our names happen to be more generally known. One of these parties, therefore, has put your name at its head, the other mine. Were we both to die today, tomorrow two other names would be in the place of ours, without any change in the motion of the machinery. Its motion is from its principle, not from you or myself." "I believe you are right," said he, "that we are but passive instruments, and should not suffer this matter to affect our personal dispositions." But he did not long retain this just view of the subject. I have always believed that the thousand calumnies which the Federalists, in bitterness of heart and mortification at their ejection, daily invented against me, were carried to him by their busy intriguers, and made some impression. When the election between Burr and myself was kept in suspense by the Federalists, and they were meditating to place the President of the Senate at the head of the government, I called on Mr. Adams with a view to have this desperate measure prevented by his negative. He grew warm in an instant, and said with a vehemence he had not used towards me before, "Sir, the event of the election is within your own power. You have only to say you will do justice to the public creditors, maintain the navy, and not disturb those holding offices, and the government will instantly be put into your hands. We know it is the wish of the people it should be so." "Mr. Adams," said I, "I know not what part of my conduct, in either public or private life, can have authorized a doubt of my fidelity to the public engagements. I say, however, I will not come into the government by capitulation. I will not enter on it, but in perfect freedom to follow the dictates of my own judgment." I had before given the same answer to the same intimation from Gouverneur Morris. "Then," said he, "things must take their course." I turned the conversa-

tion to something else, and soon took my leave. It was the first
time in our lives we had ever parted with anything like dissatisfaction. And then followed those scenes of midnight appointment, which have been condemned by all men. The last day of
his political power, the last hours, and even beyond the midnight, were employed in filling all offices, and especially permanent ones, with the bitterest Federalists, and providing for me
the alternative, either to execute the government by my enemies, whose study it would be to thwart and defeat all my
measures, or to incur the odium of such numerous removals
from office, as might bear me down. A little time and reflection
effaced in my mind this temporary dissatisfaction with Mr.
Adams, and restored me to that just estimate of his virtues and
passions, which a long acquaintance had enabled me to fix. And
my first wish became that of making his retirement easy by any
means in my power; for it was understood he was not rich. I
suggested to some Republican members of the delegation from
his State, the giving him, either directly or indirectly, an office,
the most lucrative in that State, and then offered to be resigned,
if they thought he would not deem it affrontive. They were
of opinion he would take great offense at the offer; and moreover, that the body of Republicans would consider such a step
in the outset as arguing very ill of the course I meant to pursue.
I dropped the idea, therefore, but did not cease to wish for some
opportunity of renewing our friendly understanding.

Two or three years after, having had the misfortune to lose a
daughter, between whom and Mrs. Adams there had been a
considerable attachment, she made it the occasion of writing me
a letter, in which, with the tenderest expressions of concern at
this event, she carefully avoided a single one of friendship towards myself, and even concluded it with the wishes "of her
who *once* took pleasure in subscribing herself your friend, Abigail Adams." Unpromising as was the complexion of this letter,
I determined to make an effort towards removing the cloud
from between us. This brought on a correspondence which I
now enclose for your perusal, after which be so good as to re-

turn it to me, as I have never communicated it to any mortal breathing, before. I send it to you, to convince you I have not been wanting either in the desire, or the endeavor to remove this misunderstanding. Indeed, I thought it highly disgraceful to us both, as indicating minds not sufficiently elevated to prevent a public competition from affecting our personal friendship. I soon found from the correspondence that conciliation was desperate, and yielding to an intimation in her last letter, I ceased from further explanation. I have the same good opinion of Mr. Adams which I ever had. I know him to be an honest man, an able one with his pen, and he was a powerful advocate on the floor of Congress. He has been alienated from me, by belief in the lying suggestions contrived for electioneering purposes, that I perhaps mixed in the activity and intrigues of the occasion. My most intimate friends can testify that I was perfectly passive. They would sometimes, indeed, tell me what was going on; but no man ever heard me take part in such conversations; and none ever misrepresented Mr. Adams in my presence, without my asserting his just character. With very confidential persons I have doubtless disapproved of the principles and practices of his administration. This was unavoidable. But never with those with whom it could do him any injury. Decency would have required this conduct from me, if disposition had not; and I am satisfied Mr. Adams' conduct was equally honorable towards me. But I think it part of his character to suspect foul play in those of whom he is jealous, and not easily to relinquish his suspicions.

I have gone, my dear friend, into these details, that you might know everything which had passed between us, might be fully possessed of the state of facts and dispositions, and judge for yourself whether they admit a revival of that friendly intercourse for which you are so kindly solicitous. I shall certainly not be wanting in anything on my part which may second your efforts, which will be the easier with me, inasmuch as I do not entertain a sentiment of Mr. Adams, the expression of which could give him reasonable offense. And I submit the whole to yourself, with the assurance, that whatever be the issue, my friendship and respect for yourself will remain unaltered and unalterable,

TH: JEFFERSON

To John Adams

January 21, 1812   *Monticello*

Dear Sir, I thank you before hand (for they are not yet arrived) for the specimens of homespun you have been so kind as to forward me by post. I doubt not their excellence, knowing how far you are advanced in these things in your quarter. Here we do little in the fine way, but in coarse and middling goods a great deal. Every family in the country is a manufactory within itself, and is very generally able to make within itself all the stouter and middling stuffs for its own clothing and household use. We consider a sheep for every person in the family as sufficient to clothe it, in addition to the cotton, hemp and flax which we raise ourselves. For fine stuff we shall depend on your northern manufactories. Of these, that is to say, of company establishments, we have none. We use little machinery. The spinning jenny, and loom with the flying shuttle, can be managed in a family; but nothing more complicated. The economy and thriftiness resulting from our household manufactures are such that they will never again be laid aside; and nothing more salutary for us has ever happened than the British obstructions to our demands for their manufactures. Restore free intercourse when they will, their commerce with us will have totally changed its form, and the articles we shall in future want from them will not exceed their own consumption of our produce.

A letter from you calls up recollections very dear to my mind. It carries me back to the times when, beset with difficulties and dangers, we were fellow-laborers in the same cause, struggling for what is most valuable to man, his right of self-government. Laboring always at the same oar, with some wave ever ahead, threatening to overwhelm us, and yet passing harmless under our bark, we knew not how we rode through the storm with heart and hand, and made a happy port. Still we did not expect to be without rubs and difficulties; and we have had them. First, the detention of the western posts, then the coalition of Pilnitz, outlawing our commerce with France, and the British enforcement of the outlawry. In your day, French depredations; in mine, English, and the Berlin and Milan decrees; now, the English orders of council, and the piracies they authorize. When these shall be over, it will be the impressment of our seamen or something else; and so we have gone on, and so we shall go on, puzzled and prospering beyond example in the history of man. And I do believe we shall continue to grow, to multiply and prosper until we exhibit an association, powerful, wise and happy, beyond what has yet been seen by men. As for France and England, with all their preëminence in science, the one is a den of robbers, and the other of pirates. And if science produces no better fruits than tyranny, murder, rapine and destitution of national morality, I would rather wish our country to be ignorant, honest and estimable, as our neighboring savages are. But whither is senile garrulity leading me? Into politics, of which I have taken final leave. I think little of them and say less. I have given up newspapers in exchange for Tacitus and Thucydides, for Newton and Euclid, and I find myself much the happier. Sometimes, indeed, I look back to former occurrences, in remembrance of our old friends and fellow-laborers who have fallen before us. Of the signers of the Declaration of Independence, I see now living not more than half a dozen on your side of the Potomac, and on this side, myself alone. You and I have been wonderfully spared, and myself with remarkable health, and a considerable activity of body and mind. I am on horseback three or four hours of every day; visit three or four times a year a possession I have ninety miles distant, performing the winter journey on horseback. I walk little, how-

ever, a single mile being too much for me, and I live in the
midst of my grandchildren, one of whom has lately promoted
me to be a great grandfather. I have heard with pleasure that
you also retain good health, and a greater power of exercise in
walking than I do. But I would rather have heard this from
yourself, and that, writing a letter like mine, full of egotisms,
and of details of your health, your habits, occupations and en-
joyments, I should have the pleasure of knowing that in the race
of life, you do not keep, in its physical decline, the same distance
ahead of me which you have done in political honors and
achievements. No circumstances have lessened the interest I
feel in these particulars respecting yourself; none have suspended for one moment my sincere esteem for you, and I now
salute you with unchanged affection and respect,

TH: JEFFERSON

To John Adams

June 11, 1812   *Monticello*

Dear Sir, By our post preceding that which brought your
letter of May 21st, I had received one from Mr. Malcolm on the
same subject with yours, and by the return of the post had stated
to the President my recollections of him. But both your letters
were probably too late; as the appointment had been already
made, if we may credit the newspapers.

You ask if there is any book that pretends to give any account
of the traditions of the Indians, or how one can acquire an idea
of them? Some scanty accounts of their traditions, but fuller of
their customs and characters, are given us by most of the early
travellers among them; these you know were mostly French.
Lafiteau, among them, and Adair an Englishman, have written
on this subject; the former two volumes, the latter one, all in

quarto. But unluckily Lafiteau had in his head a preconceived theory on the mythology, manners, institutions and government of the ancient nations of Europe, Asia and Africa, and seems to have entered on those of America only to fit them into the same frame, and to draw from them a confirmation of his general theory. He keeps up a perpetual parallel, in all those articles, between the Indians of America and the ancients of the other quarters of the globe. He selects, therefore, all the facts and adopts all the falsehoods which favor his theory, and very gravely retails such absurdities as zeal for a theory could alone swallow. He was a man of much classical and scriptural reading, and has rendered his book not unentertaining. He resided five years among the Northern Indians, as a missionary, but collects his matter much more from the writings of others, than from his own observation.

Adair too had his kink. He believed all the Indians of America to be descended from the Jews; the same laws, usages, rites and ceremonies, the same sacrifices, priests, prophets, fasts and festivals, almost the same religion, and that they all spoke Hebrew. For, although he writes particularly of the Southern Indians only, the Catawbas, Creeks, Cherokees, Chickasaws and Chocktaws, with whom alone he was personally acquainted, yet he generalizes whatever he found among them, and brings himself to believe that the hundred languages of America, differing fundamentally every one from every other, as much as Greek from Gothic, yet have all one common prototype. He was a trader, a man of learning, a self-taught Hebraist, a strong religionist, and of as sound a mind as Don Quixote in whatever did not touch his religious chivalry. His book contains a great deal of real instruction on its subject, only requiring the reader to be constantly on his guard against the wonderful obliquities of his theory.

The scope of your inquiry would scarcely, I suppose, take in the three folio volumes of Latin of De Bry. In these, facts and fable are mingled together, without regard to any favorite system. They are less suspicious, therefore, in their complexion, more original and authentic, than those of Lafiteau and Adair. This is a work of great curiosity, extremely rare, so as never to be bought in Europe, but on the breaking up and selling some ancient library. On one of these occasions a bookseller procured me a copy, which, unless you have one, is probably the only one in America.

You ask further, if the Indians have any order of priesthood among them, like the druids, bards or minstrels of the Celtic nations? Adair alone, determined to see what he wished to see in every object, metamorphoses their conjurers into an order of priests, and describes their sorceries as if they were the great religious ceremonies of the nation. Lafiteau called them by their proper names, jongleurs, devins, sortileges; De Bry, prestidigitators; Adair himself sometimes magi, archimagi, cunning men, seers, rain makers; and the modern Indian interpreters call them conjurers and witches. They are persons pretending to have communications with the devil and other evil spirits, to foretell future events, bring down rain, find stolen goods, raise the dead, destroy some and heal others by enchantment, lay spells, and so forth. And Adair, without departing from his parallel of the Jews and Indians, might have found their counterpart much more aptly, among the soothsayers, sorcerers and wizards of the Jews, their Gannes and Gambres, their Simon Magus, Witch of Endor, and the young damsel whose sorceries disturbed Paul so much; instead of placing them in a line with their high-priest, their chief priests, and their magnificent hierarchy generally. In the solemn ceremonies of the Indians, the persons who direct or officiate, are their chiefs, elders and warriors, in civil ceremonies or in those of war; it is the head of the cabin in their private or particular feasts or ceremonies; and sometimes the matrons, as in their corn feasts. And even here, Adair might have kept up his parallel, with ennobling his conjurers. For the ancient patriarchs, the Noahs, the Abrahams, Isaacs and Jacobs, and even after the consecration of Aaron, the Samuels and Elijahs, and we may say further, every one for himself offered sacrifices on the altars. The true line of distinction seems to be, that solemn ceremonies, whether public or private, addressed to the Great Spirit, are conducted by the worthies of the nation, men or matrons, while conjurers are resorted to only for the invocation of evil spirits. The present state of the several Indian tribes, without any public order of priests, is proof sufficient that they never had such an order. Their steady habits permit no innovations, not even those which the progress of science offers to increase the comforts, enlarge the understanding, and improve the morality of mankind. Indeed, so little idea have they of a regular order of priests that they mistake ours for their conjurers, and call them by that name.

So much in answer to your inquiries concerning Indians, a people with whom, in the early part of my life, I was very familiar, and acquired impressions of attachment and commiseration for them which have never been obliterated. Before the Revolution, they were in the habit of coming often and in great numbers to the seat of government, where I was very much with them. I knew much the great Ontassetè, the warrior and orator of the Cherokees; he was always the guest of my father, on his journeys to and from Williamsburg. I was in his camp when he made his great farewell oration to his people the evening before his departure for England. The moon was in full splendor, and to her he seemed to address himself in his prayers for his own safety on the voyage, and that of his people during his absence; his sounding voice, distinct articulation, animated action, and the solemn silence of his people at their several fires, filled me with awe and veneration, although I did not understand a word he uttered. That nation, consisting now of about 2,000 warriors, and the Creeks of about 3,000 are far advanced in civilization. They have good cabins, enclosed fields, large herds of cattle and hogs, spin and weave their own clothes of cotton, have smiths and other of the most necessary tradesmen, write and read, are on the increase in numbers, and a branch of Cherokees is now instituting a regular representative government. Some other tribes are advancing in the same line. On those who have

made any progress, English seductions will have no effect. But
the backward will yield, and be thrown further back. Those
will relapse into barbarism and misery, lose numbers by war
and want, and we shall be obliged to drive them with the beasts
of the forest into the stony mountains. They will be conquered,
however, in Canada. The possession of that country secures our
women and children forever from the tomahawk and scalping
knife, by removing those who excite them; and for this possession orders, I presume, are issued by this time; taking for
granted that the doors of Congress will re-open with a declaration of war. That this may end in indemnity for the past,
security for the future, and complete emancipation from Anglo-
many, Gallomany, and all the manias of demoralized Europe,
and that you may live in health and happiness to see all this, is
the sincere prayer of yours affectionately,

TH: JEFFERSON

To William Duane *

April 4, 1813   *Monticello*

It is true that I am tired of practical politics, and happier
while reading the history of ancient than of modern times. The
total banishment of all moral principle from the code which
governs the intercourse of nations, the melancholy reflection
that after the mean, wicked and cowardly cunning of the cabi-
nets of the age of Machiavelli had given place to the integrity
and good faith which dignified the succeeding one of a Chatham
and Turgot, that this is to be swept away again by the daring
profligacy and avowed destitution of all moral principle of a
Cartouche and a Blackbeard, sickens my soul unto death. I turn
from the contemplation with loathing, and take refuge in the

---

* Duane (1760-1835) was the editor of the Philadelphia *Aurora,* the leading
Jeffersonian newspaper, from 1798 to 1822.

histories of other times, where, if they also furnished their Tarquins, their Catilines and Caligulas, their stories are handed to us under the brand of a Livy, a Sallust and a Tacitus, and we are comforted with the reflection that the condemnation of all succeeding generations has confirmed the censures of the historian, and consigned their memories to everlasting infamy, a solace we cannot have with the Georges and Napoleons but by anticipation.

To John Adams

May 27, 1813   *Monticello*

Another of our friends of seventy-six is gone, my dear sir, another of the co-signers of the Independence of our country. And a better man than [Doctor Benjamin] Rush could not have left us, more benevolent, more learned, of finer genius, or more honest. We too must go; and that ere long. I believe we are under half a dozen at present; I mean the signers of the Declaration. Yourself, Gerry,* Carroll,† and myself, are all I know to be living. I am the only one south of the Potomac. Is Robert Treat Paine,‡ or Floyd § living? It is long since I heard of them, and yet I do not recollect to have heard of their deaths.

Moreton's deduction of the origin of our Indians from the fugitive Trojans, stated in your letter of January the 26th, and his manner of accounting for the sprinkling of their Latin with Greek, is really amusing. Adair makes them talk Hebrew. Reinold Foster derives them from the soldiers sent by Kouli Khan to conquer Japan. Brerewood, from the Tartars, as well as our bears, wolves, foxes, . . . which, he says, "must of neces-

---

* Elbridge Gerry (1744-1814) represented Massachusetts.
† Charles Carroll (1737-1832) represented Maryland.
‡ Paine (1731-1814) was another signer of the Declaration from Massachusetts.
§ William Floyd (1734-1821) represented New York.

sity fetch their beginning from Noah's ark, which rested, after the deluge, in Asia, seeing they could not proceed by the course of nature, as the imperfect sort of living creatures do, from putrefaction." Bernard Romans is of opinion that God created an original man and woman in this part of the globe. Doctor Barton thinks they are not specifically different from the Persians; but, taking afterwards a broader range, he thinks, "that in all the vast countries of America, there is but one language, nay, that it may be proven, or rendered highly probable, that all the languages of the earth bear some affinity together." This reduces it to a question of definition, in which every one is free to use his own: to wit, what constitutes identity, or difference in two things, in the common acceptation of *sameness?* All languages may be called the same, as being all made up of the same primitive sounds, expressed by the letters of the different alphabets. But, in this sense, all things on earth are the same as consisting of matter. This gives up the useful distribution into genera and species, which we form, arbitrarily indeed, for the relief of our imperfect memories. To aid the question, from whence our Indian tribes descended, some have gone into their religion, their morals, their manners, customs, habits, and physical forms. By such helps it may be learnedly proved, that our trees and plants of every kind are descended from those of Europe; because, like them, they have no locomotion, they draw nourishment from the earth, they clothe themselves with leaves in spring, of which they divest themselves in autumn for the sleep of winter. Our animals too must be descended from those of Europe, because our wolves eat lambs, our deer are gregarious, our ants hoard. But, when for convenience we distribute languages, according to common understanding, into classes originally different, as we choose to consider them, as the Hebrew, the Greek, the Celtic, the Gothic; and these again into genera, or families, as the Icelandic, German, Swedish, Danish, English; and these last into species, or dialects, as English, Scotch, Irish, we then ascribe other meanings to the terms "same" and "different." In some one of these senses, Barton, and

Adair, and Foster, and Brerewood, and Moreton, may be right, every one according to his own definition of what constitutes "identity." Romans, indeed, takes a higher stand, and supposes a separate creation. On the same unscriptural ground, he had but to mount one step higher, to suppose no creation at all, but that all things have existed without beginning in time, as they now exist, and may forever exist, producing and reproducing in a circle, without end. This would very summarily dispose of Mr. Moreton's learning, and show that the question of Indian origin, like many others, pushed to a certain height, must receive the same answer, "Ignoro."

You ask if the usage of hunting in circles has ever been known among any of our tribes of Indians? It has been practiced by them all; and is to this day, by those still remote from the settlements of the whites. But their numbers not enabling them, like Genghis Khan's seven hundred thousand, to form themselves into circles of one hundred miles diameter, they make their circle by firing the leaves fallen on the ground, which gradually forcing the animals to a centre, they there slaughter them with arrows, darts, and other missiles. This is called fire hunting, and has been practiced in this State within my time, by the white inhabitants. This is the most probable cause of the origin and extension of the vast prairies in the western country, where the grass having been of extraordinary luxuriance, has made a conflagration sufficient to kill even the old as well as the young timber.

I sincerely congratulate you on the successes of our little navy; which must be more gratifying to you than to most men, as having been the early and constant advocate of wooden walls. If I have differed with you on this ground, it was not on the principle, but the time; supposing that we cannot build or maintain a navy, which will not immediately fall into the same gulf which has swallowed not only the minor navies, but even those of the great second-rate powers of the sea. Whenever these can be resuscitated, and brought so near to a balance with England that we can turn the scale, then is my epoch for aiming at a navy. In the meantime, one competent to keep the Barbary States in order, is necessary; these being the only smaller powers disposed to quarrel with us. But I respect too much the weighty opinions of others, to be unyielding on this point, and acquiesce with the prayer *'quod felix faustumque sit;'* adding ever a sincere one for your health and happiness,

TH: JEFFERSON

To William Canby

September 18, 1813   *Monticello*

Sir, I have duly received your favor of August 27th, am sensible of the kind intentions from which it flows, and truly thankful for them. The more so as they could only be the result of a favorable estimate of my public course. During a long life, as much devoted to study as a faithful transaction of the trusts committed to me would permit, no subject has occupied more of my consideration than our relations with all the beings around us, our duties to them, and our future prospects. After reading and hearing everything which probably can be suggested respecting them, I have formed the best judgment I could as to the course they prescribe, and in the due observance of that course, I have no recollections which give me uneasiness. An eloquent preacher of your religious society, Richard Motte, in a discourse of much emotion and pathos, is said to have exclaimed aloud to his congregation, that he did not believe there was a Quaker, Presbyterian, Methodist or Baptist in heaven, having paused to give his hearers time to stare and to wonder. He added, that in heaven, God knew no distinctions, but considered all good men as his children, and as brethren of the same family. I believe, with the Quaker preacher, that he who steadily observes those moral precepts in which all religions concur, will never be questioned at the gates of heaven, as to the dogmas in which they all differ. That on entering there, all these are left behind us, and the Aristides and Catos, the Penns and Tillotsons, Presbyterians and Baptists, will find themselves united in all principles which are in concert with the reason of the supreme mind. Of all the systems of morality, ancient or modern, which have come under my observation, none appear to me so pure as that of Jesus. He who follows this steadily need not, I think, be uneasy, although he cannot comprehend the subtleties and mysteries erected on his doctrines by those who, calling themselves his special followers and favorites, would make him come into the world to lay snares for all understandings but theirs. These metaphysical heads, usurping the judgment seat of God, denounce as his enemies all who cannot perceive the geometrical logic of Euclid in the demonstrations of St. Athanasius, that three are one, and one is three; and yet that the one is not three nor the three one. In all essential points you and I are of the same religion; and I am too old to go into inquiries and changes as to the unessential.

To John Adams

October 13, 1813   *Monticello*

Dear Sir, Since mine of August the 22d, I have received your favors of August the 16th, September the 2d, 14th, 15th, and—, and Mrs. Adams' of September the 20th. I now send you, according to your request, a copy of the syllabus. To fill up this skeleton with arteries, with veins, with nerves, muscles and flesh, is really beyond my time and information. Whoever could undertake it would find great aid in Enfield's judicious abridgment of Brucker's History of Philosophy, in which he has reduced five or six quarto volumes, of one thousand pages each of Latin closely printed, to two moderate octavos of English open type.

To compare the morals of the Old, with those of the New Testament, would require an attentive study of the former, a search through all its books for its precepts, and through all its history for its practices, and the principles they prove. As commentaries, too, on these, the philosophy of the Hebrews must be inquired into, their Mishna, their Gemara, Cabbala, Jezirah, Sohar, Cosri, and their Talmud, must be examined and understood, in order to do them full justice. Brucker, it would seem, has gone deeply into these repositories of their ethics, and Enfield his epitomizer, concludes in these words: "Ethics were so little understood among the Jews, that in their whole compilation called the Talmud, there is only one treatise on moral subjects. Their books of morals chiefly consisted in a minute enumeration of duties. From the law of Moses were deduced six hundred and thirteen precepts, which were divided into two classes, affirmative and negative, two hundred and forty-eight in the former, and three hundred and sixty-five in the latter. It may serve to give the reader some idea of the low state of moral philosophy among the Jews in the middle age, to add that of the two hundred and forty-eight affirmative precepts, only three were considered as obligatory upon women, and that in order to obtain salvation, it was judged sufficient to fulfill any one single law in the hour of death; the observance of the rest being deemed necessary, only to increase the felicity of the future life. What a wretched depravity of sentiment and manners must have prevailed, before such corrupt maxims could have obtained credit! It is impossible to collect from these writings a consistent series of moral doctrine." . . . It was the reformation of this "wretched depravity" of morals which Jesus undertook. In extracting the pure principles which he taught, we should have to strip off the artificial vestments in which they have been muffled by priests, who have travestied them into various forms, as instruments of riches and power to themselves. We must dismiss the Platonists and Plotinists, the Stagyrites and Gamalielites, the Eclectics, the Gnostics and Scholastics, their essences and emanations, their logos and demiurgos, æons and dæmons, male and female, with a long train of . . . or, shall I say at once, of nonsense. We must reduce our volume to the simple evangelists, select, even from them, the very words only of Jesus, paring off the amphibologisms into which they have been led, by forgetting often, or not understanding, what had fallen from him, by giving their own misconceptions as his dicta, and expressing unintelligibly for others what they had not understood themselves. There will be found remaining the most sublime and benevolent code of morals which has ever been offered to man. I have performed this operation for my own use, by cutting verse by verse out of the printed book, and arranging the matter which is evidently his, and which is as easily distinguishable as diamonds in a dunghill. The result is an octavo of forty-six pages, of pure and unsophisticated doctrines, such as were professed and acted on by the *unlettered* Apostles, the Apostolic Fathers, and the Christians of the first century.* Their Platonizing successors, indeed, in after times, in order to legitimate the corruptions which they had incorporated into the doctrines of Jesus, found it necessary to disavow the primitive Christians, who had taken their principles from the mouth of Jesus himself, of his Apostles, and the Fathers contemporary with them. They excommunicated their followers as heretics, branding them with the opprobrious name of Ebionites or Beggars.

For a comparison of the Grecian philosophy with that of Jesus, materials might be largely drawn from the same source. Enfield gives a history and detailed account of the opinions and principles of the different sects. These relate to the Gods, their natures, grades, places and powers; the demi-Gods and dæmons, and their agency with man; the universe, its structure, extent and duration; the origin of things from the elements of fire, water, air and earth; the human soul, its essence and derivation; the *summum bonum* and *finis bonorum;* with a thousand idle

---

* See the footnote to Jefferson's letter to Charles Clay, January 29, 1815.

dreams and fancies on these and other subjects, the knowledge of which is withheld from man; leaving but a short chapter for his moral duties, and the principal section of that given to what he owes himself, to precepts for rendering him impassible, and unassailable by the evils of life, and for preserving his mind in a state of constant serenity.

Such a canvas is too broad for the age of seventy, and especially of one whose chief occupations have been in the practical business of life. We must leave, therefore, to others, younger and more learned than we are, to prepare this euthanasia for Platonic Christianity, and its restoration to the primitive simplicity of its founder. I think you give a just outline of the theism of the three religions, when you say that the principle of the Hebrew was the fear, of the Gentile the honor, and of the Christian the love of God.

An expression in your letter of September the 14th, that "the human understanding is a revelation from its maker," gives the best solution that I believe can be given of the question, "what did Socrates mean by his Dæmon?" He was too wise to believe, and too honest to pretend, that he had real and familiar converse with a superior and invisible being. He probably considered the suggestions of his conscience, or reason, as revelations or inspirations from the Supreme mind, bestowed, on important occasions, by a special superintending Providence.

I acknowledge all the merit of the hymn of Cleanthes to Jupiter, which you ascribe to it. It is as highly sublime as a chaste and correct imagination can permit itself to go. Yet in the contemplation of a being so superlative, the hyperbolic flights of the Psalmist may often be followed with approbation, even with rapture; and I have no hesitation in giving him the palm over all the hymnists of every language and of every time. Turn to the 148th Psalm, in Brady and Tate's version. Have such conceptions been ever before expressed? Their version of the 15th Psalm is more to be esteemed for its pithiness than its poetry. Even Sternhold, the leaden Sternhold, kindles, in a single instance, with the sublimity of his original, and expresses the majesty of God descending on the earth, in terms not unworthy of the subject:

> "The Lord descended from above,
> And bowed the heav'ns most high;
> And underneath his feet he cast
> The darkness of the sky.
> On Cherubim and Seraphim
> Full royally he rode;
> And on the wings of mighty winds
> Came flying all abroad."
> —Psalm xviii. 9, 10.

The best collection of these psalms is that of the Octagonian dissenters of Liverpool, in their printed form of prayer; but they are not always the best versions. Indeed, bad is the best of the English versions; not a ray of poetical genius having ever been employed on them. And how much depends on this may be seen by comparing Brady and Tate's 15th Psalm with Blacklock's *Justum et tenacem propositi virum* of Horace, quoted in Hume's history, Car. 2, ch. 65. A translation of David in this style, or in that of Pompei's Cleanthes, might give us some idea of the merit of the original. The character, too, of the poetry of these hymns is singular to us; written in monostichs, each divided into strophe and anti-strophe, the sentiment of the first member responded with amplification or antithesis in the second.

On the subject of the postscript of yours of August the 16th and of Mrs. Adams' letter, I am silent. I know the depth of the affliction it has caused, and can sympathize with it the more sensibly, inasmuch as there is no degree of affliction, produced by the loss of those dear to us, which experience has not taught me to estimate. I have ever found time and silence the only medicine, and these but assuage, they never can suppress, the deep drawn sigh which recollection forever brings up, until recollection and life are extinguished together. Ever affectionately yours,

TH: JEFFERSON

To John Adams

October 28, 1813 *Monticello*

The passage you quote from Theognis, I think has an ethical rather than a political object. * The whole piece is a moral *exhortation,* . . . and this passage particularly seems to be a reproof to man, who, while with his domestic animals he is curious to improve the race, by employing always the finest male, pays no attention to the improvement of his own race, but intermarries with the vicious, the ugly, or the old, for considerations of wealth or ambition. It is in conformity with the principle adopted afterwards by the Pythagoreans, and expressed by Ocellus . . . : (in another form; "περι δε τῆς ἐκ των αλληλων ανθρωπων γενεσεως, etc.—ουχ ηδονησ ενεκα η μιξις" which, as literally as intelligibility will admit, may be thus translated:) "concerning the interprocreation of men, how, and of whom it shall be, in a perfect manner, and according to the laws of modesty and sanctity, conjointly, this is what I think right. First, to lay it down that we do not commix for the sake of pleasure, but of the procreation of children. For the powers, the organs and desires for coition have not been given by God to man for the sake of pleasure, but for the procreation of the race. For as it were incongruous, for a mortal born to partake of divine life, the immortality of the

---

* On July 9, 1813, Adams wrote to Jefferson, mentioning a book of moral sentences from the ancient Greek poets: "In one of the oldest of them, I read in Greek, that I cannot repeat, a couplet, the sense of which was: 'Nobility in men is worth as much as it is in horses, asses, or rams; but the meanest blooded puppy in the world, if he gets a little money, is as good a man as the best of them.' Yet birth and wealth together have prevailed over virtue and talents in all ages. The many will acknowledge no other αριϛτοι."

On September 15, 1813, Adams wrote him again: "I asked you in a former letter how far advanced we were in the science of aristocracy since Theognis' stallions, jacks and rams? Have not Chancellor Livingston and Major General Humphreys introduced an hereditary aristocracy of Merino Sheep? How shall we get rid of this aristocracy? It is entailed upon us forever. And an aristocracy of land jobbers and stock jobbers is equally and irremediably entailed upon us, to endless generations." Jefferson's reply is given above.

race being taken away, God fulfilled the purpose by making the generations uninterrupted and continuous. This, therefore, we are especially to lay down as a principle, that coition is not for the sake of pleasure." But nature, not trusting to this moral and abstract motive, seems to have provided more securely for the perpetuation of the species, by making it the effect of the *oestrum* implanted in the constitution of both sexes. And not only has the commerce of love been indulged on this unhallowed impulse, but made subservient also to wealth and ambition by marriage, without regard to the beauty, the healthiness, the understanding, or virtue of the subject from which we are to breed. The selecting the best male for a harem of well chosen females also, which Theognis seems to recommend from the example of our sheep and asses, would doubtless improve the human, as it does the brute animal, and produce a race of veritable αριϛτοι. For experience proves, that the moral and physical qualities of man, whether good or evil, are transmissible in a certain degree from father to son. But I suspect that the equal rights of men will rise up against this privileged Solomon and his harem, and oblige us to continue acquiescence under the "Αμαυρωϛις γενεος αριϛτων" which Theognis complains of, and to content ourselves with the accidental aristoi produced by the fortuitous concourse of breeders. For I agree with you that there is a natural aristocracy among men. The grounds of this are virtue and talents. Formerly, bodily powers gave place among the aristoi. But since the invention of gunpowder has armed the weak as well as the strong with missile death, bodily strength, like beauty, good humor, politeness and other accomplishments, has become but an auxiliary ground of distinction. There is also an artificial aristocracy, founded on wealth and birth, without either virtue or talents; for with these it would belong to the first class. The natural aristocracy I consider as the most precious gift of nature, for the instruction, the trusts, and government of society. And, indeed, it would have been inconsistent in creation to have formed man for the social state, and not to have provided virtue and wisdom enough to manage the concerns of the society. May we not even say, that that form of government is the best, which provides the most effectually for a pure selection of these natural aristoi into the offices of government? The artificial aristocracy is a mischievous ingredient in government, and provision should be made to prevent its ascendency. On the question, what is the best provision, you and I differ; but we differ as rational friends, using the free exercise of our own reason, and mutually indulging its errors. You think it best to put the pseudo-aristoi into a separate chamber of legislation, where they may be hindered from doing mischief by their co-ordinate branches, and where, also, they may be a protection to wealth against the agrarian and plundering enterprises of the majority of the people. I think that to give them power in order to prevent them from doing mischief, is arming them for it, and increasing instead of remedying the evil. For if the co-ordinate branches can arrest their action, so may they that of the co-ordinates. Mischief may be done negatively as well as positively. Of this, a cabal in the Senate of the United States has furnished many proofs. Nor do I believe them necessary to protect the wealthy; because enough of these will find their way into every branch of the legislation, to protect themselves. From fifteen to twenty legislatures of our own, in action for thirty years past, have proved that no fears of an equalization of property are to be apprehended from them. I think the best remedy is exactly that provided by all our constitutions, to leave to the citizens the free election and separation of the aristoi from the pseudo-aristoi, of the wheat from the chaff. In general they will elect the really good and wise. In some instances, wealth may corrupt, and birth blind them; but not in sufficient degree to endanger the society.

It is probable that our difference of opinion may, in some measure, be produced by a difference of character in those among whom we live. From what I have seen of Massachusetts and Connecticut myself, and still more from what I have heard, and the character given of the former by yourself, . . . who know them so much better, there seems to be in those two States a traditionary reverence for certain families, which has rendered the offices of the government nearly hereditary in those families. I presume that from an early period of your history, members of those families happening to possess virtue and talents, have honestly exercised them for the good of the people, and by their services have endeared their names to them. In coupling Connecticut with you, I mean it politically only, not morally. For having made the Bible the common law of their land, they seem to have modeled their morality on the story of Jacob and Laban. But although this hereditary succession to office with you, may, in some degree, be founded in real family merit, yet in a much higher degree, it has proceeded from your strict alliance of Church and State. These families are canonized in the eyes of the people on common principles, "you tickle me, and I will tickle you." In Virginia we have nothing of this. Our clergy, before the Revolution, having been secured against rivalship by fixed salaries, did not give themselves the trouble of acquiring influence over the people. Of wealth, there were great accumulations in particular families, handed down from generation to generation, under the English law of entails. But the only object of ambition for the wealthy was a seat in the King's Council. All their court then was paid to the crown and its creatures; and they Philipized in all collisions between the King and the people. Hence they were unpopular; and that unpopularity continues attached to their names. A Randolph, a Carter, or a Burwell must have great personal superiority over a common competitor to be elected by the people even at this day. At the first session of our legislature after the Declaration of Independence, we passed a law abolishing entails. And this was followed by one abolishing the privilege of primogeniture, and dividing the lands of intestates equally among all their children, or other representatives. These laws, drawn by myself, laid the axe to the foot of pseudo-aristocracy. And had another which I prepared been adopted by the legislature, our work would have been complete. It was a bill for the more general diffusion of learning. This proposed to divide every county into wards of five or six miles square, like your townships; to establish in each ward a free school for reading, writing and common arithmetic; to provide for the annual selection of the best subjects from these schools, who might receive, at the public expense, a higher degree of education at a district school; and from these district schools to select a certain number of the most promising subjects, to be completed at a University, where all the useful sciences should be taught. Worth and genius would thus have been sought out from every condition of life, and completely prepared by education for defeating the competition of wealth and birth for public trusts. My proposition had, for a further object, to impart to these wards those portions of self-government for which they are best qualified, by confiding to them the care of their poor, their roads, police, elections, the nomination of jurors, administration of justice in small cases, elementary exercises of militia; in short, to have made them little republics, with a warden at the head of each, for all those concerns which, being under their eye, they would better manage than the larger republics of the county or State. A general call of ward meetings by their wardens on the same day through the State, would at any time produce the genuine sense of the people on any required point, and would enable the State to act in mass, as your people have so often done, and with so much effect by their town meetings. The law for religious freedom, which made a part of this system, having put down the aristocracy of the clergy and restored to the citizen the freedom of the mind, and those of entails and descents nurturing an equality of condition among them, this on education would have raised the mass of the people to the high ground of moral respectability necessary to their own safety, and to orderly government; and would have completed the great object of qualifying them to select the veritable aristoi, for the trusts of government, to the exclusion of the pseudalists; and the same Theognis who has furnished the epigraphs of your two letters, assures us that "Ουδεμιαν πω,

Κυρν', αγαθοι πολιν ωλεσαν ανδρες." Although this law has not yet been acted on but in a small and inefficient degree, it is still considered as before the legislature, with other bills of the revised code, not yet taken up, and I have great hope that some patriotic spirit will, at a favorable moment, call it up, and make it the key-stone of the arch of our government.

With respect to aristocracy, we should further consider, that before the establishment of the American States, nothing was known to history but the man of the old world, crowded within limits either small or overcharged, and steeped in the vices which that situation generates. A government adapted to such men would be one thing; but a very different one, that for the man of these States. Here everyone may have land to labor for himself, if he chooses; or, preferring the exercise of any other industry, may exact for it such compensation as not only to afford a comfortable subsistence, but wherewith to provide for a cessation from labor in old age. Everyone, by his property, or by his satisfactory situation, is interested in the support of law and order. And such men may safely and advantageously reserve to themselves a wholesome control over their public affairs, and a degree of freedom, which, in the hands of the *canaille* of the cities of Europe, would be instantly perverted to the demolition and destruction of everything public and private. The history of the last twenty-five years of France, and of the last forty years in America, nay of its last two hundred years, proves the truth of both parts of this observation.

But even in Europe a change has sensibly taken place in the mind of man. Science had liberated the ideas of those who read and reflect, and the American example had kindled feelings of right in the people. An insurrection has consequently begun, of science, talents, and courage, against rank and birth, which have fallen into contempt. It has failed in its first effort, because the mobs of the cities, the instrument used for its accomplishment, debased by ignorance, poverty, and vice, could not be restrained to rational action. But the world will recover from the panic of this first catastrophe. Science is progressive, and talents and enterprise on the alert. Resort may be had to the people of the country, a more governable power from their principles and subordination; and rank, and birth, and tinsel-aristocracy will finally shrink into insignificance, even there. This, however, we have no right to meddle with. It suffices for us, if the moral and physical condition of our own citizens qualifies them to select the able and good for the direction of their government, with a recurrence of elections at such short periods as will enable them to displace an unfaithful servant, before the mischief he mediates may be irremediable.

I have thus stated my opinion on a point on which we differ, not with a view to controversy, for we are both too old to change opinions which are the result of a long life of inquiry and reflection; but on the suggestions of a former letter of yours, that we ought not to die before we have explained ourselves to each other. We acted in perfect harmony, through a long and perilous contest for our liberty and independence. A constitution has been acquired, which, though neither of us thinks perfect, yet both consider as competent to render our fellow citizens the happiest and the securest on whom the sun has ever shone. If we do not think exactly alike as to its imperfections, it matters little to our country, which, after devoting to it long lives of disinterested labor, we have delivered over to our successors in life, who will be able to take care of it and of themselves.

Of the pamphlet on aristocracy which has been sent to you, or who may be its author, I have heard nothing but through your letter. If the person you suspect, it may be known from the quaint, mystical, and hyperbolical ideas, involved in affected, new-fangled and pedantic terms which stamp his writings. Whatever it be, I hope your quiet is not to be affected at this day by the rudeness or intemperance of scribblers; but that you may continue in tranquillity to live and to rejoice in the prosperity of our country, until it shall be your own wish to take your seat among the aristoi who have gone before you. Ever and affectionately yours,

TH: JEFFERSON

To Alexander von Humboldt *

December 6, 1813   *Monticello*

My dear friend and baron,—I have to acknowledge your two letters of December 20 and 26, 1811, by Mr. Correa, and am first to thank you for making me acquainted with that most excellent character. He was so kind as to visit me at Monticello, and I found him one of the most learned and amiable of men. It was a subject of deep regret to separate from so much worth in the moment of its becoming known to us.

The livraison of your astronomical observations, and the 6th and 7th on the subject of New Spain, with the corresponding atlases, are duly received, as had been the preceding cahiers. For these treasures of a learning so interesting to us, accept my sincere thanks. I think it most fortunate that your travels in those countries were so timed as to make them known to the world in the moment they were about to become actors on its stage. That they will throw off their European depend- ence I have no doubt; but in what kind of government their revolution will end I am not so certain. History, I believe, furnishes no example of a priest-ridden people maintaining a free civil government. This marks the lowest grade of ig- norance, of which their civil as well as religious leaders will always avail themselves for their own purposes. The vicinity of New Spain to the United States, and their consequent inter- course, may furnish schools for the higher, and example for the lower classes of their citizens. And Mexico, where we learn

---

* Humboldt (1769-1859) was a famous German explorer and philosopher.

from you that men of science are not wanting, may revolution-
ize itself under better auspices than the Southern provinces.
These last, I fear, must end in military despotisms. The
different casts of their inhabitants, their mutual hatreds and
jealousies, their profound ignorance and bigotry, will be played
off by cunning leaders, and each be made the instrument of
enslaving the others. But of all this you can best judge, for
in truth we have little knowledge of them to be depended
on, but through you. But in whatever governments they end
they will be *American* governments, no longer to be involved
in the never-ceasing broils of Europe. The European nations
constitute a separate division of the globe; their localities
make them part of a distinct system; they have a set of interests
of their own in which it is our business never to engage ourselves. America has a hemisphere to itself. It must have its
separate system of interests, which must not be subordinated
to those of Europe. The insulated state in which nature has
placed the American continent, should so far avail it that no
spark of war kindled in the other quarters of the globe should
be wafted across the wide oceans which separate us from them.
And it will be so. In fifty years more the United States alone
will contain fifty millions of inhabitants, and fifty years are soon
gone over. The peace of 1763 is within that period. I was then
twenty years old, and of course remember well all the transactions of the war preceding it. And you will live to see the
epoch now equally ahead of us; and the numbers which will
then be spread over the other parts of the American hemisphere, catching long before that the principles of our portion
of it, and concurring with us in the maintenance of the same
system. You see how readily we run into ages beyond the
grave; and even those of us to whom that grave is already
opening its quiet bosom. I am anticipating events of which
you will be the bearer to me in the Elysian fields fifty years
hence.

You know, my friend, the benevolent plan we were pursuing
here for the happiness of the aboriginal inhabitants in our

vicinities. We spared nothing to keep them at peace with one another, to teach them agriculture and the rudiments of the most necessary arts, and to encourage industry by establishing among them separate property. In this way they would have been enabled to subsist and multiply on a moderate scale of landed possession. They would have mixed their blood with ours, and been amalgamated and identified with us within no distant period of time. On the commencement of our present war, we pressed on them the observance of peace and neutrality, but the interested and unprincipled policy of England has defeated all our labors for the salvation of these unfortunate people. They have seduced the greater part of the tribes within our neighborhood, to take up the hatchet against us, and the cruel massacres they have committed on the women and children of our frontiers taken by surprise, will oblige us now to pursue them to extermination, or drive them to new seats beyond our reach. Already we have driven their patrons and seducers into Montreal, and the opening season will force them to their last refuge, the walls of Quebec. We have cut off all possibility of intercourse and of mutual aid, and may pursue at our leisure whatever plan we find necessary to secure ourselves against the future effects of their savage and ruthless warfare. The confirmed brutalization, if not the extermination, of this race in our America, is therefore to form an additional chapter in the English history of the same colored man in Asia, and of the brethren of their own color in Ireland, and wherever else Anglo-mercantile cupidity can find a two-penny interest in deluging the earth with human blood. But let us turn from the loathsome contemplation of the degrading effects of commercial avarice.

That their Arrowsmith should have stolen your Map of Mexico, was in the piratical spirit of his country. But I should be sincerely sorry if our Pike has made an ungenerous use of your candid communications here; and the more so as he died in the arms of victory gained over the enemies of his country. Whatever he did was on a principle of enlarging knowledge, and not for filthy shillings and pence of which he made none from that work. If what he has borrowed has any effect, it will be to excite an appeal in his readers from his defective information to the copious volumes of it with which you have enriched the world. I am sorry he omitted even to acknowledge the source of his information. It has been an oversight, and not at all in the spirit of his generous nature. Let me solicit your forgiveness then of a deceased hero, of an honest and zealous patriot, who lived and died for his country.

You will find it inconceivable that Lewis's journey to the Pacific should not yet have appeared; nor is it in my power to tell you the reason. The measures taken by his surviving companion, Clarke, for the publication, have not answered our wishes in point of dispatch. I think, however, from what I have heard, that the mere journal will be out within a few weeks in two volumes 8vo. These I will take care to send you with the tobacco seed you desired, if it be possible for them to escape the thousand ships of our enemies spread over the ocean. The botanical and zoological discoveries of Lewis will probably experience greater delay, and become known to the world through other channels before that volume will be ready. The Atlas, I believe, waits on the leisure of the engraver.

Although I do not know whether you are now at Paris or ranging the regions of Asia to acquire more knowledge for the use of men, I cannot deny myself the gratification of an endeavor to recall myself to your recollection, and of assuring you of my constant attachment, and of renewing to you the just tribute of my affectionate esteem and high respect and consideration,

TH: JEFFERSON

To Walter Jones *

January 2, 1814   *Monticello*

You say that in taking General Washington on your shoulders, to bear him harmless through the federal coalition, you encounter a perilous topic. I do not think so. You have given the genuine history of the course of his mind through the trying scenes in which it was engaged, and of the seductions by which it was deceived, but not depraved. I think I knew General Washington intimately and thoroughly; and were I called on to delineate his character, it should be in terms like these.

His mind was great and powerful, without being of the very first order; his penetration strong, though not so acute as that of a Newton, Bacon, or Locke; and as far as he saw, no judgment was ever sounder. It was slow in operation, being little aided by invention or imagination, but sure in conclusion. Hence the common remark of his officers, of the advantage he derived from councils of war, where, hearing all suggestions, he selected whatever was best; and certainly no general ever planned his battles more judiciously. But if deranged during the course of the action, if any member of his plan was dislocated by sudden circumstances, he was slow in a readjustment. The consequence was that he often failed in the field, and rarely against an enemy in station, as at Boston and York. He was incapable of fear, meeting personal dangers with the calmest unconcern. Perhaps the strongest feature in his character was prudence, never acting until every circumstance, every consideration, was maturely weighed; refraining if he saw a doubt, but, when once decided, going through with his purpose, whatever obstacles opposed. His integrity was most pure, his justice the most inflexible I have ever known, no motives

---

* Jones (1745-1815) was a Virginia physician and member of Congress from 1797 to 1799 and from 1803 to 1811.

of interest or consanguinity, of friendship or hatred, being able to bias his decision. He was, indeed, in every sense of the words, a wise, a good, and a great man. His temper was naturally irritable and high-toned; but reflection and resolution had obtained a firm and habitual ascendency over it. If ever, however, it broke its bonds, he was most tremendous in his wrath. In his expenses he was honorable, but exact; liberal in contributions to whatever promised utility; but frowning and unyielding on all visionary projects, and all unworthy calls on his charity. His heart was not warm in its affections; but he exactly calculated every man's value, and gave him a solid esteem proportioned to it. His person, you know, was fine, his stature exactly what one would wish, his deportment easy, erect and noble; the best horseman of his age, and the most graceful figure that could be seen on horseback. Although, in the circle of his friends, where he might be unreserved with safety, he took a free share in conversation, his colloquial talents were not above mediocrity, possessing neither copiousness of ideas, nor fluency of words. In public, when called on for a sudden opinion, he was unready, short, and embarrassed. Yet he wrote readily, rather diffusely, in an easy and correct style. This he had acquired by conversation with the world, for his education was merely reading, writing, and common arithmetic, to which he added surveying at a later day. His time was employed in action chiefly, reading little, and that only in agriculture and English history. His correspondence became necessarily extensive, and, with journalizing his agricultural proceedings, occupied most of his leisure hours within doors. On the whole, his character was, in its mass, perfect, in nothing bad, in few points indifferent; and it may truly be said, that never did nature and fortune combine more perfectly to make a man great, and to place him in the same constellation with whatever worthies have merited from man an everlasting remembrance. For his was the singular destiny and merit, of leading the armies of his country successfully through an arduous war, for the establishment of its independence; of conducting its councils through the birth of a government, new in its forms and principles, until it had settled down into a quiet and orderly train; and of scrupulously obeying the laws through the whole of his career, civil and military, of which the history of the world furnishes no other example.

How, then, can it be perilous for you to take such a man on your shoulders? I am satisfied the great body of Republicans think of him as I do. We were, indeed, dissatisfied with him on his ratification of the British treaty. But this was short lived. We knew his honesty, the wiles with which he was encompassed, and that age had already begun to relax the firmness of his purposes; and I am convinced he is more deeply seated in the love and gratitude of the Republicans, than in the Pharisaical homage of the Federal monarchists. For he was no monarchist from preference of his judgment. The soundness of that gave him correct views of the rights of man, and his severe justice devoted him to them. He has often declared to me that he considered our new Constitution as an experiment on the practicability of republican government, and with what dose of liberty man could be trusted for his own good; that he was determined the experiment should have a fair trial, and would lose the last drop of his blood in support of it. And these declarations he repeated to me the oftener and more pointedly, because he knew my suspicions of Colonel Hamilton's views, and probably had heard from him the same declarations which I had, to wit, "that the British constitution, with its unequal representation, corruption, and other existing abuses, was the most perfect government which had ever been established on earth, and that a reformation of those abuses would make it an impracticable government." I do believe that General Washington had not a firm confidence in the durability of our government. He was naturally distrustful of men, and inclined to gloomy apprehensions; and I was ever persuaded that a belief that we must at length end in something like a British constitution, had some weight in his adoption of the ceremonies of levees, birthdays, pompous meetings with Congress, and other forms of the same character, calculated to prepare us gradually for a change which he believed possible, and to let it come on with as little shock as might be to the public mind.

These are my opinions of General Washington, which I would vouch at the judgment-seat of God, having been formed on an acquaintance of thirty years. I served with him in the Virginia Legislature from 1769 to the Revolutionary war, and again, a short time in Congress, until he left us to take command of the army. During the war and after it we corresponded occasionally, and in the four years of my continuance in the office of Secretary of State, our intercourse was daily, confidential, and cordial. After I retired from that office, great and malignant pains were taken by our federal monarchists, and not entirely without effect, to make him view me as a theorist, holding French principles of government, which would lead infallibly to licentiousness and anarchy. And to this he listened the more easily, from my known disapprobation of the British treaty. I never saw him afterwards, or these malignant insinuations should have been dissipated before his just judgment, as mists before the sun. I felt on his death, with my countrymen, that "verily a great man hath fallen this day in Israel."

More time and recollection would enable me to add many other traits of his character; but why add them to you, who knew him well? And I cannot justify to myself a longer detention of your paper.

Vale, proprieque tuum, me esse tibi persuadeas,

TH: JEFFERSON

To Thomas Law *

June 13, 1814 *Monticello*

Of all the theories on this question, the most whimsical seems to have been that of Wollaston, † who considers *truth* as the foundation of morality. The thief who steals your guinea does wrong only inasmuch as he acts a lie in using your guinea as if it were his own. Truth is certainly a branch of morality, and a very important one to society. But presented as its foundation, it is as if a tree taken up by the roots had its stem reversed in the air, and one of its branches planted in the ground. Some have made the *love of God* the foundation of morality. This, too, is but a branch of our moral duties, which are generally divided into duties to God and duties to man. If we did a good act merely from the love of God and a belief that it is pleasing to Him, whence arises the morality of the atheist? It is idle to say, as some do, that no such being exists. We have the same evidence of the fact as of most of those we act on, to wit: their own affirmations, and their reasonings in support of them. I have observed, indeed, generally, that while in Protestant countries the defections from the Platonic Christianity of the priests is to Deism, in Catholic countries they are to Atheism. Diderot, D'Alembert, D'Holbach, Condorcet, are known to have been among the most virtuous of men. Their virtue, then, must have had some other foundation than the love of God.

The Τὸ καλὸν of others is founded in a different faculty, that of taste, which is not even a branch of morality. We have indeed an innate sense of what we call beautiful, but that is exercised chiefly on subjects addressed to the fancy, whether

---

* Law (1759-1834), a writer on economic subjects, was born in England and in 1793 settled in the U. S., where he married Eliza Parke Custis, Martha Washington's granddaughter.

† William Wollaston (1650-1724), an English philosophical writer, was the author of books on religion, including *The Religion of Nature Delineated* (1722).

through the eye in visible forms, as landscape, animal figure, dress, drapery, architecture, the composition of colors . . . or to the imagination directly, as imagery, style, or measure in prose or poetry, or whatever else constitutes the domain of criticism or taste, a faculty entirely distinct from the moral one. Self-interest, or rather self-love, or *egoism,* has been more plausibly substituted as the basis of morality. But I consider our relations with others as constituting the boundaries of morality. With ourselves we stand on the ground of identity, not of relation, which last, requiring two subjects, excludes self-love confined to a single one. To ourselves, in strict language, we can owe no duties, obligation requiring also two parties. Self-love, therefore, is no part of morality. Indeed it is exactly its counterpart. It is the sole antagonist of virtue, leading us constantly by our propensities to self-gratification in violation of our moral duties to others. Accordingly, it is against this enemy that are erected the batteries of moralists and religionists, as the only obstacle to the practice of morality. Take from man his selfish propensities, and he can have nothing to seduce him from the practice of virtue. Or subdue those propensities by education, instruction or restraint, and virtue remains without a competitor. Egoism, in a broader sense, has been thus presented as the source of moral action. It has been said that we feed the hungry, clothe the naked, bind up the wounds of the man beaten by thieves, pour oil and wine into them, set him on our own beast and bring him to the inn, because we receive ourselves pleasure from these acts. So Helvetius, one of the best men on earth, and the most ingenious advocate of this principle, after defining "interest" to mean not merely that which is pecuniary, but whatever may procure us pleasure or withdraw us from pain, [*De l'esprit* 2, 1,] says, [*ib.* 2, 2,] " the humane man is he to whom the sight of misfortune is insupportable, and who to rescue himself from this spectacle, is forced to succor the unfortunate object." This indeed is true. But it is one step short of the ultimate question. These good acts give us pleasure, but how happens it that they give us pleasure? Because nature hath implanted in our breasts a love of others, a sense of duty to them, a moral instinct, in short, which prompts us irresistibly to feel and to succor their distresses, and protests against the language of Helvetius, [*ib.* 2, 5,] "what other motive than self-interest could determine a man to generous actions? It is as impossible for him to love what is good for the sake of good, as to love evil for the sake of evil." The Creator would indeed have been a bungling artist, had he intended man for a social animal, without planting in him social dispositions. It is true they are not planted in every man, because there is no rule without exceptions; but it is false reasoning which converts exceptions into the general rule. Some men are born without the organs of sight, or of hearing, or without hands. Yet it would be wrong to say that man is born without these faculties, and sight, hearing, and hands may with truth enter into the general definition of man. The want or imperfection of the moral sense in some men, like the want or imperfection of the senses of sight and hearing in others, is no proof that it is a general characteristic of the species. When it is wanting, we endeavor to supply the defect by education, by appeals to reason and calculation, by presenting to the being so unhappily conformed, other motives to do good and to eschew evil, such as the love, or the hatred, or rejection of those among whom he lives, and whose society is necessary to his happiness and even existence; demonstrations by sound calculation that honesty promotes interest in the long run; the rewards and penalties established by the laws; and ultimately the prospects of a future state of retribution for the evil as well as the good done while here. These are the correctives which are supplied by education, and which exercise the functions of the moralist, the preacher, and legislator; and they lead into a course of correct action all those whose disparity is not too profound to be eradicated. Some have argued against the existence of a moral sense, by saying that if nature had given us such a sense, impelling us to virtuous actions, and warning us against those which are vicious, then nature would also have designated, by some particular ear-marks, the two sets of actions which are, in themselves, the one virtuous and the other vicious. Whereas, we find, in fact, that the same actions are deemed virtuous in one country and vicious in another. The answer is that nature has constituted *utility* to man the standard and best of virtue. Men living in different countries, under different circumstances, different habits and regimens, may have different utilities; the same act, therefore, may be useful, and consequently virtuous in one country which is injurious and vicious in another differently circumstanced. I sincerely, then, believe with you in the general existence of a moral instinct. I think it the brightest gem with which the human character is studded, and the want of it as more degrading than the most hideous of the bodily deformities. I am happy in reviewing the roll of associates in this principle which you present in your second letter, some of which I had not before met with. To these might be added Lord Kames,* one of the ablest of our advocates, who goes so far as to say, in his Principles of Natural Religion,† that a man owes no duty to which he is not urged by some impulsive feeling. This is correct, if referred to the standard of general feeling in the given case, and not to the feeling of a single individual. Perhaps I may misquote him, it being fifty years since I read his book.

To John Adams

July 5, 1814   *Monticello*

I learned with great regret the serious illness mentioned in your letter . . . Our machines have now been running seventy or eighty years, and we must expect that, worn as they

---

* Henry Home, Lord Kames (1696-1782), was a Scottish jurist and philosopher.
† *Essays on the Principles of Morality and Natural Religion,* published in 1751.

are, here a pivot, there a wheel, now a pinion, next a spring, will be giving way; and however we may tinker them up for a while, all will at length surcease motion. Our watches, with works of brass and steel, wear out within that period. Shall you and I last to see the course the seven-fold wonders of the times will take? The Attila of the age dethroned, * the ruthless destroyer of ten millions of the human race, whose thirst for blood appeared unquenchable, the great oppressor of the rights and liberties of the world, shut up within the circle of a little island of the Mediterranean, † and dwindled to the condition of an humble and degraded pensioner on the bounty of those he had most injured. How miserably, how meanly, has he closed his inflated career! What a sample of the bathos will his history present! He should have perished on the swords of his enemies, under the walls of Paris . . .

But Bonaparte was a lion in the field only. In civil life, a cold-blooded, calculating, unprincipled usurper, without a virtue: no statesman, knowing nothing of commerce, political economy, or civil government, and supplying ignorance by bold presumption. I had supposed him a great man until his entrance into the Assembly *des cinq cents,* eighteen Brumaire (an 8). From that date, however, I set him down as a great scoundrel only . . .

I amused myself with reading seriously Plato's Republic. I am wrong, however, in calling it amusement, for it was the heaviest task-work I ever went through. I had occasionally before taken up some of his other works, but scarcely ever had patience to go through a whole dialogue. While wading through the whimsies, the puerilities, and unintelligible jargon of this work, I laid it down often to ask myself how it could have been that the world should have so long consented to give reputation to such nonsense as this? How the *soi-disant* Christian world, indeed, should have done it, is a piece of historical curiosity.

---

* On April 4, 1814, Napoleon, whom Jefferson despised as a tyrant and hated as a militarist, was forced to abdicate his throne.

† The reference is to Elba, where Napoleon arrived as an exile on May 4, 1814.

But how could the Roman good sense do it? And particularly, how could Cicero bestow such eulogies on Plato? Although Cicero did not wield the dense logic of Demosthenes, yet he was able, learned, laborious, practiced in the business of the world, and honest. He could not be the dupe of mere style, of which he was himself the first master in the world. With the moderns, I think, it is rather a matter of fashion and authority. Education is chiefly in the hands of persons who, from their profession, have an interest in the reputation and the dreams of Plato. They give the tone while at school, and few in their after years have occasion to revise their college opinions. But fashion and authority apart, and bringing Plato to the test of reason, take from him his sophisms, futilities and incomprehensibilities, and what remains? In truth, he is one of the race of genuine sophists, who has escaped the oblivion of his brethren, first, by the elegance of his diction, but chiefly, by the adoption and incorporation of his whimsies into the body of artificial Christianity. His foggy mind is forever presenting the semblances of objects which, half seen through a mist, can be defined neither in form nor dimensions. Yet this, which should have consigned him to early oblivion, really procured him immortality of fame and reverence. The Christian priesthood, finding the doctrines of Christ levelled to every understanding, and too plain to need explanation, saw in the mysticism of Plato materials with which they might build up an artificial system, which might, from its indistinctness, admit everlasting controversy, give employment for their order, and introduce it to profit, power and pre-eminence. The doctrines which flowed from the lips of Jesus himself are within the comprehension of a child; but thousands of volumes have not yet explained the Platonisms engrafted on them; and for this obvious reason, that nonsense can never be explained. Their purposes, however, are answered. Plato is canonized; and it is now deemed as impious to question his merits as those of an Apostle of Jesus. He is peculiarly appealed to as an advocate of the immortality of the soul; and yet I will venture to say, that were there no better arguments than his in proof of it, not a man in the world would believe it. It is fortunate for us, that Platonic republicanism has not obtained the same favor as Platonic Christianity; or we should now have been all living, men, women and children, pell-mell together, like beasts of the field or forest. Yet "Plato is a great philosopher," said La Fontaine. But, says Fontenelle, "do you find his ideas very clear?" "Oh no! he is of an obscurity impenetrable." "Do you not find him full of contradictions?" "Certainly," replied La Fontaine, "he is but a sophist." Yet immediately after, he exclaims again, "Oh, Plato was a great philosopher." Socrates had reason, indeed, to complain of the misrepresentations of Plato; for in truth, his dialogues are libels on Socrates,

TH: JEFFERSON

To Peter Carr

September 7, 1814   *Monticello*

Dear sir, on the subject of the academy or college pro-posed to be established in our neighborhood, I promised the trustees that I would prepare for them a plan, adapted, in the first instance, to our slender funds, but susceptible of being enlarged, either by their own growth or by accession from other quarters.

I have long entertained the hope that this, our native State, would take up the subject of education, and make an establish-ment, either with or without incorporation into that of William and Mary, where every branch of science, deemed useful at this day, should be taught in its highest degree. With this view, I have lost no occasion of making myself acquainted with the organization of the best seminaries in other countries, and with the opinions of the most enlightened individuals, on the subject of the sciences worthy of a place in such an institution.

In order to prepare what I have promised our trustees, I have lately revised these several plans with attention; and I am struck with the diversity of arrangement observable in them —no two alike. Yet, I have no doubt that these several arrangements have been the subject of mature reflection, by wise and learned men, who, contemplating local circumstances, have adopted them to the conditions of the section of society for which they have been framed. I am strengthened in this conclusion by an examination of each separately, and a conviction that no one of them, if adopted without change, would be suited to the circumstances and pursuit of our country. The example they set, then, is authority for us to select from their different institutions the materials which are good for us, and, with them, to erect a structure, whose arrangement shall correspond with our own social condition, and shall admit of enlargement in proportion to the encouragement it may merit and receive. As I may not be able to attend the meetings of the trustees, I will make you the depository of my ideas on the subject, which may be corrected, as you proceed, by the better view of others, and adapted, from time to time, to the prospects which open upon us, and which cannot be specifically seen and provided for.

In the first place, we must ascertain with precision the object of our institution, by taking a survey of the general field of science, and marking out the portion we mean to occupy at first, and the ultimate extension of our views beyond that, should we be enabled to render it, in the end, as comprehensive as we would wish.

1. Elementary schools.

It is highly interesting to our country, and it is the duty of its functionaries, to provide that every citizen in it should receive an education proportioned to the condition and pursuits of his life. The mass of our citizens may be divided into two classes— the laboring and the learned. The laboring will need the first grade of education to qualify them for their pursuits and duties; the learned will need it as a foundation for further acquirements. A plan was formerly proposed to the legislature of this State for laying off every county into hundreds or wards of five or six miles square, within each of which should be a school for the education of the children of the ward, wherein they should receive three years' instruction gratis, in reading, writing, arithmetic as far as fractions, the roots and ratios, and geography. The Legislature at one time tried an ineffectual expedient for introducing this plan, which having failed, it is hoped they will some day resume it in a more promising form.

2. General schools.

At the discharging of the pupils from the elementary schools, the two classes separate—those destined for labor will engage in the business of agriculture, or enter into apprenticeships to such handicraft art as may be their choice; their companions, destined to the pursuits of science, will proceed to the college, which will consist, 1st of general schools; and, 2d, of professional schools. The general schools will constitute the second grade of education.

The learned class may still be subdivided into two sections: 1, Those who are destined for learned professions, as means of livelihood; and, 2, the wealthy, who, possessing independent fortunes, may aspire to share in conducting the affairs of the nation, or to live with usefulness and respect in the private ranks of life. Both of these sections will require instruction in all the higher branches of science; the wealthy to qualify them for either public or private life; the professional section will need those branches, especially, which are the basis of their future profession, and a general knowledge of the others, as auxiliary to that, and necessary to their standing and association with the scientific class. All the branches, then, of useful science, ought to be taught in the general schools, to a competent degree, in the first instance. These sciences may be arranged into three departments, not rigorously scientific, indeed, but sufficiently so for our purposes. These are, I. language; II. mathematics; III. philosophy.

I. Language. In the first department, I would arrange a distinct science. 1, Languages and history, ancient and modern; 2, grammar; 3, belles lettres; 4, rhetoric and oratory; 5, a school for the deaf, dumb and blind. History is here associated with languages, not as a kindred subject, but on the principle of economy, because both may be attained by the same course of reading, if books are selected with that view.

II. Mathematics. In the department of mathematics, I should give place distinctly: 1, mathematics pure; 2, physico-mathematics; 3, physics; 4, chemistry; 5, natural history, to wit: mineralogy; 6, botany; and 7, zoology; 8, anatomy; 9, the theory of medicine.

III. Philosophy. In the philosophical department, I should distinguish: 1, ideology; 2, ethics; 3, the law of nature and nations; 4, government; 5, political economy.

But, some of these terms being used by different writers, in different degrees of extension, I shall define exactly what I mean to comprehend in each of them.

I. 3. Within the term of belles lettres I include poetry and composition generally, and criticism.

II. 1. I consider pure mathematics as the science of, 1, numbers, and 2, measure in the abstract; that of numbers comprehending arithmetic, algebra and fluxions; that of measure (under the general appellation of geometry), comprehending trigonometry, plane and spherical, conic sections, and transcendental curves.

II. 2. Physico-mathematics treat of physical subjects by the aid of mathematical calculation. These are mechanics, statics, hydrostatics, hydrodynamics, navigation, astronomy, geography, optics, pneumatics, acoustics.

II. 3. Physics, or natural philosophy (not entering the limits of chemistry), treat of natural substances, their properties, mutual relations and action. They particularly examine the subjects of motion, action, magnetism, electricity, galvanism, light, meteorology, with an etc. not easily enumerated. These definitions and specifications render immaterial the question whether I use the generic terms in the exact degree of comprehension in which others use them; to be understood is all that is necessary to the present object.

3. Professional schools.

At the close of this course the students separate; the wealthy retiring, with a sufficient stock of knowledge, to improve themselves to any degree to which their views may lead them, and the professional section to the professional schools, constituting the third grade of education, and teaching the particular sciences which the individuals of this section mean to pursue with more minuteness and detail than was within the scope of the general schools for the second grade of instruction. In these professional schools each science is to be taught in the highest degree it has yet attained. They are to be the

1st Department, the fine arts, to wit: civil architecture, gardening, painting, sculpture, and the theory of music; the

2d Department, architecture, military and naval; projectiles, rural economy (comprehending agriculture, horticulture and veterinary), technical philosophy, the practice of medicine, materia medica, pharmacy and surgery. In the

3d Department, theology and ecclesiastical history; law, municipal and foreign.

To these professional schools will come those who separated at the close of their first elementary course, to wit:

The lawyer to the school of law.

The ecclesiastic to that of theology and ecclesiastical history.

The physician to those of medicine, materia medica, pharmacy and surgery.

The miltary man to that of military and naval architecture and projectiles.

The agricultor to that of rural economy.

The gentleman, the architect, the pleasure gardener, painter and musician to the school of fine arts.

And to that of technical philosophy will come the mariner, carpenter, shipwright, pumpmaker, clockmaker, machinist, optician, metallurgist, founder, cutler, druggist, brewer, vintner, distiller, dyer, painter, bleacher, soapmaker, tanner, powdermaker, saltmaker, glassmaker, to learn as much as shall be necessary to pursue their art understandingly, of the sciences of geometry, mechanics, statics, hydrostatics, hydraulics, hydro-dynamics, navigation, astronomy, geography, optics, pneumatics, physics, chemistry, natural history, botany, mineralogy and pharmacy.

The school of technical philosophy will differ essentially in its functions from the other professional schools. The others are instituted to ramify and dilate the particular sciences taught in the schools of the second grade on a general scale only. The technical school is to abridge those which were taught there too much *in extenso* for the limited wants of the artificer or practical man. These artificers must be grouped together, according to the particular branch of science in which they need elementary and practical instruction; and a special lecture or lectures should be prepared for each group. And these lectures should be given in the evening, so as not to interrupt the labors of the day. The school, particularly, should be maintained wholly at the public expense, on the same principles with that of the ward schools. Through the whole of the collegiate course, at the hours of recreation on certain days, all the students should be taught the manual exercise; military evolutions and maneuvers should be under a standing organization as a military corps, and with proper officers to train and command them.

A tabular statement of this distribution of the sciences will place the system of instruction more particularly in view:

1st, or Elementary grade in the ward schools.
Reading, writing, arithmetic, geography.

2d, or General Grade.

1. Language and history, ancient and modern.
2. Mathematics, *viz.*: mathematics pure, physico-mathematics, physics, chemistry, anatomy, theory of medicine, zoology, botany and mineralogy.
3. Philosophy, *viz.*: ideology, and ethics, law of nature and nations, government, political economy.

3d, or Professional Grades.

Theology and ecclesiastical history; law, municipal and foreign; practice of medicine; materia medica and pharmacy; surgery; architecture, military and naval, and projectiles; technical philosophy; rural economy; fine arts.

On this survey of the field of science, I recur to the question, what portion of it we mark out for the occupation of our institution? With the first grade of education we shall have nothing to do. The sciences of the second grade are our first object; and, to adapt them to our slender beginnings, we must separate them into groups, comprehending many sciences each, and greatly more, in the first instance, than ought to be imposed on, or can be competently conducted by a single professor permanently. They must be subdivided from time to time, as our means increase, until each professor shall have no more under his care than he can attend to with advantage to his pupils and ease to himself. For the present, we may group the sciences into professorships, as follows, subject, however, to be changed, according to the qualifications of the persons we may be able to engage.

I. Professorship.

Languages and history, ancient and modern.
Belles-lettres, rhetoric and oratory.

II. Professorship.

Mathematics pure, physico-mathematics.
Physics, anatomy, medicine, theory.

III. Professorship.

Chemistry, zoology, botany, mineralogy.

IV. Professorship.

Philosophy.

The organization of the branch of the institution which respects its government, police and economy, depending on principles which have no affinity with those of its institution, may be the subject of separate and subsequent consideration.

To Samuel Harrison Smith *

September 21, 1814   *Monticello*

Dear Sir, I learn from the newspapers that the vandalism of our enemy has triumphed at Washington over science as well as the arts, by the destruction of the public library with the noble edifice in which it was deposited.† Of this transaction, as of that of Copenhagen,‡ the world will entertain but one sentiment. They will see a nation suddenly withdrawn from a great war, full armed and full handed, taking advantage of another whom they had recently forced into it, unarmed, and unprepared, to indulge themselves in acts of barbarism which do not belong to a civilized age. When Van Ghent destroyed their shipping at Chatham, and De Ruyter rode triumphantly up the Thames, he might in like manner, by the acknowledgment of their own historians, have forced all their ships up to London bridge, and there have burnt them, the tower, and city, had these examples been then set. London, when thus menaced, was near a thousand years old, Washington is but in its teens.

I presume it will be among the early objects of Congress to re-commence their collection. This will be difficult while the war continues, and intercourse with Europe is attended with so much risk. You know my collection, its condition and extent. I have been fifty years making it, and have spared no pains, opportunity or expense, to make it what it is. While residing in Paris, I devoted every afternoon I was disengaged, for a sum-

---

* Samuel Harrison Smith (1772-1845) was a newspaper publisher who, upon the advice and encouragement of Jefferson, moved his printing establishment from Philadelphia to Washington, where he published the semi-official *Washington Intelligencer.*

† On August 24, 1814, the British took Washington and deliberately burned all the public buildings in the young capital, including the government books.

‡ In the summer of 1807, a British fleet of over 100 vessels sailed up to Copenhagen and, without declaration of war, bombarded the city and killed 2,000 civilians; this was done on the excuse of keeping Danish ships from falling into Napoleon's hands.

mer or two, in examining all the principal bookstores, turning over every book with my own hand, and putting by everything which related to America, and indeed whatever was rare and valuable in every science. Besides this, I had standing orders during the whole time I was in Europe, on its principal book-marts, particularly Amsterdam, Frankfort, Madrid and London, for such works relating to America as could not be found in Paris. So that in that department particularly, such a collection was made as probably can never again be effected, because it is hardly probable that the same opportunities, the same time, industry, perseverance and expense, with some knowledge of the bibliography of the subject, would again happen to be in concurrence. During the same period, and after my return to America, I was led to procure, also, whatever related to the duties of those in the high concerns of the nation. So that the collection, which I suppose is of between nine and ten thousand volumes, while it includes what is chiefly valuable in science and literature generally, extends more particularly to whatever belongs to the American statesman. In the diplomatic and parliamentary branches, it is particularly full. It is long since I have been sensible it ought not to continue private property, and had provided that at my death, Congress should have the refusal of it at their own price.* But the loss they have now incurred, makes the present the proper moment for their accommodation, without regard to the small remnant of time and the barren use of my enjoying it. I ask of your friendship, therefore, to make for me the tender of it to the library committee of Congress, not knowing myself of whom the committee consists. I enclose you the catalogue, which will enable them to judge of its contents. Nearly the whole are well bound, abundance of them elegantly, and of the choicest editions existing. They may be valued by persons named by themselves, and the payment made convenient to the public. It may be, for instance, in such annual installments as the law of Congress has left at

---

* Congress accepted the offer and paid Jefferson $25,000 for his great and rare collection, which became the nucleus of the Library of Congress.

their disposal, or in stock of any of their late loans, or of any loan they may institute at this session, so as to spare the present calls of our country, and await its days of peace and prosperity. They may enter, nevertheless, into immediate use of it, as eighteen or twenty wagons would place it in Washington in a single trip of a fortnight. I should be willing, indeed, to retain a few of the books, to amuse the time I have yet to pass, which might be valued with the rest, but not included in the sum of valuation until they should be restored at my death, which I would carefully provide for, so that the whole library as it stands in the catalogue at this moment should be theirs without any garbling. Those I should like to retain would be chiefly classical and mathematical. Some few in other branches, and particularly one of the five encyclopedias in the catalogue. But this, if not acceptable, would not be urged. I must add that I have not revised the library since I came home to live, so that it is probable some of the books may be missing, except in the chapters of Law and Divinity, which have been revised and stand exactly as in the catalogue. The return of the catalogue will of course be needed, whether the tender be accepted or not. I do not know that it contains any branch of science which Congress would wish to exclude from their collection; there is, in fact, no subject to which a member of Congress may not have occasion to refer. But such a wish would not correspond with my views of preventing its dismemberment. My desire is either to place it in their hands entire, or to preserve it so here. I am engaged in making an alphabetical index of the authors' names, to be annexed to the catalogue, which I will forward to you as soon as completed. Any agreement you shall be so good as to take the trouble of entering into with the committee, I hereby confirm. Accept the assurance of my great esteem and respect,

TH: JEFFERSON

To Charles Clay *

January 29, 1815   *Monticello*

Dear Sir, Of publishing a book on religion, my dear sir, I never had an idea. I should as soon think of writing for the reformation of Bedlam, as of the world of religious sects. Of these there must be, at least, ten thousand, every individual of every one of which believes all wrong but his own. To undertake to bring them all right, would be like undertaking, single-handed, to fell the forests of America. Probably you have heard me say I had taken the four evangelists, had cut out from them every text they had recorded of the moral precepts of Jesus, and arranged them in a certain order,† and although they appeared but as fragments, yet fragments of the most sublime edifice of morality which had ever been exhibited to man. This I have probably mentioned to you, because it is true; and the idea of its publication may have suggested itself as an inference of your own mind.

I not only write nothing on religion, but rarely permit myself to speak on it, and never but in a reasonable society. I have probably said more to you than to any other person, because we have had more hours of conversation in *duetto* in our meetings at the Forest. I abuse the priests,‡ indeed, who have so much abused the pure and holy doctrines of their master, and who have laid me under no obligations of reticence as to the tricks of their trade. The genuine system of Jesus, and the artificial

---

* The Rev. Charles Clay had been rector of St. Anne's Parish, in Albemarle County, Va., of which Jefferson was nominally a vestryman.

† This selection of passages, "extracted textually" from the Gospels, has been published under the title of *The Life and Morals of Jesus of Nazareth*. Several editions have come out, the most recent, with an historic introduction, being that of The Beacon Press in 1951. See also Jefferson's letters to Charles Thomson, January 9, 1816, and the one to William Short, October 31, 1819.

‡ See also Jefferson's letter to Benjamin Rush, September 23, 1800, with its famous passage:—"I have sworn upon the altar of God, eternal hostility against every form of tyranny over the mind of man."

structures they have erected to make them the instruments of wealth, power, and preëminence to themselves, are as distinct things in my view as light and darkness; and while I have classed them with soothsayers and necromancers, I place him among the greatest reformers of morals, and scourges of priest-craft that have ever existed. They felt him as such, and never rested until they had silenced him by death. But his heresies against Judaism prevailing in the long run, the priests have tacked about, and rebuilt upon them the temple which he destroyed, as splendid, as profitable, and as imposing as that.

Government, as well as religion, has furnished its schisms, its persecutions, and its devices for fattening idleness on the earnings of the people. It has its hierarchy of emperors, kings, princes, and nobles, as that has of popes, cardinals, archbishops, bishops, and priests. In short, cannibals are not to be found in the wilds of America only, but are revelling on the blood of every living people. Turning, then, from this loathsome combination of church and state, and weeping over the follies of our fellow men, who yield themselves the willing dupes and drudges of these mountebanks, I consider reformation and redress as desperate, and abandon them to the Quixotism of more enthusiastic minds.

I have received from Philadelphia, by mail, the spectacles you had desired, and now forward them by the same conveyance, as equally safe and more in time than were they to await my own going. In a separate case is a complete set of glasses, from early use to old age. I think the pair now in the frames will suit your eyes, but should they not, you will easily change them by the screws. I believe the largest numbers are the smallest magnifiers, but am not certain. Trial will readily ascertain it. You must do me the favor to accept them as a token of my friendship, and with them the assurance of my great esteem and respect,

Th: Jefferson

To Francis C. Gray *

March 4, 1815   *Monticello*

You asked me in conversation, what constituted a mulatto by our law? And I believe I told you four crossings with the whites. I looked afterwards into our law, and found it to be in these words: "Every person, other than a Negro, of whose grandfathers or grandmothers anyone shall have been a Negro, shall be deemed a mulatto, and so every such person who shall have one-fourth part or more of Negro blood, shall in like manner be deemed a mulatto;" L. Virgà 1792, December 17: the case put in the first member of this paragraph of the law is *exempli gratiâ*. The latter contains the true canon, which is that one-fourth of Negro blood, mixed with any portion of white, constitutes the mulatto. As the issue has one-half of the blood of each parent, and the blood of each of these may be made up of a variety of fractional mixtures, the estimate of their compound in some cases may be intricate, it becomes a mathematical problem of the same class with those on the mixtures of different liquors or different metals; as in these, therefore, the algebraical notation is the most convenient and intelligible. Let us express the pure blood of the white in the capital letters of the printed alphabet, the pure blood of the Negro in the small letters of the printed alphabet, and any given mixture of either, by way of abridgment in MS. letters.

Let the first crossing be of *a*, pure Negro, with A, pure white. The unit of blood of the issue being composed of the half of that of each parent, will be $\frac{a}{2} + \frac{A}{2}$. Call it, for abbreviation, *h* (half blood).

Let the second crossing be of *h* and B, the blood of the issue

---

will be $\dfrac{h}{2} + \dfrac{B}{2}$, or substituting for $\dfrac{h}{2}$ its equivalent, it will be $\dfrac{a}{4} + \dfrac{A}{4} + \dfrac{B}{2}$ call it q (quarteroon) being ¼ Negro blood.

Let the third crossing be of q and C, their offspring will be $\dfrac{q}{2} + \dfrac{C}{2} = \dfrac{a}{8} + \dfrac{A}{8} + \dfrac{B}{4} + \dfrac{C}{2}$, call this e (eighth), who having less than ¼ of a, or of pure Negro blood, to wit ⅛ only, is no longer a mulatto, so that a third cross clears the blood.

From these elements let us examine their compounds. For example, let h and q cohabit, their issue will be $\dfrac{h}{2} + \dfrac{q}{2} = \dfrac{a}{4} + \dfrac{A}{4} + \dfrac{a}{8} + \dfrac{A}{8} + \dfrac{B}{4} = \dfrac{^3a}{8} + \dfrac{^3A}{8} + \dfrac{B}{4}$ wherein we find ⅜ of a, or Negro blood.

Let h and e cohabit, their issue will be $\dfrac{h}{2} + \dfrac{e}{2} = \dfrac{a}{4} + \dfrac{A}{4} + \dfrac{a}{16} + \dfrac{A}{16} + \dfrac{B}{8} + \dfrac{c}{4} = \dfrac{^5a}{16} + \dfrac{^5A}{16} + \dfrac{B}{8} + \dfrac{c}{4}$, wherein $\tfrac{5}{16}$ a makes still a mulatto.

Let q and e cohabit, the half of the blood of each will be $\dfrac{q}{2} + \dfrac{e}{2} = \dfrac{a}{8} + \dfrac{A}{8} + \dfrac{B}{4} + \dfrac{a}{16} + \dfrac{A}{16} + \dfrac{B}{8} + \dfrac{C}{4} = \dfrac{^3a}{16} + \dfrac{^3A}{16} + \dfrac{^3B}{8} + \dfrac{C}{4}$, wherein $\tfrac{3}{16}$ of a is no longer a mulatto, and thus may every compound be noted and summed, the sum of the fractions composing the blood of the issue being always equal to unit. It is understood in natural history that a fourth cross of one race of animals with another gives an issue equivalent for all sensible purposes to the original blood. Thus a Merino ram being crossed, first with a country ewe, second with his daughter, third with his granddaughter, and fourth with the great-granddaughter, the last issue is deemed pure Merino, having in fact but $\tfrac{1}{16}$ of the country blood. Our canon considers two crosses with the pure white, and a third with any degree of mixture, however small, as clearing the issue of the Negro blood. But observe, that this does not re-establish freedom, which depends on the condition of the mother, the principle of the civil law, *partus sequitur ventrem,* being adopted here. But if *e* emancipated, he becomes a free *white* man, and a citizen of the United States to all intents and purposes. So much for this trifle by way of correction.

To Charles Thomson

January 9, 1816   *Monticello*

My dear and ancient friend, An acquaintance of fifty-two years, for I think ours dates from 1764, calls for an interchange of notice now and then, that we remain in existence, the monuments of another age, and examples of a friendship unaffected by the jarring elements by which we have been surrounded, of revolutions of government, of party and of opinion. I am reminded of this duty by the receipt, through our friend Doctor Patterson, of your synopsis of the four Evangelists. I had procured it as soon as I saw it advertised, and had become familiar with its use; but this copy is the more valued as it comes from your hand. This work bears the stamp of that accuracy which marks everything from you, and will be useful to those who, not taking things on trust, recur for themselves to the fountain of pure morals. I, too, have made a wee-little book from the same materials, which I call the Philosophy of Jesus; it is a paradigma of his doctrines, made by cutting the texts out of the book, and arranging them on the pages of a blank book, in a certain order of time or subject.* A more beautiful or precious morsel of ethics I have never seen; it is a document in proof that *I* † am a *real Christian,*† that is to say, a disciple of the doctrines of Jesus, very different from the Platonists, who call *me* † infidel and *themselves* † Christians and preachers of

---

* See the footnote to Jefferson's letter to Charles Clay, January 29, 1815.
† Underlined by Jefferson in the original.

the Gospel, while they draw all their characteristic dogmas from what its author never said nor saw. They have compounded from the heathen mysteries a system beyond the comprehension of man, of which the great reformer of the vicious ethics and deism of the Jews, were he to return on earth, would not recognize one feature. If I had time I would add to my little book the Greek, Latin and French texts, in columns side by side. And I wish I could subjoin a translation of Gassendi's Syntagma of the doctrines of Epicurus, which, notwithstanding the calumnies of the Stoics and caricatures of Cicero, is the most rational system remaining of the philosophy of the ancients, as frugal of vicious indulgence, and fruitful of virtue as the hyperbolical extravagances of his rival sects.

I retain good health, am rather feeble to walk much, but ride with ease, passing two or three hours a day on horseback, and every three or four months taking in a carriage a journey of ninety miles to a distant possession, where I pass a good deal of my time. My eyes need the aid of glasses by night, and with small print in the day also; my hearing is not quite so sensible as it used to be; no tooth shaking yet, but shivering and shrinking in body from the cold we now experience, my thermometer having been as low as 12° this morning. My greatest oppression is a correspondence afflictingly laborious, the extent of which I have been long endeavoring to curtail. This keeps me at the drudgery of the writing-table all the prime hours of the day, leaving for the gratification of my appetite for reading, only what I can steal from the hours of sleep. Could I reduce this epistolary corvée within the limits of my friends and affairs, and give the time redeemed from it to reading and reflection, to history, ethics, mathematics, my life would be as happy as the infirmities of age would admit, and I should look on its consummation with the composure of one *"qui summum nec metuit diem nec optat."*

So much as to myself, and I have given you this string of egotisms in the hope of drawing a similar one from yourself. I have heard from others that you retain your health, a good degree of activity, and all the vivacity and cheerfulness of your mind, but I wish to learn it more minutely from yourself. How has time affected your health and spirits? What are your amusements, literary and social? Tell me everything about yourself, because all will be interesting to me who retains for you ever the same constant and affectionate friendship and respect,

TH: JEFFERSON

To Benjamin Austin *

January 9, 1816   *Monticello*

Dear Sir, Your favor of December 21st has been received, and I am first to thank you for the pamphlet it covered. The same description of persons which is the subject of that is so much multiplied here too, as to be almost a grievance, and by their numbers in the public councils, have wrested from the public hand the direction of the pruning knife. But with us as a body, they are republican, and mostly moderate in their views; so far, therefore, less objects of jealousy than with you. Your opinions on the events which have taken place in France, are entirely just, so far as these events are yet developed. But they have not reached their ultimate termination. There is still an awful void between the present and what is to be the last chapter of that history; and I fear it is to be filled with abominations as frightful as those which have already disgraced it. That nation is too high-minded, has too much innate force, intelligence and elasticity, to remain under its present compression. Samson will arise in his strength, as of old, and as of old will burst asunder the withes and the cords, and the webs of the Philistines. But what are to be the scenes of havoc and horror, and how widely they may spread between brethren of

---

* Austin (1752-1820) was a Jeffersonian political leader in Boston.

the same house, our ignorance of the interior feuds and antipathies of the country places beyond our ken. It will end, nevertheless, in a representative government, in a government in which the will of the people will be an effective ingredient. This important element has taken root in the European mind, and will have its growth; their despots, sensible of this, are already offering this modification of their governments, as if of their own accord. Instead of the parricide treason of Bonaparte, in perverting the means confided to him as a republican magistrate, to the subversion of that republic and erection of a military despotism for himself and his family, had he used it honestly for the establishment and support of a free government in his own country, France would now have been in freedom and rest; and her example operating in a contrary direction, every nation in Europe would have had a government over which the will of the people would have had some control. His atrocious egotism has checked the salutary progress of principle, and deluged it with rivers of blood which are not yet run out. To the vast sum of devastation and of human misery, of which he has been the guilty cause, much is still to be added. But the object is fixed in the eye of nations, and they will press on to its accomplishment and to the general amelioration of the condition of man. What a germ have we planted, and how faithfully should we cherish the parent tree at home!

You tell me I am quoted by those who wish to continue our dependence on England for manufactures. There was a time when I might have been so quoted with more candor, but within the thirty years which have since elapsed, how are circumstances changed! We were then in peace. Our independent place among nations was acknowledged. A commerce which offered the raw material in exchange for the same material after receiving the last touch of industry, was worthy of welcome to all nations. It was expected that those especially to whom manufacturing industry was important, would cherish the friendship of such customers by every favor, by every inducement, and particularly cultivate their peace by every act of justice and friendship. Under this prospect the question seemed legitimate, whether, with such an immensity of unimproved land, courting the hand of husbandry, the industry of agriculture, or that of manufacturers, would add most to the national wealth? And the doubt was entertained on this consideration chiefly, that to the labor of the husbandman a vast addition is made by the spontaneous energies of the earth on which it is employed: for one grain of wheat committed to the earth, she renders twenty, thirty, and even fifty fold, whereas to the labor of the manufacturer nothing is added. Pounds of flax, in his hands, yield, on the contrary, but pennyweights of lace. This exchange, too, laborious as it might seem, what a field did it promise for the occupations of the ocean; what a nursery for that class of citizens who were to exercise and maintain our equal rights on that element? This was the state of things in 1785, when the "Notes on Virginia" were first printed; when, the ocean being open to all nations, and their common right in it acknowledged and exercised under regulations sanctioned by the assent and usage of all, it was thought that the doubt might claim some consideration. But who in 1785 could foresee the rapid depravity which was to render the close of that century the disgrace of the history of man? Who could have imagined that the two most distinguished in the rank of nations, for science and civilization, would have suddenly descended from that honorable eminence, and setting at defiance all those moral laws established by the Author of nature between nation and nation, as between man and man, would cover earth and sea with robberies and piracies, merely because strong enough to do it with temporal impunity; and that under this disbandment of nations from social order, we should have been despoiled of a thousand ships, and have thousands of our citizens reduced to Algerine slavery. Yet all this has taken place. One of these nations interdicted to our vessels all harbors of the globe without having first proceeded to some one of hers, there paid a tribute proportioned to the cargo, and obtained her license to proceed to the port of destination. The other declared them to be lawful prize if they had touched at the port, or been visited by a ship of the enemy nation. Thus were we completely excluded from the ocean. Compare this state of things with that of '85, and say whether an opinion founded in the circumstances of that day can be fairly applied to those of the present. We have experienced what we did not then believe, that there exists both profligacy and power enough to exclude us from the field of interchange with other nations: that to be independent for the comforts of life we must fabricate them ourselves. We must now place the manufacturer by the side of the agriculturist. The former question is suppressed, or rather assumes a new form. Shall we make our own comforts, or go without them, at the will of a foreign nation? He, therefore, who is now against domestic manufacture, must be for reducing us either to dependence on that foreign nation, or to be clothed in skins, and to live like wild beasts in dens and caverns. I am not one of these; experience has taught me that manufactures are now as necessary to our independence as to our comfort; and if those who quote me as of a different opinion, will keep pace with me in purchasing nothing foreign where an equivalent of domestic fabric can be obtained, without regard to difference of price, it will not be our fault if we do not soon have a supply at home equal to our demand, and wrest that weapon of distress from the hand which has wielded it. If it shall be proposed to go beyond our own supply, the question of '85 will then recur, will our *surplus* labor be then most beneficially employed in the culture of the earth, or in the fabrications of art? We have time yet for consideration, before that question will press upon us; and the maxim to be applied will depend on the circumstances which shall then exist; for in so complicated a science as political economy, no one axiom can be laid down as wise and expedient for all times and circumstances, and for their contraries.

To John Adams

January 11, 1816 *Monticello*

Dear Sir, Of the last five months I have passed four at my other domicile, for such it is in a considerable degree. No letters are forwarded to me there, because the cross post to that place is circuitous and uncertain; during my absence, therefore, they are accumulating here, and awaiting acknowledgments. This has been the fate of your favor of November 13th.

I agree with you in all its eulogies on the eighteenth century. It certainly witnessed the sciences and arts, manners and morals, advanced to a higher degree than the world had ever before seen. And might we not go back to the era of the Borgias, by which time the barbarous ages had reduced national morality to its lowest point of depravity, and observe that the arts and sciences, rising from that point, advanced gradually through all the sixteenth, seventeenth and eighteenth centuries, softening and correcting the manners and morals of man? I think, too, we may add to the great honor of science and the arts, that their natural effect is, by illuminating public opinion, to erect it into a censor, before which the most exalted tremble for their future, as well as present fame. With some exceptions only, through the seventeenth and eighteenth centuries, morality occupied an honorable chapter in the political code of nations. You must have observed while in Europe, as I thought I did, that those who administered the governments of the greater powers at least, had a respect to faith, and considered the dignity of their government as involved in its integrity. A wound indeed was inflicted on this character of honor in the eighteenth century by the partition of Poland. But this was the atrocity of a barbarous government chiefly, in conjunction with a smaller one still scrambling to become great, while one only of those already great, and having character to lose, descended to the baseness of an accomplice in the crime. France, England,

Spain shared in it only inasmuch as they stood aloof and permitted its perpetration.

How then has it happened that these nations, France especially and England, so great, so dignified, so distinguished by science and the arts, plunged all at once into all the depths of human enormity, threw off suddenly and openly all the restraints of morality, all sensation to character, and unblushingly avowed and acted on the principle that power was right? Can this sudden apostasy from national rectitude be accounted for? The treaty of Pilnitz seems to have begun it, suggested perhaps by the baneful precedent of Poland. Was it from the terror of monarchs, alarmed at the light returning on them from the west, and kindling a volcano under their thrones? Was it a combination to extinguish that light, and to bring back, as their best auxiliaries, those enumerated by you, the Sorbonne, the Inquisition, the Index Expurgatorius, and the knights of Loyola? Whatever it was, the close of the century saw the moral world thrown back again to the age of the Borgias, to the point from which it had departed three hundred years before. France, after crushing and punishing the conspiracy of Pilnitz, went herself deeper and deeper into the crimes she had been chastising. I say France and not Bonaparte; for, although he was the head and mouth, the nation furnished the hands which executed his enormities. England, although in opposition, kept full pace with France, not indeed by the manly force of her own arms, but by oppressing the weak and bribing the strong. At length the whole choir joined and divided the weaker nations among them. Your prophecies to Doctor Price proved truer than mine; and yet fell short of the fact, for instead of a million, the destruction of eight or ten millions of human beings has probably been the effect of these convulsions. I did not, in '89, believe they would have lasted so long, nor have cost so much blood. But although your prophecy has proved true so far, I hope it does not preclude a better final result. That same light from our west seems to have spread and illuminated the very engines employed to extinguish it.

It has given them a glimmering of their rights and their power. The idea of representative government has taken root and growth among them. Their masters feel it, and are saving themselves by timely offers of this modification of their powers. Belgium, Prussia, Poland, Lombardy . . . are now offered a representative organization; illusive probably at first, but it will grow into power in the end. Opinion is power, and that opinion will come. Even France will yet attain representative government. You observe it makes the basis of every constitution which has been demanded or offered—of that demanded by their Senate; of that offered by Bonaparte; and of that granted by Louis XVIII. The idea then is rooted, and will be established, although rivers of blood may yet flow between them and their object. The allied armies now couching upon them are first to be destroyed, and destroyed they will surely be. A nation united can never be conquered. We have seen what the ignorant, bigoted and unarmed Spaniards could do against the disciplined veterans of their invaders. What then may we not expect from the power and character of the French nation? The oppressors may cut off heads after heads, but like those of the Hydra they multiply at every stroke. The recruits within a nation's own limits are prompt and without number; while those of their invaders from a distance are slow, limited, and must come to an end. I think, too, we perceive that all these allies do not see the same interest in the annihilation of the power of France. There are certainly some symptoms of foresight in Alexander that France might produce a salutary diversion of force were Austria and Prussia to become her enemies. France, too, is the neutral ally of the Turk, as having no interfering interests, and might be useful in neutralizing and perhaps turning that power on Austria. That a re-acting jealousy, too, exists with Austria and Prussia, I think their late strict alliance indicates; and I should not wonder if Spain should discover a sympathy with them. Italy is so divided as to be nothing. Here then we see new coalitions in embryo, which, after France shall in turn have suffered a just punishment for her crimes, will not only raise her from the earth on which she is prostrate, but give her an opportunity to establish a government of as much liberty as she can bear—enough to ensure her happiness and prosperity. When insurrection begins, be it where it will, all the partitioned countries will rush to arms, and Europe again become an arena of gladiators. And what is the definite object they will propose? A restoration certainly of the *status quo prius,* of the state of possession of '89. I see no other principle on which Europe can ever again settle down in lasting peace. I hope your prophecies will go thus far, as my wishes do, and that they, like the former, will prove to have been the sober dictates of a superior understanding, and a sound calculation of effects from causes well understood.

To Peter Wilson *

January 20, 1816   *Monticello*

Sir, of the last five months, I have been absent four from home, which must apologize for so very late an acknowledgment of your favor of November 22d, and I wish the delay could be compensated by the matter of the answer. But an unfortunate accident puts that out of my power. During the course of my public life, and from a very early period of it, I omitted no opportunity of procuring vocabularies of the Indian languages, and for that purpose formed a model expressing such objects in nature as must be familiar to every people, savage or civilized. This being made the standard to which all were brought, would exhibit readily whatever affinities of language there be between the several tribes. It was my intention, on retiring from public business, to have digested

---

* Wilson (1746-1825), a Scotch-born philologist, was professor of Greek and Latin at Columbia College from 1797 to his retirement in 1820.

these into some order, so as to show not only what relations of language existed among our own aborigines, but by a collation with the great Russian vocabulary of the languages of Europe and Asia, whether there were any between them and the other nations of the continent. On my removal from Washington, the package in which this collection was coming by water was stolen and destroyed. It consisted of between thirty and forty vocabularies, of which I can, from memory, say nothing particular; but that I am certain more than half of them differed as radically, each from every other, as the Greek, the Latin, and Icelandic. And even of those which seemed to be derived from the same radix, the departure was such that the tribes speaking them could not probably understand one another. Single words, or two or three together, might perhaps be understood, but not a whole sentence of any extent or construction. I think, therefore, the pious missionaries who shall go to the several tribes to instruct them in the Christian religion will have to learn a language for every tribe they go to; nay, more, that they will have to create a new language for every one, that is to say, to add to theirs new words for the new ideas they will have to communicate. Law, medicine, chemistry, mathematics, every science has a language of its own, and divinity not less than others. Their barren vocabularies cannot be vehicles for ideas of the fall of man, his redemption, the triune composition of the Godhead, and other mystical doctrines considered by most Christians of the present date as essential elements of faith. The enterprise is therefore arduous, but the more inviting perhaps to missionary zeal, in proportion as the merit of surmounting it will be greater. Again repeating my regrets that I am able to give so little satisfaction on the subject of your inquiry, I pray you to accept the assurance of my great consideration and esteem,

TH: JEFFERSON

To Joseph C. Cabell *

February 2, 1816   *Monticello*

No, my friend, the way to have good and safe government, is not to trust it all to one, but to divide it among the many, distributing to every one exactly the functions he is competent to. Let the national government be entrusted with the defense of the nation, and its foreign and federal relations; the State governments with the civil rights, laws, police, and administration of what concerns the State generally; the counties with the local concerns of the counties, and each ward direct the interests within itself. It is by dividing and subdividing these republics from the great national one down through all its subordinations, until it ends in the administration of every man's farm by himself; by placing under every one what his own eye may superintend, that all will be done for the best. What has destroyed liberty and the rights of man in every government which has ever existed under the sun? The generalizing and concentrating all cares and powers into one body, no matter whether of the autocrats of Russia or France, or of the aristocrats of a Venetian senate. And I do believe that if the Almighty has not decreed that man shall never be free, (and it is a blasphemy to believe it,) that the secret will be found to be in the making himself the depository of the powers respecting himself, so far as he is competent to them, and delegating only what is beyond his competence by a synthetical process, to higher and higher orders of functionaries, so as to trust fewer and fewer powers in proportion as the trustees become more and more oligarchical. The elementary republics of the wards, the county republics, the State republics, and the republic of the union, would form a gradation of authorities, standing each on the

---

* Cabell (1778-1856) was co-founder with Jefferson of the University of Virginia.

basis of law, holding every one its delegated share of powers, and constituting truly a system of fundamental balances and checks for the government. Where every man is a sharer in the direction of his ward-republic, or of some of the higher ones, and feels that he is a participator in the government of affairs, not merely at an election one day in the year, but every day; when there shall not be a man in the State who will not be a member of some one of its councils, great or small, he will let the heart be torn out of his body sooner than his power be wrested from him by a Cæsar or a Bonaparte. How powerfully did we feel the energy of this organization in the case of embargo? I felt the foundations of the government shaken under my feet by the New England townships. There was not an individual in their States whose body was not thrown with all its momentum into action; and although the whole of the other States were known to be in favor of the measure, yet the organization of this little selfish minority enabled it to overrule the union. What would the unwieldy counties of the middle, the south, and the west do? Call a county meeting, and the drunken loungers at and about the court houses would have collected, the distances being too great for the good people and the industrious generally to attend. The character of those who really met would have been the measure of the weight they would have had in the scale of public opinion. As Cato, then, concluded every speech with the words, *"Carthago delenda est,"* so do I every opinion, with the injunction, "divide the counties into wards." Begin them only for a single purpose; they will soon show for what others they are the best instruments. God bless you, and all our rulers, and give them the wisdom, as I am sure they have the will, to fortify us against the degeneracy of one government, and the concentration of all its powers in the hands of the one, the few, the well-born or the many.

To James Monroe *

February 4, 1816   *Monticello*

Dear Sir, Your letter concerning that of General Scott
is received, and his is now returned. I am very thankful for
these communications. From forty years' experience of the
wretched guess-work of the newspapers of what is not done in
open daylight, and of their falsehood even as to that, I rarely
think them worth reading, and almost never worth notice.
A ray, therefore, now and then, from the fountain of light, is
like sight restored to the blind. It tells me where I am; and
that to a mariner who has long been without sight of land
or sun, is a rallying of reckoning which places him at ease.
The ground you have taken with Spain is sound in every part.
It is the true ground, especially, as to the South Americans.
When subjects are able to maintain themselves in the
field, they are then an independent power as to all neutral
nations, are entitled to their commerce, and to protection
within their limits. Every kindness which can be shown the
South Americans, every friendly office and aid within the limits
of the law of nations, I would extend to them, without fearing
Spain or her Swiss auxiliaries. For this is but an assertion of
our own independence. But to join in their war, as General
Scott proposes, and to which even some members of Congress
seem to squint, is what we ought not to do as yet. On the
question of our interest in their independence, were that alone
a sufficient motive of action, much may be said on both sides.
When they are free, they will drive every article of our produce
from every market, by underselling it, and change the condition
of our existence, forcing us into other habits and pursuits. We
shall, indeed, have in exchange some commerce with them, but
in what I know not, for we shall have nothing to offer which

---

* Secretary of State in Madison's Administration, Monroe was President of
the United States from 1817 to 1825.

they cannot raise cheaper; and their separation from Spain seals
our everlasting peace with her. On the other hand, so long as
they are dependent, Spain, from her jealousy, is our natural
enemy, and always in either open or secret hostility with us.
These countries, too, in war, will be a powerful weight in her
scale, and, in peace, totally shut to us. Interest then, on the
whole, would wish their independence, and justice makes
the wish a duty. They have a right to be free, and we a right
to aid them, as a strong man has a right to assist a weak one
assailed by a robber or murderer. That a war is brewing
between us and Spain cannot be doubted. When that disposition is matured on both sides, and open rupture can no
longer be deferred, then will be the time for our joining the
South Americans, and entering into treaties of alliance with
them. There will then be but one opinion, at home or abroad,
that we shall be justifiable in choosing to have them with us,
rather than against us. In the meantime, they will have organized regular governments, and perhaps have formed themselves into one or more confederacies; more than one I hope,
as in single mass they would be a very formidable neighbor.
The geography of their country seems to indicate three: 1,
What is north of the Isthmus. 2, What is south of it on the
Atlantic; and 3, The southern part on the Pacific. In this form,
we might be the balancing power.

To Benjamin Austin

February 9, 1816   *Monticello*

Sir, Your favor of January 25th is just now received. I
am in general extremely unwilling to be carried into the newspapers, no matter what the subject; the whole pack of the Essex
kennel would open upon me. With respect, however, to so much

of my letter of January 9th as relates to manufactures, I have less repugnance, because there is perhaps a degree of duty to avow a change of opinion called for by a change of circumstances, and especially on a point now become peculiarly interesting.

What relates to Bonaparte stands on different ground. You think it will silence the misrepresentations of my enemies as to my opinions of him. No, sir; it will not silence them. They had no ground either in my words or actions for these misrepresentations before, and cannot have less afterwards; nor will they calumniate less. There is, however, a consideration respecting our own friends, which may merit attention. I have grieved to see even good republicans so infatuated as to this man, as to consider his downfall as calamitous to the cause of liberty. In their indignation against England which is just, they seem to consider all *her* enemies as *our* friends, when it is well known there was not a being on earth who bore us so deadly a hatred. In fact, he saw nothing in this world but himself, and looked on the people under him as cattle, beasts for burden and slaughter. Promises cost him nothing when they could serve his purpose. On his return from Elba, what did he not promise? But those who had credited them a little, soon saw their total insignificance, and, satisfied they could not fall under worse hands, refused every effort after the defeat of Waterloo. Their present sufferings will have a term; his iron despotism would have had none. France has now a family of fools at its head, from whom, whenever it can shake off its foreign riders, it will extort a free constitution, or dismount them and establish some other on the solid basis of national right. To whine after this exorcised demon is a disgrace to republicans, and must have arisen either from want of reflection, or the indulgence of passion against principle. If anything I have said could lead them to take correcter views, to rally to the polar principles of genuine republicanism, I could consent that that part of my letter also should go into a newspaper. This I leave to yourself and such candid friends as you may consult. There is one word in the letter, however, which decency towards the allied sovereigns requires should be softened. Instead of *despots,* call them *rulers.* The first paragraph, too, of seven or eight lines, must be wholly omitted. Trusting all the rest to your discretion, I salute you with great esteem and respect,

TH: JEFFERSON

To John Adams

April 8, 1816   *Monticello*

Dear Sir, I have to acknowledge your two favors of February the 16th and March the 2d, and to join sincerely in the sentiment of Mrs. Adams, and regret that distance separates us so widely. An hour of conversation would be worth a volume of letters. But we must take things as they come.

You ask, if I would agree to live my seventy or rather seventy-three years over again? * To which I say, yea. I think with you, that it is a good world on the whole; that it has been framed on a principle of benevolence, and more pleasure than pain dealt out to us. There are, indeed, (who might say nay) gloomy and hypochondriac minds, inhabitants of diseased bodies, disgusted with the present, and despairing of the future; always counting that the worst will happen, because it may happen. To these I say, how much pain have cost us the evils which have never happened! My temperament is sanguine. I steer my bark with hope in the head, leaving fear astern. My hopes, indeed, sometimes fail; but not oftener than the forebodings of the gloomy. There are, I acknowledge, even in the happiest life, some terrible convulsions, heavy set-offs against the opposite page of the account. I have often wondered for

---

* On March 2, 1816, Adams wrote to Jefferson: "I am about to write you the most frivolous letter you ever read. Would you go back to your cradle and live over again your seventy years? I believe you would return me a New England answer, by asking me another question."

what good end the sensations of grief could be intended. All
our other passions, within proper bounds, have an useful
object. And the perfection of the moral character is, not in a
stoical apathy, so hypocritically vaunted, and so untruly too,
because impossible, but in a just equilibrium of all the passions.
I wish the pathologists then would tell us what is the use of
grief in the economy, and of what good it is the cause, proximate or remote.

Did I know Baron Grimm while at Paris? Yes, most intimately. He was the pleasantest and most conversable member
of the diplomatic corps while I was there; a man of good fancy,
acuteness, irony, cunning and egoism. No heart, not much of
any science, yet enough of every one to speak its language; his
forte was belles-lettres, painting and sculpture. In these he was
the oracle of society, and as such, was the Empress Catherine's
private correspondent and factor, in all things not diplomatic. It
was through him I got her permission for poor Ledyard to go to
Kamchatka, and cross over thence to the western coast of
America, in order to penetrate across our continent in the opposite direction to that afterwards adopted for Lewis and Clarke;
which permission she withdrew after he had got within two
hundred miles of Kamchatka, had him seized, brought back,
and set down in Poland. Although I never heard Grimm express the opinion directly, yet I always supposed him to be of
the school of Diderot, D'Alembert, D'Holbach; the first of
whom committed his system of atheism to writing in *"Le
bon sens,"* and the last in his *"Systeme de la Nature."* It was
a numerous school in the Catholic countries, while the infidelity
of the Protestant took generally the form of theism. The former always insisted that it was a mere question of definition
between them, the hypostasis of which, on both sides, was *"Nature,"* or *"the Universe;"* that both agreed in the order of the
existing system, but the one supposed it from eternity, the other
as having begun in time. And when the atheist descanted on
the unceasing motion and circulation of matter through the
animal, vegetable and mineral kingdoms, never resting, never

annihilated, always changing form, and under all forms gifted with the power of reproduction; the theist, pointing "to the heavens above, and to the earth beneath, and to the waters under the earth," asked, if these did not proclaim a first cause, possessing intelligence and power; power in the production, and intelligence in the design and constant preservation of the system; urged the palpable existence of final causes; that the eye was made to see, and the ear to hear, and not that we see because we have eyes, and hear because we have ears; an answer obvious to the senses, as that of walking across the room, was to the philosopher demonstrating the non-existence of motion. It was in D'Holbach's conventicles that Rousseau imagined all the machinations against him were contrived; and he left, in his *Confessions*, the most biting anecdotes of Grimm. These appeared after I left France; but I have heard that poor Grimm was so much afflicted by them, that he kept his bed several weeks. I have never seen the Memoirs of Grimm. Their volume has kept them out of our market.

I have lately been amusing myself with Levi's book, in answer to Doctor Priestley. It is a curious and tough work. His style is inelegant and incorrect, harsh and petulant to his adversary, and his reasoning flimsy enough. Some of his doctrines were new to me, particularly that of his two resurrections; the first, a particular one of all the dead, in body as well as soul, who are to live over again, the Jews in a state of perfect obedience to God, the other nations in a state of corporeal punishment for the sufferings they have inflicted on the Jews. And he explains this resurrection of the bodies to be only of the original stamen of Leibnitz, or the human *calus* in *semine masculino*, considering that as a mathematical point, insusceptible of separation or division. The second resurrection, a general one of souls and bodies, eternally to enjoy divine glory in the presence of the Supreme Being. He alleges that the Jews alone preserve the doctrine of the unity of God. Yet their God would be deemed a very indifferent man with us; and it was to correct their anamorphosis of the Deity, that Jesus preached, as well as to establish the doctrine of a future state. However, Levi insists, that that was taught in the Old Testament, and even by Moses himself and the prophets. He agrees that an anointed prince was prophesied and promised; but denies that the character and history of Jesus had any analogy with that of the person promised. He must be fearfully embarrassing to the Hierophants of fabricated Christianity; because it is their own armor in which he clothes himself for the attack. For example, he takes passages of scripture from their context (which would give them a very different meaning), strings them together, and makes them point towards what object he pleases; he interprets them figuratively, typically, analogically, hyperbolically; he calls in the aid of emendation, transposition, ellipse, metonymy, and every other figure of rhetoric; the name of one man is taken for another, one place for another, days and weeks for months and years; and finally, he avails himself all his advantage over his adversaries by his superior knowledge of the Hebrew, speaking in the very language of the divine communication, while they can only fumble on with conflicting and disputed translations. Such is this war of giants. And how can such pigmies as you and I decide between them? For myself, I confess that my head is not formed *tantas componere lites.* And as you began yours of March the 2d, with a declaration that you were about to write me the most frivolous letter I had ever read, so I will close mine by saying, I have written you a full match for it, and by adding my affectionate respects to Mrs. Adams, and the assurance of my constant attachment and consideration for yourself,

TH: JEFFERSON

To Dupont de Nemours

April 24, 1816   *Poplar Forest*

I received, my dear friend, your letter covering the constitution for your equinoctial republics, just as I was setting out for this place. I brought it with me, and have read it with great satisfaction. I suppose it well formed for those for whom it was intended, and the excellence of every government is its adaptation to the state of those to be governed by it. For us it would not do. Distinguishing between the structure of the government and the moral principles on which you prescribe its administration, with the latter we concur cordially, with the former we should not. We of the United States, you know, are constitutionally and conscientiously democrats. We consider society as one of the natural wants with which man has been created; that he has been endowed with faculties and qualities to effect its satisfaction by concurrence of others having the same want; that when, by the exercise of these faculties, he has procured a state of society, it is one of his acquisitions which he has a right to regulate and control, jointly indeed with all those who have concurred in the procurement, whom he cannot exclude from its use or direction more than they him. We think experience has proved it safer, for the mass of individuals composing the society, to reserve to themselves personally the exercise of all rightful powers to which they are competent, and to delegate those to which they are not competent to deputies named, and removable for unfaithful conduct, by themselves immediately. Hence, with us, the people (by which is meant the mass of individuals composing the society) being competent to judge of the facts occurring in ordinary life, they have retained the functions of judges of facts, under the name of jurors; but being unqualified for the management of affairs requiring intelligence above the common level, yet competent judges of human character, they chose, for their management, representatives, some by themselves immediately, others by electors chosen by themselves. Thus our President is chosen by ourselves, directly in *practice,* for we vote for A as elector only on the condition he will vote for B, our representatives by ourselves immediately, our Senate and judges of law through electors chosen by ourselves. And we believe that this proximate choice and power of removal is the best security which experience has sanctioned for ensuring an honest conduct in the functionaries of society. Your three or four alembications have indeed a seducing appearance. We should conceive, *primâ facie,* that the last extract would be the pure alcohol of the substance, three or four times rectified. But in proportion as they are more and more sublimated, they are also farther and farther removed from the control of the society; and the human character, we believe, requires in general constant and immediate control, to prevent its being biased from right by the seductions of self-love. Your process produces therefore a structure of government from which the fundamental principle of ours is excluded. You first set down as zeros all individuals not having lands, which are the greater number in every society of long standing. Those holding lands are permitted to manage in person the small affairs of their commune or corporation, and to elect a deputy for the canton; in which election, too, every one's vote is to be a unit, a plurality, or a fraction, in proportion to his landed possessions. The assemblies of cantons, then, elect for the districts; those of districts for circles; and those of circles for the national assemblies. Some of these highest councils, too, are in a considerable degree self-elected, the regency partially, the judiciary entirely, and some are for life. Whenever, therefore, an *esprit de corps,* or of party, gets possession of them, which experience shows to be inevitable, there are no means of breaking it up, for they will never elect but those of their own spirit. Juries are allowed in criminal cases only. I acknowledge myself strong in affection to our own form, yet both of us act and think from the same motive, we both consider the people as our children, and love them with parental affection. But you love them as infants whom you are afraid to trust without nurses; and I as adults whom I freely leave to self-government. And you are right in the case referred to you; my criticism being built on a state of society not under your contemplation. It is, in fact, like a critic on Homer by the laws of the drama.

But when we come to the moral principles on which the government is to be administered, we come to what is proper for all conditions of society. I meet you there in all the benevolence and rectitude of your native character; and I love myself always most where I concur most with you. Liberty, truth, probity, honor, are declared to be the four cardinal principles of your society. I believe with you that morality, compassion, generosity, are innate elements of the human constitution; that there exists a right independent of force; that a right to property is founded in our natural wants, in the means with which we are endowed to satisfy these wants, and the right to what we acquire by those means without violating the similar rights of other sensible beings; that no one has a right to obstruct another, exercising his faculties innocently for the relief of sensibilities made a part of his nature; that justice is the fundamental law of society; that the majority, oppressing an individual, is guilty of a crime, abuses its strength, and by acting on the law of the strongest breaks up the foundations of society; that action by the citizens in person, in affairs within their reach and competence, and in all others by representatives, chosen immediately, and removable by themselves, constitutes the essence of a republic; that all governments are more or less republican in proportion as this principle enters more or less into their composition; and that a government by representation is capable of extension over a greater surface of country than one of any other form. These, my friend, are the essentials in which you and I agree; however, in our zeal for their maintenance, we may be perplexed and divaricate as to the structure of society most likely to secure them.

In the constitution of Spain, as proposed by the late Cortes,

there was a principle entirely new to me, and not noticed in
yours, that no person, born after that day, should ever acquire
the rights of citizenship until he could read and write. It is
impossible sufficiently to estimate the wisdom of this provision.
Of all those which have been thought of for securing fidelity in
the administration of the government, constant ralliance to the
principles of the constitution, and progressive amendments with
the progressive advances of the human mind, or changes in
human affairs, it is the most effectual. Enlighten the people
generally, and tyranny and oppressions of body and mind will
vanish like evil spirits at the dawn of day. Although I do not,
with some enthusiasts, believe that the human condition will
ever advance to such a state of perfection as that there shall no
longer be pain or vice in the world, yet I believe it susceptible
of much improvement, and most of all, in matters of government and religion; and that the diffusion of knowledge among
the people is to be the instrument by which it is to be effected.
The constitution of the Cortes had defects enough; but when I
saw in it this amendatory provision, I was satisfied all would
come right in time, under its salutary operation. No people have
more need of a similar provision than those for whom you have
felt so much interest. No mortal wishes them more success than
I do. But if what I have heard of the ignorance and bigotry of
the mass be true, I doubt their capacity to understand and to
support a free government; and fear that their emancipation
from the foreign tyranny of Spain, will result in a military
despotism at home. Palacios may be great; others may be great;
but it is the multitude which possesses force; and wisdom must
yield to that. For such a condition of society, the constitution
you have devised is probably the best imaginable. It is certainly
calculated to elicit the best talents; although perhaps not well
guarded against the egoism of its functionaries. But that egoism
will be light in comparison with the pressure of a military
despot, and his army of janissaries. Like Solon to the Athenians,
you have given to your Columbians, not the best possible
government, but the best they can bear. By-the-bye, I wish

you had called them the Columbian republics, to distinguish them from our American republics. Theirs would be the most honorable name, and they best entitled to it; for Columbus discovered their continent, but never saw ours.

To them liberty and happiness; to you the meed of wisdom and goodness in teaching them how to attain them, with the affectionate respect and friendship of,

TH: JEFFERSON

To Francis Eppes *

May 21, 1816   *Monticello*

I send you, my dear Francis, a Greek grammar, the best I know for the use of schools. It is the one now the most generally used in the United States. I expect you will begin it soon after your arrival at the New London Academy. You might, while at home, amuse yourself with learning the letters, and spelling and reading the Greek words, so that you may not be stopped by that when Mr. Mitchell puts you into the grammar. I think you will like him, and old Mr. and Mrs. Deshavens, from the character I have of them. I am sure Mr. Mitchell will do everything for you he can, and I have no fear that you will not do full justice to his instruction. But, while you endeavor, by a good store of learning, to prepare yourself to become a useful and distinguished member of your country, you must remember that this can never be, without uniting merit with your learning. Honesty, disinterestedness, and good nature are indispensable to procure the esteem and confidence of those with whom we live, and on whose esteem our happiness depends. Never suffer a thought to be harbored in your mind which you would not avow openly. When tempted to do anything in secret, ask yourself if you would do it in public; if

---

* Jefferson's grandson.

you would not, be sure it is wrong. In little disputes with your companions, give way rather than insist on trifles, for their love and the approbation of others will be worth more to you than the trifle in dispute. Above all things, and at all times, practice yourself in good humor; this of all human qualities is the most amiable and endearing to society. Whenever you feel a warmth of temper rising, check it at once, and suppress it, recollecting it would make you unhappy within yourself, and disliked by others. Nothing gives one person so great an advantage over another, under all circumstances. Think of these things, practice them, and you will be rewarded by the love and confidence of the world. I have some expectation of being at Poplar Forest the third week of June, when I hope I shall see you going on cleverly, and already beloved by your tutors, curators, and companions, as you are by yours affectionately,

TH: JEFFERSON

To John Taylor *

May 28, 1816   *Monticello*

Dear Sir, On my return from a long journey and considerable absence from home, I found here the copy of your "Enquiry into the Principles of Our Government," † which you

---

* John Taylor "of Caroline" (1753-1824) was a Virginia aristocrat, agrarian philosopher, democratic statesman, and agricultural pioneer whose book *Ararat* became a standard guide for Virginia farmers.

† The correct title was *An Inquiry into the Principles and Policy of the Government of the United States,* published at Fredericksburg, Va., in 1814. Of this prolix but original work, Parrington (*Main Currents in American Thought,* II, 15) wrote: "It summed up adequately the agrarian argument against capitalism, analyzed the current tendencies, and provided a convenient handbook for the Jacksonian movement, from which the latter drew freely in the dispute over the Bank." Charles Beard (*Economic Origins of Jeffersonian Democracy, 323*) thought it worthy "to rank among the two or three really historic contributions to political science which have been produced in the United States." But a contemporary, John Randolph, described it as "forcible, concise, perspicuous, feeble, tedious, obscure, unintelligible."

had been so kind as to send me; and for which I pray you to accept my thanks. The difficulties of getting new works in our situation, inland and without a single bookstore, are such as had prevented my obtaining a copy before; and letters which had accumulated during my absence, and were calling for answers, have not yet permitted me to give to the whole a thorough reading; yet certain that you and I could not think differently on the fundamentals of rightful government, I was impatient, and availed myself of the intervals of repose from the writing table, to obtain a cursory idea of the body of the work.

I see in it much matter for profound reflection; much which should confirm our adhesion, in practice, to the good principles of our constitution, and fix our attention on what is yet to be made good. The sixth section on the good moral principles of our government, I found so interesting and replete with sound principles, as to postpone my letter-writing to its thorough perusal and consideration. Besides much other good matter, it settles unanswerably the right of instructing representatives, and their duty to obey. The system of banking we have both equally and ever reprobated. I contemplate it as a blot left in all our constitutions, which, if not covered, will end in their destruction, which is already hit by the gamblers in corruption, and is sweeping away in its progress the fortunes and morals of our citizens. Funding I consider as limited, rightfully, to a redemption of the debt within the lives of a majority of the generation contracting it; every generation coming equally, by the laws of the Creator of the world, to the free possession of the earth he made for their subsistence, unencumbered by their predecessors, who, like them, were but tenants for life. You have successfully and completely pulverized Mr. Adams' system of orders, and his opening the mantle of republicanism to every government of laws, whether consistent or not with natural right. Indeed, it must be acknowledged, that the term *republic* is of very vague application in every language. Witness the self-styled republics of Holland, Switzerland, Genoa, Venice,

Poland. Were I to assign to this term a precise and definite idea, I would say, purely and simply, it means a government by its citizens in mass, acting directly and personally, according to rules established by the majority; and that every other government is more or less republican, in proportion as it has in its composition more or less of this ingredient of the direct action of the citizens. Such a government is evidently restrained to very narrow limits of space and population. I doubt if it would be practicable beyond the extent of a New England township. The first shade from this pure element, which, like that of pure vital air, cannot sustain life of itself, would be where the powers of the government, being divided, should be exercised each by representatives chosen either *pro hac vice,* or for such short terms as should render secure the duty of expressing the will of their constituents. This I should consider as the nearest approach to a pure republic, which is practicable on a large scale of country or population. And we have examples of it in some of our State constitutions, which, if not poisoned by priestcraft, would prove its excellence over all mixtures with other elements; and, with only equal doses of poison, would still be the best. Other shades of republicanism may be found in other forms of government, where the executive, judiciary and legislative functions, and the different branches of the latter, are chosen by the people more or less directly, for longer terms of years, or for life, or made hereditary; or where there are mixtures of authorities, some dependent on, and others independent of the people. The further the departure from direct and constant control by the citizens, the less has the government of the ingredient of republicanism; evidently none where the authorities are hereditary, as in France, Venice . . . or self-chosen, as in Holland; and little, where for life, in proportion as the life continues in being after the act of election.

The purest republican feature in the government of our own State, is the House of Representatives. The Senate is equally so the first year, less the second, and so on. The executive still less, because not chosen by the people directly. The judiciary seriously anti-republican, because for life; and the national arm wielded, as you observe, by military leaders, irresponsible but to themselves. Add to this the vicious constitution of our county courts (to whom the justice, the executive administration, the taxation, police, the military appointments of the county, and nearly all our daily concerns are confided), self-appointed, self-continued, holding their authorities for life, and with an impossibility of breaking in on the perpetual succession of any faction once possessed of the bench. They are in truth, the executive, the judiciary, and the military of their respective counties, and the sum of the counties makes the State. And add, also, that one half of our brethren who fight and pay taxes, are excluded, like Helots, from the rights of representation, as if society were instituted for the soil, and not for the men inhabiting it; or one half of these could dispose of the rights and the will of the other half, without their consent.

> "What constitutes a State?
> Not high-raised battlements, or labor'd mound,
> Thick wall, or moated gate;
> Not cities proud, with spires and turrets crown'd;
> No: men, high minded men;
> Men, who their duties know;
> But know their rights; and knowing, dare maintain.
> These constitute a State."

In the general government, the House of Representatives is mainly republican; the Senate scarcely so at all, as not elected by the people directly, and so long secured even against those who do elect them; the executive more republican than the Senate, from its shorter term, its election by the people, in *practice,* (for they vote for A only on an assurance that he will vote for B), and because, *in practice also,* a principle of rotation seems to be in a course of establishment; the judiciary independent of the nation, their coercion by impeachment being found nugatory.

If, then, the control of the people over the organs of their government be the measure of its republicanism, and I confess I know no other measure, it must be agreed that our governments have much less of republicanism than ought to have been expected; in other words, that the people have less regular control over their agents, than their rights and their interests require. And this I ascribe, not to any want of republican dispositions in those who formed these constitutions, but to a submission of true principle to European authorities, to speculators on government, whose fears of the people have been inspired by the populace of their own great cities, and were unjustly entertained against the independent, the happy, and therefore orderly citizens of the United States. Much I apprehend that the golden moment is past for reforming these heresies. The functionaries of public power rarely strengthen in their dispositions to abridge it, and an unorganized call for timely amendment is not likely to prevail against an organized opposition to it. We are always told that things are going on well; why change them? *"Chi sta bene, non si muove,"* said the Italian, "let him who stands well, stand still." This is true; and I verily believe they would go on well with us under an absolute monarch, while our present character remains, of order, industry and love of peace, and restrained, as he would be, by the proper spirit of the people. But it is while it remains such, we should provide against the consequences of its deterioration. And let us rest in the hope that it will yet be done, and spare ourselves the pain of evils which may never happen.

On this view of the import of the term *republic,* instead of saying, as has been said, "that it may mean anything or nothing," we may say with truth and meaning, that governments are more or less republican, as they have more or less of the element of popular election and control in their composition; and believing, as I do, that the mass of the citizens is the safest depository of their own rights, and especially, that the evils flowing from the duperies of the people, are less injurious than those from the egoism of their agents. I am a friend to that composition of government which has in it the most of this ingredient. And I sincerely believe, with you, that banking establishments are more dangerous than standing armies; and that the principle of spending money to be paid by posterity, under the name of funding, is but swindling futurity on a large scale.

I salute you with constant friendship and respect,

TH: JEFFERSON

To Samuel Kercheval

July 12, 1816   *Monticello*

Some men look at constitutions with sanctimonious reverence, and deem them like the ark of the covenant, too sacred to be touched. They ascribe to the men of the preceding age a wisdom more than human, and suppose what they did to be beyond amendment. I knew that age well; I belonged to it, and labored with it. It deserved well of its country. It was very like the present, but without the experience of the present; and forty years of experience in government is worth a century of book-reading; and this they would say themselves, were they to rise from the dead. I am certainly not an advocate for frequent and untried changes in laws and constitutions. I think moderate imperfections had better be borne with; because, when once known, we accommodate ourselves to them, and find practical means of correcting their ill effects. But I know also, that laws and institutions must go hand in hand with the progress of the human mind. As that becomes more developed, more enlightened, as new discoveries are made, new truths disclosed, and manners and opinions change with the change of circumstances, institutions must advance also, and keep pace with the times. We might as well require a man to wear still the coat which fitted him when a boy, as civilized society to remain ever under the regimen of their barbarous ancestors. It is this preposterous idea which has lately deluged Europe in blood. Their monarchs, instead of wisely yielding to the gradual change of circumstances, of favoring progressive accommodation to progressive improvement, have clung to old abuses, entrenched themselves behind steady habits, and obliged their subjects to seek through blood and violence rash and ruinous innovations, which, had they been referred to the peaceful deliberations and collected wisdom of the nation, would have been put into acceptable and salutary forms. Let us follow no such examples, nor weakly believe that one generation is not as capable as another of taking care of itself, and of ordering its own affairs. Let us, as our sister States have done, avail ourselves of our reason and experience, to correct the crude essays of our first and unexperienced, although wise, virtuous, and well-meaning councils. And lastly, let us provide in our constitution for its revision at stated periods. What these periods should be, nature herself indicates. By the European tables of mortality, of the adults living at any one moment of time, a majority will be dead in about nineteen years. At the end of that period then, a new majority is come into place; or, in other words, a new generation. Each generation is as independent of the one preceding, as that was of all which had gone before. It has then, like them, a right to choose for itself the form of government it believes most promotive of its own happiness; consequently, to accommodate to the circumstances in which it finds itself, that received from its predecessors; and it is for the peace and good of mankind, that a solemn opportunity of doing this every nineteen or twenty years, should be provided by the constitution; so that it may be handed on, with periodical repairs, from generation to generation, to the end of time, if anything human can so long endure. It is now forty years since the constitution of Virginia was formed. The same tables inform us, that, within that period, two-thirds of the adults then living are now dead. Have then the remaining third, even if they had the wish, the right to hold in obedience to their will, and to laws heretofore made by them, the other two-thirds, who, with themselves, compose the present mass of adults? If they have not, who has? The dead? But the dead have no rights. They are nothing; and nothing cannot own something. Where there is no substance, there can be no accident. This corporeal globe, and everything upon it, belong to its present corporeal inhabitants, during their generation. They alone have a right to direct what is the concern of themselves alone, and to declare the law of that direction; and this declaration can only be made by their majority. That majority, then, has a right to depute representatives to a convention, and to make the constitution what they think will be the best for themselves. But how collect their voice? This is the real difficulty. If invited by private authority, or county or district meetings, these divisions are so large that few will attend; and their voice will be imperfectly, or falsely pronounced. Here, then, would be one of the advantages of the ward divisions I have proposed. The mayor of every ward, on a question like the present, would call his ward together, take the simple yea or nay of its members, convey these to the county court, who would hand on those of all its wards to the proper general authority; and the voice of the whole people would be thus fairly, full, and peaceably expressed, discussed, and decided by the common reason of the society. If this avenue be shut to the call of sufferance, it will make itself heard through that of force, and we shall go on, as other nations are doing, in the endless circle of oppression, rebellion, reformation; and oppression, rebellion, reformation, again; and so on forever.

These, sir, are my opinions of the governments we see among men, and of the principles by which alone we may prevent our own from falling into the same dreadful track. I have given them at greater length than your letter called for. But I cannot say things by halves; and I confide them to your honor, so to use them as to preserve me from the gridiron of the public papers. If you shall approve and enforce them, as you have done that of equal representation, they may do some good. If not, keep them to yourself as the effusions of withered age and useless time. I shall, with not the less truth, assure you of my great respect and consideration.

To Mrs. Samuel Harrison Smith *

August 6, 1816   *Monticello*

I recognize the same motives of goodness in the solicitude you express on the rumor supposed to proceed from a letter of mine to Charles Thomson, on the subject of the Christian religion. It is true that, in writing to the translator of the Bible and Testament, that subject was mentioned; but equally so that no adherence to any particular mode of Christianity was there expressed; nor any change of opinions suggested. A change from what? The priests, indeed, have heretofore thought proper to ascribe to me religious, or rather anti-religious sentiments of their own fabric, but such as soothed their resentments against the Act of Virginia for establishing religious freedom. They wished him to be thought atheist, deist, or devil, who could advocate freedom from their religious dictations, but I have ever thought religion a concern purely between our God and our consciences, for which we were accountable to Him, and not to the priests. I never told my own religion, nor scrutinized that of another. I never attempted to make a convert, nor wished to change another's creed. I have ever judged of the religion of others by their lives; and by this test, my dear madam, I have been satisfied yours must be an excellent one, to have produced a life of such exemplary virtue and correctness, for it is in our lives and not from our words, that our religion must be read. By the same test the world must judge me.

---

* Wife of the publisher of the pro-Jeffersonian Washington *Universal Gazette,* as well as the *National Intelligencer and Washington Advertiser.*

But this does not satisfy the priesthood. They must have a positive, a declared assent to all their interested absurdities. My opinion is that there would never have been an infidel, if there had never been a priest. The artificial structures they have built on the purest of all moral systems, for the purpose of deriving from it pence and power, revolt those who think for themselves and who read in that system only what is really there. These, therefore, they brand with such nicknames as their enmity chooses gratuitously to impute. I have left the world in silence, to judge causes from their effects; and I am consoled in this course, my dear friend, when I perceive the candor with which I am judged by your justice and discernment; and that, notwithstanding the slanders of the saints, my fellow citizens have thought me worthy of trust. The imputations of irreligion having spent their force, they think an imputation of change might now be turned to account as a bolster for their duperies. I shall leave them, as heretofore, to grope on in the dark.

To Abigail Adams

January 11, 1817   *Monticello*

I owe you, dear madam, a thousand thanks for the letters communicated in your favor of December 15th, and now returned. They give me more information than I possessed before, of the family of Mr. Tracy. But what is infinitely interesting, is the scene of the exchange of Louis XVIII for Bonaparte. What lessons of wisdom Mr. Adams must have read in that short space of time! More than fall to the lot of others in the course of a long life. Man, and the man of Paris, under those circumstances, must have been a subject of profound speculation! It would be a singular addition to that spectacle, to see the same beast in the cage of St. Helena, like a lion in

the tower. That is probably the closing verse of the chapter of
his crimes. But not so with Louis. He has other vicissitudes to
go through.

I communicated the letters, according to your permission,
to my grand-daughter, Ellen Randolph,* who read them with
pleasure and edification. She is justly sensible of, and flattered
by your kind notice of her; and additionally so, by the favorable recollections of our northern visiting friends. If Monticello has anything which has merited their remembrance, it gives
it a value the more in our estimation; and could I, in the spirit
of your wish, count backwards a score of years, it would not be
long before Ellen and myself would pay our homage personally
to Quincy. But those twenty years! Alas! where are they? With
those beyond the flood. Our next meeting must then be in the
country to which they have flown—a country for us not now
very distant. For this journey we shall need neither gold nor
silver in our purse, nor scrip, nor coats, nor staves. Nor is the
provision for it more easy than the preparation has been kind.
Nothing proves more than this, that the Being who presides
over the world is essentially benevolent. Stealing from us, one
by one, the faculties of enjoyment, searing our sensibilities,
leading us, like the horse in his mill, round and round the same
beaten circle,

> —To see what we have seen,
> To taste the tasted, and at each return
> Less tasteful; o'er our palates to decant
> Another vintage—

until satiated and fatigued with this leaden iteration, we ask
our own *congé*. I heard once a very old friend, who had troubled himself with neither poets nor philosophers, say the same
thing in plain prose, that he was tired of pulling off his shoes
and stockings at night, and putting them on again in the morning. The wish to stay here is thus gradually extinguished; but
not so easily that of returning once in a while, to see how things

* Mrs. Joseph Coolidge, of Boston.

have gone on. Perhaps, however, one of the elements of future felicity is to be a constant and unimpassioned view of what is passing here. If so, this may well supply the wish of occasional visits. Mercier has given us a vision of the year 2440; but prophecy is one thing, and history another. On the whole, however, perhaps it is wise and well to be contented with the good things which the master of the feast places before us, and to be thankful for what we have, rather than thoughtful about what we have not. You and I, dear madam, have already had more than an ordinary portion of life, and more, too, of health than the general measure. On this score I owe boundless thankfulness. Your health was, some time ago, not so good as it has been; and I perceive in the letters communicated, some complaints still. I hope it is restored; and that life and health may be continued to you as many years as yourself shall wish, is the sincere prayer of your affectionate and respectful friend,

TH: JEFFERSON

To Charles Thomson

January 29, 1817   *Monticello*

My very dear and ancient friend, I learnt from your last letter, with much affliction, the severe and singular attack, your health has lately sustained, but its equally singular and sudden restoration confirms my confidence in the strength of your constitution of body and mind and my conclusions that neither has received hurt, and that you are still ours for a long time to come. We have both much to be thankful for in the soundness of our physical organization, and something for self approbation in the order and regularity of life by which it has been preserved. Your preceding letter had given me no cause to doubt the continued strength of your mind, and were it not that I am always peculiarly gratified by hearing from you, I

should regret you had thought the incident with Mr. Delaplaine * worth an explanation. He wrote me on the subject of
my letter to you of January 9, 1816, and asked me questions
which I answer only to one Being. To himself, therefore, I
replied: "Say nothing of my religion: it is known to my God
and myself alone; its evidence before the world is to be sought
in my life; if that has been honest and dutiful to society the
religion which has regulated it cannot be a bad one." It is a
singular anxiety which some people have that we should all
think alike. Would the world be more beautiful were all our
faces alike? were our tempers, our talents, our tastes, our forms,
our wishes, aversions and pursuits cast exactly in the same
mould? If no varieties existed in the animal, vegetable or
mineral creation, but all moved strictly uniform, catholic and
orthodox, what a world of physical and moral monotony would
it be! These are the absurdities into which those run who usurp
the throne of God and dictate to Him what He should have
done. May they with all their metaphysical riddles appear before that tribunal with as clean hands and hearts as you and
I shall. There, suspended in the scales of eternal justice, faith
and works will show their worth by their weight. God bless
you and preserve you long in life and health,

TH: JEFFERSON

To Joseph Delaplaine †

April 12, 1817   *Monticello*

Dear Sir, My repugnance is so invincible to be saying
anything of my own history as if worthy to occupy the public
attention that I have suffered your letter of March 17, but not
received till March 28, to lie thus long without resolution

---

* See Jefferson's letter to Delaplaine, April 12, 1817.
† Delaplaine (1777-1824) was a Philadelphia publisher and historian.

enough to take it up. I indulged myself at some length on a former occasion because it was to repel a calumny still sometimes repeated after the death of its numerous brethren, by which a party at one time thought they could vote me down, deeming even science itself as well as my affection for it a fit object of ridicule and a disqualification for the affairs of government. I still think that many of the objects of our inquiry are too minute for public notice. The number of names and ages of my children, grandchildren, great-grandchildren, etc., would produce fatigue and disgust to your readers of which I would be an unwilling instrument; it will certainly be enough to say that from one daughter living and another deceased, I have a numerous family of grandchildren and an increasing one of great-grandchildren.

I was married on New Year's day of 1772, and Mrs. J. died in the autumn of 1782. I was educated at William and Mary College, in Williamsburg. I read Greek, Latin, French, Italian, Spanish and English of course, with something of its radics, the Anglo-Saxon. I became a member of the legislature of Virginia in 1769 at the accession of Lord Botetourt to our government. I could not readily make a statement of the literary societies of which I am a member, they are many and would be long to enumerate and would savor too much of vanity and pedantry. Would it not be better to say merely that I am a member of many literary societies in Europe and America.

Your statements of the corrections of the Declaration of Independence by Dr. Franklin and Mr. Adams are neither of them at all exact. I should think it better to say generally that the rough draft was communicated to those two gentlemen, who each of them made two or three short and verbal alterations only, but even this is laying more stress on mere composition than it merits, for that alone was mine. The sentiments were of all America. I already possess a portrait of Mr. Adams, done by our countryman Brown when we were both in England, and have no occasion, therefore, for the copy you propose to me. Accept my apologies for not going more fully into the minutiæ of your letter. With my friendly and respectful salutations,

TH: JEFFERSON

To Lafayette

May 14, 1817   *Monticello*

Although, dear sir, much retired from the world, and meddling little in its concerns, yet I think it almost a religious duty to salute at times my old friends, were it only to say and to know that "all's well. . . ."

I wish I could give better hopes of our southern brethren. The achievement of their independence of Spain is no longer a question. But it is a very serious one, what will then become of them? Ignorance and bigotry, like other insanities, are incapable of self-government. They will fall under military despotism, and become the murderous tools of the ambition of their respective Bonapartes; and whether this will be for their greater happiness, the rule of one only has taught us to judge. No one, I hope, can doubt my wish to see them and all mankind exercising self-government, and capable of exercising it. But the question is not what we wish, but what is practicable? As their sincere friend and brother then, I do believe the best thing for them, would be for themselves to come to an accord with Spain, under the guarantee of France, Russia, Holland, and the United States, allowing to Spain a nominal supremacy, with authority only to keep the peace among them, leaving them otherwise all the powers of self-government, until their experience in them, their emanicpation from their priests, and advancement in information, shall prepare them for complete independence. I exclude England from this confederacy, because her selfish principles render her incapable of honorable patronage or disinterested co-operation.

To Alexander von Humboldt

June 13, 1817   *Monticello*

The issue of its [South America's] struggles, as they respect Spain, is no longer matter of doubt. As it respects their
own liberty, peace and happiness, we cannot be quite so certain.
Whether the blinds of bigotry, the shackles of the priesthood,
and the fascinating glare of rank and wealth, give fair play to
the common sense of the mass of their people, so far as to
qualify them for self-government, is what we do not know. Perhaps our wishes may be stronger than our hopes. The first principle of republicanism is, that the *lex majoris partis* is the
fundamental law of every society of individuals of equal rights;
to consider the will of the society enounced by the majority of
a single vote, as sacred as if unanimous, is the first of all lessons
in importance, yet the last which is thoroughly learnt. This law
once disregarded, no other remains but that of force, which
ends necessarily in military despotism. This has been the history
of the French Revolution, and I wish the understanding of our
Southern brethren may be sufficiently enlarged and firm to see
that their fate depends on its sacred observance.

To Francis Adrian van der Kemp *

February 9, 1818   *Monticello*

Dear Sir, Your favor of January 7 has been some time at
hand. Age, which lethargizes all our movements, makes me a
slow correspondent also, and revolts me strongly from the la-

---

* Van der Kemp (1752-1829) was a Dutch-born pastor, scholar and author
who settled in the United States in 1788.

bors of the writing table. Reading when I can be indulged in it, is the elysium of my present life.

You suppose I may possess essays and scraps, on various subjects committed to paper, and lying buried in my desk. No, sir, I have nothing of the sort. My life has been one of unremitting labor, and that in a line entirely foreign to the sciences. It was my lot to be cast into being at the period of the commencement of a political convulsion, which has continued since to agitate the whole civilized globe. That commencement was in my own country, and under circumstances which placed in a state of requisition all the energies of the body and mind of every citizen. Its necessities dragged me from a life of retirement and contemplation, to which my natural propensities strongly inclined, to one of action and contention, and in the field of politics from which I was most averse. In this I have never had leisure to turn to right or left, to indulge for a moment in speculative meditations, much less to commit them to writing.

I return you the paper on incestuous marriages, in which you have proved beyond question that neither under the Mosaic, nor natural law is a man forbidden to take in second marriage the sister of his first. Early in our revolution the legislature of Virginia thought it necessary that their code of laws should be revised, and made homogeneous with their new situation. This task was committed to Mr. Wythe, Mr. Pendleton and myself. Among others, the law regulating marriages came under consideration. We thought it most orthodox and correct to copy into our bill the very words of Levitical law. After continuing in force for some years, the permission to marry a wife's sister was thought to produce in practice jealousies and heartburnings in families, and even temptations to crime; and it was therefore repealed, not as in itself intrinsic guilt, but independent as leading to guilt. This depends much on the family habits and intercourse of each country.

Not having replaced my set of the philosophical transactions, I am not able to turn to the paper from which you quote the words "the movements of nature are in a never-ending ciricle"

. . . but I suppose they were in that which I wrote on the discovery of the bones of the Megalonyx. This animal was pronounced to be extinct, but I thought it might be doubted whether any particular species of animals or vegetables, which ever did exist, has ceased to exist. This doubt is suggested by the consideration that if one species of organized matter might become extinct, so might also a second, a third and so on to the last: and thus all organized bodies might disappear, and the earth be left without life or intellect, for the habitation of which it is so peculiarly prepared. A particular species of unorganized matter might disappear for a while, and be restored by the fortuitous concourse and combination of the elements which compose it, but organized being cannot be restored by accidental aggregation of its elements. It is reproduced only by its seed. Against its loss therefore nature has made ample provision, by a profusion of seed, some of which, however inauspiciously scattered, may be sure to take effect. Thus, the tree produces a seed, and the seed produces a tree. A bird produces an egg, and the egg a bird. An animal or vegetable body, after thus reproducing more or fewer individuals of its own species, perishes, is decomposed, and its particles of matter pass into other forms. Not one is lost or left unemployed. The universe is now made up of exactly the same particles of matter, not a single one more or less, which it had in its original creation. So sung truly the poetical disciple of Pythagoras:

"Nec perit in tanto quicquam (mihi credite) mundo."

This is the never-ending circle in which I observed that animal and vegetable natures are circulated and secured against failure through indefinite time.

Extending our views to the heavenly bodies, we know that certain movements of theirs, heretofore deemed anomalous and erratic, have been considered as indications of disorder, affecting the equilibrium of the powers of impulse and attraction which restrain them in their orbits, and threatening consequently their crush and destruction in time. Yet De Laplace has now demonstrated that these supposed irregularities are strictly in obedience to the general laws of motion, that they are periodical and secular; and that these members of the universe also may continue moving in their orbits through indefinite time. Yet I have not seen this demonstration of a possibility condemned by orthodoxy either of religion or philosphy. Its only result is that if a time is to be when these bodies shall be brought to an end, it will not be from any defect in the laws of their continuance, but by another "Sta Sol" of the Creator, by an arrest of their motion from the hand which first impressed it. Nor indeed do I know that a belief in the eternity of the world is against the sound doctrines of the Christian faith. The eternity of two beings is not more incomprehensible to us than that of one. The eternity of the universe, and that of the being who regulates its order, preserves its course, and superintends the action of all its parts, may stand together, as well as either of them alone. And the most eminent divines have considered this coeternity as not inconsistent with the relation of the two beings as cause and effect. Where effect is produced by motion of parts, there they admit there must be priority and posteriority. But where effect is the result of will alone, they are simultaneous and coeval. And they maintain that the Creator must have willed the creation of the world from all eternity.

I have said so much on this subject that I am afraid you will imagine I have been defending an *opinion*. Not at all. It is a *doubt* only which I have been vindicating from the charge of puerility imputed to it by a writer, whose greater ripeness of judgment was offended by the doubt. For it was expressed merely as a doubt whether any race of animals which ever did exist, has ceased to exist? For example the sphinx, cyclops, centaur, satyr, faun, mermaid, dragon, phoenix? Cuvier indeed has proved to us by anatomizing their remains, that several animals have existed, now unknown to us. But then follows the second inquiry, is it known that they are extinct? Have all parts of the earth been sufficiently explored to authorize a confident assertion—the interior parts of North and South America, the interior of Africa, the polar regions Arctic and Antarctic, the Austrasian division of the earth, for we are no longer to talk of its quarters? Of this latter division, a small portion of its margin only has been explored: and yet what singular and un-known animals have been found there! Had a skeleton of one of these floated to our shores half a century ago, it would have been enrolled in the catalogue of "species extinct."

I think therefore still, there is reason to doubt whether any species of animal has become extinct; that this does not involve as a necessary consequence the eternity of the world; and, if it did, that we are authorized by the fathers of our faith to say there would be nothing unlawful in this consequence, and I have quoted the authorities of theologians, rather than of philosophers, because the former consider these as their natural enemies. For these quotations I am indebted to M. D'Argens.

You ask whether I have seen Cuvier's "Essai sur la Théorie de la Terre," or Brieslau's "Introduction à la Geologie?" I have seen neither: and in truth I am disposed to place all these hypothetical theories of the earth in a line with Ovid's

> "Ante mare et terras et quod tegit omnia coelum
> Unus erat toto naturae vultus in orbe,
> Quem dixere Chaos; rudis indigestaque moles."

for all their theories require the original hand of a Creator: and if his intervention is necessary, why should we suppose him to throw together a rude and undigested mass of matter, and leave it in chaos, unfinished, for millions of years, to work its own way by mechanical fusions and aggregations, and by chemi-cal affinities and fermentations into mineral forms, and animal and vegetable life? Could not he, with the same ease, have created the earth at once, in all the perfection in which it now exists? And were the Genesis of the earth by Moses tradition, not revelation, instead of employing the Creator in detail through six days of labor, in one of which he says "let there be light and there was light," it would have better filled our ideas of his exalted power and wisdom, to have summed the whole in the single fiat of "Let the world be, and it was."

I am afraid that a letter, extended to such inordinate length, will make you doubt the truth with which it began, that I am averse to the labors of the writing-table. Yet it is a real truth. But my subject sometimes runs away with me, without control or discretion, until my reader as well as myself, is ready to welcome with gladness the valedictory assurance of my great esteem and respect,

TH: JEFFERSON

To Benjamin Waterhouse *

March 3, 1818   *Monticello*

Dear Sir, I have just received your favor of February 20th, in which you observe that Mr. Wirt, on page forty-seven of his "Life of Patrick Henry," quotes me as saying that "Mr. Henry certainly gave the first impulse to the ball of revolution." I well recollect to have used some such expression in a letter to him, and am tolerably certain that our own State being the subject under contemplation, I must have used it with respect to that only. . . . But the question, who commenced the Revolution? is as difficult as that of the first inventors of a thousand good things. For example, who first discovered the principle of gravity? Not Newton; for Galileo, who died the year that Newton was born, had measured its force in the descent of gravid bodies. Who invented the Lavoisierian chemistry? The English say Doctor Black, by the preparatory discovery of latent heat. Who invented the steamboat? Was it Gerbert, the Marquis of Worcester, Newcomen, Savery, Papin, Fitch, Fulton?

---

* Waterhouse (1754-1846) was a physician, professor of medicine at Harvard, author, pioneer in vaccination, and a follower of Jefferson in politics.

The fact is, that one new idea leads to another, that to a third, and so on through a course of time until some one, with whom no one of these ideas was original, combines all together, and produces what is justly called a new invention. I suppose it would be as difficult to trace our Revolution to its first embryo.

To Nathaniel Burwell

March 14, 1818   *Monticello*

A plan of female education has never been a subject of systematic contemplation with me. It has occupied my attention so far only as the education of my own daughters occasionally required. Considering that they would be placed in a country situation where little aid could be obtained from abroad, I thought it essential to give them a solid education, which might enable them, when become mothers, to educate their own daughters, and even to direct the course for sons, should their fathers be lost, or incapable, or inattentive. My surviving daughter accordingly, the mother of many daughters as well as sons, has made their education the object of her life, and being a better judge of the practical part than myself, it is with her aid and that of one of her *élèves,* that I shall subjoin a catalogue of the books for such a course of reading as we have practiced.

A great obstacle to good education is the inordinate passion prevalent for novels, and the time lost in that reading which should be instructively employed. When this poison infects the mind, it destroys its tone and revolts it against wholesome reading. Reason and fact, plain and unadorned, are rejected. Nothing can engage attention unless dressed in all the figments of fancy, and nothing so bedecked comes amiss. The result is a bloated imagination, sickly judgment, and disgust towards all the real businesses of life. This mass of trash, however, is not without some distinction; some few modeling their narratives, although fictitious, on the incidents of real life, have been able to make them interesting and useful vehicles of a sound morality. Such, I think, are Marmontel's new moral tales, but not his old ones, which are really immoral. Such are the writings of Miss Edgeworth, and some of those of Madame Genlis. For a like reason, too, much poetry should not be indulged. Some is useful for forming style and taste. Pope, Dryden, Thomson, Shakespeare, and of the French, Molière, Racine, the Corneilles, may be read with pleasure and improvement.

The French language, become that of the general intercourse of nations, and from their extraordinary advances, now the depository of all science, is an indispensable part of education for both sexes. In the subjoined catalogue, therefore, I have placed the books of both languages indifferently, according as the one or the other offers what is best.

The ornaments, too, and the amusements of life, are entitled to their portion of attention. These, for a female, are dancing, drawing, and music. The first is a healthy exercise, elegant, and very attractive for young people. Every affectionate parent would be pleased to see his daughter qualified to participate with her companions and without awkwardness at least, in the circles of festivity, of which she occasionally becomes a part. It is a necessary accomplishment, therefore, although of short use; for the French rule is wise, that no lady dances after marriage. This is founded in solid physical reasons, gestation and nursing leaving little time to a married lady when this exercise can be either safe or innocent. Drawing is thought less of in this country than in Europe. It is an innocent and engaging amusement, often useful, and a qualification not to be neglected in one who is to become a mother and an instructor. Music is invaluable where a person has an ear. Where they have not, it should not be attempted. It furnishes a delightful recreation for the hours of respite from the cares of the day, and lasts us through life. The taste of this country, too, calls for this accomplishment more strongly than for either of the others.

I need say nothing of household economy, in which the mothers of our country are generally skilled, and generally careful to instruct their daughters. We all know its value, and that diligence and dexterity in all its processes are inestimable treasures. The order and economy of a house are as honorable to the mistress as those of the farm to the master, and if either be neglected, ruin follows, and children destitute of the means of living.

This, sir, is offered as a summary sketch on a subject on which I have not thought much. It probably contains nothing but what has already occurred to yourself, and claims your acceptance on no other ground than as a testimony of my respect for your wishes, and of my great esteem and respect,

TH: JEFFERSON

To John Adams

November 13, 1818   *Monticello*

The public papers, my dear friend, announce the fatal event * of which your letter of October the 20th had given me ominous foreboding. Tried myself in the school of affliction by the loss of every form of connection which can rive the human heart, I know well, and feel what you have lost, what you have suffered, are suffering, and have yet to endure. The same trials have taught me that for ills so immeasurable, time and silence are the only medicine. I will not, therefore, by useless condolences, open afresh the sluices of your grief, nor although mingling sincerely my tears with yours, will I say a word more where words are vain, but that it is of some comfort to us both that the term is not very distant, at which we are to deposit in the same cerement, our sorrows and suffering bodies, and to ascend in essence to an ecstatic meeting with the friends we

---

* The death of Mrs. Adams.

have loved and lost, and whom we shall still love and never lose
again. God bless you and support you under your heavy affliction,

TH: JEFFERSON

To Robert Walsh *

December 4, 1818   *Monticello*

When the Declaration of Independence was under the
consideration of Congress, there were two or three unlucky expressions in it which gave offense to some members. The words
"Scotch and other foreign auxiliaries" excited the ire of a gentleman or two of that country. Severe strictures on the conduct
of the British King, in negativing our repeated repeals of the
law which permitted the importation of slaves, were disapproved by some southern gentlemen, whose reflections were
not yet matured to the full abhorrence of that traffic. Although
the offensive expressions were immediately yielded, these gentlemen continued their depredations on other parts of the instrument.

I was sitting by Doctor Franklin, who perceived that I was
not insensible to these mutilations. "I have made it a rule,"
said he, "whenever in my power, to avoid becoming the drafts-
man of papers to be reviewed by a public body. I took my lesson
from an incident which I will relate to you. When I was a
journeyman printer, one of my companions, an apprentice
hatter, having served out his time, was about to open shop for
himself. His first concern was to have a handsome sign-board,
with a proper inscription. He composed it in these words, 'John
Thompson, *Hatter, makes and sells hats for ready money,*'
with a figure of a hat subjoined; but he thought he would submit it to his friends for their amendments. The first he showed

---

* Walsh (1784-1859), a Baltimore author and editor, published in 1811 the
first United States quarterly, *The American Review of History and Politics.*

it to thought the word '*Hatter*' tautologous, because followed by the words 'makes hats,' which show he was a hatter. It was struck out. The next observed that the word '*makes*' might as well be omitted, because his customers would not care who made the hats. If good and to their mind, they would buy by whomsoever made. He struck it out. A third said he thought the words '*for ready money*' were useless, as it was not the custom of the place to sell on credit. Every one who purchased expected to pay. They were parted with, and the inscription now stood, 'John Thompson sells hats.' '*Sells hats!*' says his next friend: 'why, nobody will expect you to give them away; what then is the use of that word?' It was stricken out, and '*hats*' followed it, the rather as there was one painted on the board. So the inscription was reduced ultimately to 'John Thompson,' with the figure of a hat subjoined."

To Hyde de Neuville *

December 13, 1818   *Monticello*

    I rejoice, as a moralist, at the prospect of a reduction of the duties on wine, by our national legislature. It is an error to view a tax on that liquor as merely a tax on the rich. It is a prohibition of its use to the middling class of our citizens, and a condemnation of them to the poison of whiskey, which is desolating their houses. No nation is drunken where wine is cheap; and none sober, where the dearness of wine substitutes ardent spirits as the common beverage. It is, in truth, the only antidote to the bane of whiskey. Fix but the duty at the rate of other merchandise, and we can drink wine here as cheap as we do grog; and who will not prefer it? Its extended use will carry

---

* Baron Jean-Guillaume Hyde de Neuville (1776-1857), a French politician and diplomat, was France's minister to the U. S. from 1816 to 1821.

health and comfort to a much enlarged circle. Every one in easy circumstances (as the bulk of our citizens are) will prefer it to the poison to which they are now driven by their government. And the treasury itself will find that a penny apiece from a dozen is more than a groat from a single one. This reformation, however, will require time. Our merchants know nothing of the infinite variety of cheap and good wines to be had in Europe; and particularly in France, in Italy, and the Grecian Islands.

To Vine Utley

March 21, 1819   *Monticello*

Sir, Your letter of February the 18th came to hand on the 1st and the request of the history of my physical habits would have puzzled me not a little, had it not been for the model with which you accompanied it, of Doctor Rush's answer to a similar inquiry. I live so much like other people, that I might refer to ordinary life as the history of my own. Like my friend the Doctor, I have lived temperately, eating little animal food, and that not as an aliment so much as a condiment for the vegetables, which constitute my principal diet. I double, however, the Doctor's glass and a half of wine, and even treble it with a friend; but halve its effects by drinking the weak wines only. The ardent wines I cannot drink, nor do I use ardent spirits in any form. Malt liquors and cider are my table drinks, and my breakfast, like that also of my friend, is of tea and coffee. I have been blest with organs of digestion which accept and concoct, without ever murmuring, whatever the palate chooses to consign to them, and I have not yet lost a tooth by age. I was a hard student until I entered on the business of life, the duties of which leave no idle time to those disposed to fulfill them; and now, retired, and at the age of seventy-six, I am again a hard student. Indeed, my fondness for reading and study revolts me from the drudgery of letter writing. And a stiff wrist, the consequence of an early dislocation, makes writing both slow and painful. I am not so regular in my sleep as the Doctor says he was, devoting to it from five to eight hours, according as my company or the book I am reading interests me; *and I never go to bed without an hour, or half an hour's previous reading of something moral, whereon to ruminate in the intervals of sleep.* But whether I retire to bed early or late, I rise with the sun. I use spectacles at night, but not necessarily in the day, unless in reading small print. My hearing is distinct in particular conversation, but confused when several voices cross each other, which unfits me for the society of the table. I have been more fortunate than my friend in the article of health. So free from catarrhs that I have not had one (in the breast, I mean) on an average of eight or ten years through life. I ascribe this exemption partly to the habit of bathing my feet in cold water every morning, for sixty years past. A fever of more than twenty-four hours I have not had above two or three times in my life. A periodical headache has afflicted me occasionally, once, perhaps, in six or eight years, for two or three weeks at a time, which seems now to have left me; and, except on a late occasion of indisposition, I enjoy good health; too feeble, indeed, to walk much, but riding without fatigue six or eight miles a day, and sometimes thirty or forty. I may end these egotisms, therefore, as I began, by saying that my life has been so much like that of other people, that I might say with Horace, to every one *"nomine mutato, narratur fabula de te."* I must not end, however, without due thanks for the kind sentiments of regard you are so good as to express towards myself; and with my acknowledgments for these, be pleased to accept the assurances of my respect and esteem,

TH: JEFFERSON

To John Brazer *

August 24, 1819   *Monticello*

You ask my opinion on the extent to which classical learning should be carried in our country. A sickly condition permits me to think and a rheumatic hand to write too briefly on this litigated question. The utilities we derive from the remains of the Greek and Latin languages are, first, as models of pure taste in writing. To these we are certainly indebted for the national and chaste style of modern composition which so much distinguishes the nations to whom these languages are familiar. Without these models we should probably have continued the inflated style of our northern ancestors, or the hyperbolical and vague one of the east. Second, among the values of classical learning, I estimate the luxury of reading the Greek and Roman authors in all the beauties of their originals. And why should not this innocent and elegant luxury take its pre-eminent stand ahead of all those addressed merely to the senses? I think myself more indebted to my father for this than for all the other luxuries his cares and affections have placed within my reach; and more now than when younger, and more susceptible of delights from other sources. When the decays of age have enfeebled the useful energies of the mind, the classic pages fill up the vacuum of *ennui,* and become sweet composers to that rest of the grave into which we are all sooner or later to descend. A third value is in the stores of real science deposited and transmitted us in these languages, to-wit: in history, ethics, arithmetic, geometry, astronomy, and natural history.

But to whom are these things useful? Certainly not to all men. There are conditions of life to which they must be forever estranged, and there are epochs of life too, after which the endeavor to attain them would be a great misemployment of

---

* Brazer (1789-1846), professor of Latin at Harvard, resigned in 1820 to become Unitarian pastor at Salem.

time. Their acquisition should be the occupation of our early years only, when the memory is susceptible of deep and lasting impressions, and reason and judgment not yet strong enough for abstract speculations. To the moralist they are valuable, because they furnish ethical writings highly and justly esteemed: although in my own opinion, the moderns are far advanced beyond them in this line of science, the divine finds in the Greek language a translation of his primary code, of more importance to him than the original because better understood; and, in the same language, the newer code, with the doctrines of the earliest fathers, who lived and wrote before the simple precepts of the founder of this most benign and pure of all systems of morality became frittered into subtleties and mysteries, and hidden under jargons incomprehensible to the human mind. To these original sources he must now, therefore, return, to recover the virgin purity of his religion. The lawyer finds in the Latin language the system of civil law most conformable with the principles of justice of any which has ever yet been established among men, and from which much has been incorporated into our own. The physician as good a code of his art as has been given us to this day. Theories and systems of medicine, indeed, have been in perpetual change from the days of the good Hippocrates to the days of the good Rush, but which of them is the true one? The present, to be sure, as long as it is the present, but to yield its place in turn to the next novelty, which is then to become the true system, and is to mark the vast advance of medicine since the days of Hippocrates. Our situation is certainly benefited by the discovery of some new and very valuable medicines; and substituting those for some of his with the treasure of facts, and of sound observations recorded by him (mixed to be sure with anilities of his day) and we shall have nearly the present sum of the healing art. The statesman will find in these languages history, politics, mathematics, ethics, eloquence, love of country, to which he must add the sciences of his own day, for which of them should be unknown to him? And all the sciences must recur to the classical languages for the etymon, and sound understanding of their fundamental terms. For the merchant I should not say that the languages are a necessary. Ethics, mathematics, geography, political economy, history, seem to constitute the immediate foundations of his calling. The agriculturist needs ethics, mathematics, chemistry and natural philosophy. The mechanic the same. To them the languages are but ornament and comfort. I know it is often said there have been shining examples of men of great abilities in all the businesses of life, without any other science than what they had gathered from conversations and intercourse with the world. But who can say what these men would not have been had they started in the science on the shoulders of a Demosthenes or Cicero, of a Locke or Bacon, or a Newton? To sum the whole, therefore, it may truly be said that the classical languages are a solid basis for most, and an ornament to all the sciences.

To William Short *

October 31, 1819   *Monticello*

As you say of yourself, I too am an Epicurean. I consider the genuine (not the imputed) doctrines of Epicurus as containing everything rational in moral philosophy which Greece and Rome have left us. Epictetus, indeed, has given us what was good of the Stoics; all beyond, of their dogmas, being hypocrisy and grimace. Their great crime was in their calumnies of Epicurus and misrepresentations of his doctrines; in which we lament to see the candid character of Cicero engaging as an accomplice. Diffuse, vapid, rhetorical, but enchanting. His prototype Plato, eloquent as himself, dealing out mysticisms incomprehensible to the human mind, has been deified by certain

---

* Short (1759-1849), Jefferson's friend and one-time secretary, was an American diplomat.

sects usurping the name of Christians; because, in his foggy conceptions, they found a basis of impenetrable darkness whereon to rear fabrications as delirious, of their own invention. These they fathered blasphemously on him whom they claimed as their founder, but who would disclaim them with the indignation which their caricatures of his religion so justly excite. Of Socrates we have nothing genuine but in the Memorabilia of Xenophon; for Plato makes him one of his collocutors merely to cover his own whimsies under the mantle of his name; a liberty of which we are told Socrates himself complained. Seneca is indeed a fine moralist, disfiguring his work at times with some stoicisms, and affecting too much of antithesis and point, yet giving us on the whole a great deal of sound and practical morality. But the greatest of all the reformers of the depraved religion of his own country, was Jesus of Nazareth. Abstracting what is really his from the rubbish in which it is buried, easily distinguished by its luster from the dross of his biographers, and as separable from that as the diamond from the dunghill, we have the outlines of a system of the most sublime morality which has ever fallen from the lips of man; outlines which it is lamentable he did not live to fill up.* Epictetus and Epicurus give laws for governing ourselves, Jesus a supplement of the duties and charities we owe to others. The establishment of the innocent and genuine character of this benevolent moralist, and the rescuing it from the imputation of imposture, which has resulted from artificial systems,† invented by ultra-Christian sects, unauthorized by a single word ever uttered by him, is a most desirable object, and one to which Priestley ‡ has successfully devoted his labors and learning. It would in time, it is to be hoped, effect a quiet euthanasia of

---

* See also Jefferson's letter to Charles Clay, January 29, 1815, and the footnote.

† E.g. The immaculate conception of Jesus, his deification, the creation of the world by him, his miraculous powers, his resurrection and visible ascension, his corporeal presence in the Eucharist, the Trinity; original sin, atonement, regeneration, election, orders of Hierarchy. . . .–T.J.

‡ Jefferson's friend, the scientist Joseph Priestley, organized the first Unitarian Church in the United States and wrote many philosophical works on religion.

the heresies of bigotry and fanaticism which have so long triumphed over human reason, and so generally and deeply afflicted mankind; but this work is to be begun by winnowing the grain from the chaff of the historians of his life. I have sometimes thought of translating Epictetus (for he has never been tolerably translated into English) by adding the genuine doctrines of Epicurus from the Syntagma of Gassendi, and an abstract from the Evangelists of whatever has the stamp of the eloquence and fine imagination of Jesus. The last I attempted too hastily some twelve or fifteen years ago. It was the work of two or three nights only, at Washington, after getting through the evening task of reading the letters and papers of the day.* But with one foot in the grave, these are now idle projects for me. My business is to beguile the wearisomeness of declining life, as I endeavor to do, by the delights of classical reading and of mathematical truths, and by the consolations of a sound philosophy, equally indifferent to hope and fear.

I take the liberty of observing that you are not a true disciple of our master Epicurus, in indulging the indolence to which you say you are yielding. One of his canons, you know, was that "the indulgence which prevents a greater pleasure, or produces a greater pain, is to be avoided." Your love of repose will lead, in its progress, to a suspension of healthy exercise, a relaxation of mind, an indifference to everything around you, and finally to a debility of body, and hebetude of mind, the farthest of all things from the happiness which the well-regulated indulgences of Epicurus ensure; fortitude, you know, is one of his four cardinal virtues. That teaches us to meet and surmount difficulties; not to fly from them, like cowards; and to fly, too, in vain, for they will meet and arrest us at every turn of our road. Weigh this matter well; brace yourself up.

_____
* See the footnote to Jefferson's letter to Charles Clay, January 29, 1815.

To John Adams

Dear Sir, I have to acknowledge the receipt of your favor of November the 23d. The banks, bankrupt law, manufactures, Spanish treaty, are nothing. These are occurrences which, like waves in a storm, will pass under the ship. But the Missouri question is a breaker on which we lose the Missouri country by revolt, and what more, God only knows. From the battle of Bunker's Hill to the Treaty of Paris, we never had so ominous a question. It even damps the joy with which I hear of your high health, and welcomes to me the consequences of my want of it. I thank God that I shall not live to witness its issue. *Sed haec hactenus.*

I have been amusing myself latterly with reading the voluminous letters of Cicero. They certainly breathe the purest effusions of an exalted patriot, while the parricide Caesar is lost in odious contrast. When the enthusiasm, however, kindled by Cicero's pen and principles, subsides into cool reflection, I ask myself, what was that government which the virtues of Cicero were so zealous to restore, and the ambition of Caesar to subvert? And if Caesar had been as virtuous as he was daring and sagacious, what could he, even in the plenitude of his usurped power, have done to lead his fellow citizens into good government? I do not say to *restore it,* because they never had it, from the rape of the Sabines to the ravages of the Caesars. If their people indeed had been, like ourselves, enlightened, peaceable, and really free, the answer would be obvious. "Restore independence to all your foreign conquests, relieve Italy from the government of the rabble of Rome, consult it as a nation entitled to self-government, and do its will." But steeped in corruption, vice and venality, as the whole nation was (and nobody had done more than Caesar to corrupt it), what could even Cicero, Cato, Brutus have done, had it been referred

to them to establish a good government for their country?
They had no ideas of government themselves, but of their
degenerate Senate, nor the people of liberty, but of the factious
opposition of their tribunes. They had afterwards their Tituses,
their Trajans and Antoninuses, who had the will to make
them happy, and the power to mold their government into a
good and permanent form. But it would seem as if they could
not see their way clearly to do it. No government can continue
good, but under the control of the people; and their people
were so demoralized and depraved, as to be incapable of exercising a wholesome control. Their reformation then was to be
taken up *ab incunabulis*. Their minds were to be informed by
education what is right and what wrong; to be encouraged
in habits of virtue, and deterred from those of vice by the
dread of punishments, proportioned indeed, but irremissible;
in all cases, to follow truth as the only safe guide, and to
eschew error, which bewilders us in one false consequence
after another, in endless succession. These are the inculcations
necessary to render the people a sure basis for the structure
of order and good government. But this would have been an
operation of a generation or two, at least, within which period
would have succeeded many Neros and Commoduses, who
would have quashed the whole process. I confess then, I
can neither see what Cicero, Cato, and Brutus, united and
uncontrolled, could have devised to lead their people into
good government, nor how this enigma can be solved, nor
how further shown why it has been the fate of that delightful country never to have known, to this day, and through a
course of five and twenty hundred years, the history of which
we possess, one single day of free and rational government.
Your intimacy with their history, ancient, middle and modern,
your familiarity with the improvements in the science of government at this time, will enable you, if anybody, to go back
with our principles and opinions to the times of Cicero, Cato,
and Brutus, and tell us by what process these great and virtuous
men could have led so unenlightened and vitiated a people into

freedom and good government, *et eris mihi magnus Apollo.
Cura ut valeas, et tibi persuadeas carissimum te mihi esse,*

TH: JEFFERSON

To William Short

April 13, 1820   *Monticello*

Dear Sir, Your favor of March the 27th is received, and
as you request, a copy of the syllabus is now inclosed. It was
originally written to Doctor Rush. On his death, fearing that
the inquisition of the public might get hold of it, I asked the
return of it from the family, which they kindly complied with.
At the request of another friend, I had given him a copy. He
lent it to *his* friend to read, who copied it, and in a few months
it appeared in the Theological Magazine of London. Happily
that repository is scarcely known in this country; and the syllabus, therefore, is still a secret, and in your hands I am sure it
will continue so.

But while this syllabus is meant to place the character of
Jesus in its true and high light, as no imposter himself, but a
great reformer of the Hebrew code of religion, it is not to be
understood that I am with him in all his doctrines. I am a materialist; he takes the side of spiritualism; he preaches the efficacy
of repentance towards forgiveness of sin; I require a counter-
poise of good works to redeem it. . . . It is the innocence of his
character, the purity and sublimity of his moral precepts, the
eloquence of his inculcations, the beauty of the apologues in
which he conveys them, that I so much admire; sometimes, indeed, needing indulgence to eastern hyperbolism. My eulogies,
too, may be founded on a postulate which all may not be ready
to grant. Among the sayings and discourses imputed to him by
his biographers, I find many passages of fine imagination, correct morality, and of the most lovely benevolence; and others,

again, of so much ignorance, so much absurdity, so much untruth, charlatanism and imposture, as to pronounce it impossible that such contradictions should have proceeded from the
same being. I separate, therefore, the gold from the dross; restore to him the former, and leave the latter to the stupidity
of some, and roguery of others of his disciples. Of this band of
dupes and imposters, Paul was the great Coryphaeus, and first
corruptor of the doctrines of Jesus. These palpable interpola-
tions and falsifications of his doctrines, led me to try to sift
them apart. I found the work obvious and easy, and that his
past composed the most beautiful morsel of morality which has
been given to us by man. The syllabus is therefore of *his* doctrines, not *all* of *mine:* I read them as I do those of other ancient and modern moralists, with a mixture of approbation and
dissent.

To John Holmes *

April 22, 1820　　　　　　　　　　　　　　　　　　*Monticello*

I thank you, dear sir, for the copy you have been so kind
as to send me of the letter to your constituents on the Missouri
question. It is a perfect justification to them. I had for a long
time ceased to read newspapers, or pay any attention to public
affairs, confident they were in good hands, and content to be a
passenger in our bark to the shore from which I am not distant.
But this momentous question, like a fire-bell in the night,
awakened and filled me with terror. I considered it at once as
the knell of the union. It is hushed, indeed, for the moment.
But this is a reprieve only, not a final sentence. A geographical
line, coinciding with a marked principle, moral and political,

* Holmes (1773-1843), a former Federalist who became a Democrat, was elected
U. S. Senator from Maine in 1813.

once conceived and held up to the angry passions of men, will never be obliterated; and every new irritation will mark it deeper and deeper. I can say, with conscious truth, that there is not a man on earth who would sacrifice more than I would to relieve us from this heavy reproach, in any *practicable* way. The cession of that kind of property, for so it is misnamed, is a bagatelle which would not cost me a second thought, if, in that way, a general emancipation and *expatriation* could be effected: and, gradually, and with due sacrifices, I think it might be. But as it is, we have the wolf by the ears, and we can neither hold him, nor safely let him go. Justice is in one scale, and self-preservation in the other. Of one thing I am certain, that as the passage of slaves from one state to another, would not make a slave of a single human being who would not be so without it, so their diffusion over a greater surface would make them individually happier, and proportionally facilitate the accomplishment of their emancipation, by dividing the burden on a greater number of coadjutors. An abstinence, too, from this act of power, would remove the jealousy excited by the undertaking of Congress to regulate the condition of the different descriptions of men composing a State. This certainly is the exclusive right of every State which nothing in the Constitution has taken from them and given to the general government. Could Congress, for example, say, that the non-freemen of Connecticut shall be freemen, or that they shall not emigrate into any other State?

I regret that I am now to die in the belief, that the useless sacrifice of themselves by the generation of 1776, to acquire self-government and happiness to their country, is to be thrown away by the unwise and unworthy passions of their sons, and that my only consolation is to be, that I live not to weep over it. If they would but dispassionately weigh the blessings they will throw away, against an abstract principle more likely to be effected by union than by scission, they would pause before they would perpetrate this act of suicide on themselves, and of treason against the hopes of the world. To yourself, as the faithful advocate of the union, I tender the offering of my high esteem and respect,

TH: JEFFERSON

To James Madison

January 13, 1821   *Monticello*

I am sorry to hear of the situation of your family, and the more so as that species of fever is dangerous in the hands of our medical boys. I am not a physician and still less a quack but I may relate a fact. While I was at Paris, both my daughters were taken with what we formerly called a nervous fever, now a typhus, distinguished very certainly by a thread-like pulse, low, quick and every now and then fluttering. Doctor Gem, an English physician, old and of great experience, and certainly the ablest I ever met with, attended them. The one was about five or six weeks ill, the other, ten years old, was eight or ten weeks. He never gave them a single dose of physic. He told me it was a disease which tended with certainty to wear itself off, but so slowly that the strength of patient might first fail if not kept up. That this alone was the object to be attended to by nourishment and stimulus. He forced them to eat a cup of rice, or panada, or gruel, or of some of the farinaceous substances of easy digestion every two hours and to drink a glass of Madeira. The youngest took a pint of Madeira a day without feeling it, and that for many weeks. For costiveness, injections were used; and he observed that a single dose of medicine taken into the stomach and consuming any of the strength of the patient was often fatal. He was attending a grandson of Madame Helvetius, of ten years old, at the same time, and under the same disease. The boy got so low that the old lady became alarmed and wished to call in another physician for consultation. Gem consented, that physician gave a gentle purgative, but it exhausted what remained of strength, and the patient expired in a few hours.

I have had this fever in my family three or four times since I have lived at home, and have carried between twenty and thirty patients through it without losing a single one, by a rigorous observance of Doctor Gem's plan and principle. Instead of Madeira I have used toddy of French brandy about as strong as Madeira. Brown preferred this stimulus to Madeira. I rarely had a case, if taken in hand early, to last above one, two, or three weeks, except a single one of seven weeks, in whom when I thought him near his last, I discovered a change in his pulse to regularity, and in twelve hours he was out of danger. I vouch for these facts only, not for their theory. You may on their authority, think it expedient to try a single case before it has shewn signs of danger,

TH: JEFFERSON

P. S. I should have observed that the same typhus fever prevailed in my neighborhood at the same time as in my family, and that it was very fatal in the hands of our Philadelphia tyros.

To Francis Eppes

January 19, 1821   *Monticello*

You ask my opinion of Lord Bolingbroke and Thomas Paine. They were alike in making bitter enemies of the priests and pharisees of their day. Both were honest men; both advocates for human liberty. Paine wrote for a country which permitted him to push his reasoning to whatever length it would go. Lord Bolingbroke in one restrained by a constitution, and by public opinion. He was called indeed a tory; but his writings prove him a stronger advocate for liberty than any of his countrymen, the Whigs of the present day. Irritated by his exile, he committed one act unworthy of him, in connecting himself momentarily with a prince rejected by his country. But he redeemed that single act by his establishment of the principles which proved it to be wrong. These two persons differed remarkably in the style of their writing, each leaving a model of what is most perfect in both extremes of the simple and the sublime. No writer has exceeded Paine in ease and familiarity of style, in perspicuity of expression, happiness of elucidation, and in simple and unassuming language. In this he may be compared with Doctor Franklin; and indeed his *Common Sense* was, for a while, believed to have been written by Doctor Franklin, and published under the borrowed name of Paine, who had come over with him from England. Lord Bolingbroke's, on the other hand, is a style of the highest order. The lofty, rhythmical, full-flowing eloquence of Cicero. Periods of just measure, their members proportioned, their close full and round. His conceptions, too, are bold and strong, his diction copious, polished and commanding as his subject. His writings are certainly the finest samples in the English language, of the eloquence proper for the Senate. His political tracts are safe reading for the most timid religionist, his philosophical, for those who are not afraid to trust their reason with discussions of right and wrong.

You have asked my opinion of these persons, and, *to you,* I have given it freely. But, remember, that I am old, that I wish not to make new enemies, nor to give offense to those who would consider a difference of opinion as sufficient ground for unfriendly dispositions. God bless you, and make you what I wish you to be,

TH: JEFFERSON

To John Adams

June 1, 1822 *Monticello*

It is very long, my dear sir, since I have written to you. My dislocated wrist is now become so stiff that I write slow and with pain, and therefore write as little as I can. Yet it is due to mutual friendship to ask once in a while how we do. The papers tell us that General Stark * is off at the age of ninety-three. Charles Thomson still lives at about the same age, cheerful, slender as a grasshopper, and so much without memory that he scarcely recognizes the members of his household. An intimate friend of his called on him not long since; it was difficult to make him recollect who he was, and, sitting one hour, he told him the same story four times over. Is this life?

> "With lab'ring step
> To tread our former footsteps? pace the round
> Eternal?—to beat and beat
> The beaten track? to see what we have seen,
> To taste the tasted? o'er our palates to decant
> Another vintage?"

It is at most but the life of a cabbage; surely not worth a wish. When all our faculties have left, or are leaving us, one by one— sight, hearing, memory—every avenue of pleasing sensation is closed, and athumy, † debility, and malaise left in their places—when friends of our youth are all gone, and a generation is risen around us whom we know not, is death an evil?

> "When one by one our ties are torn,
> And friend from friend is snatched forlorn,
> When man is left alone to mourn,
> Oh! then how sweet it is to die!

---

* John Stark (1728-1822) was an officer in the Revolutionary War.
† Athymia (?).

> When trembling limbs refuse their weight,
> And films slow gathering dim the sight,
> When clouds obscure the mental light
> 'Tis nature's kindest boon to die!"

I really think so. I have ever dreaded a doting old age; and my health has been generally so good, and is now so good, that I dread it still. The rapid decline of my strength during the last winter has made me hope sometimes that I see land. During summer I enjoy its temperature, but I shudder at the approach of winter, and wish I could sleep through it with the dormouse, and only wake with him in spring, if ever. They say that Stark could walk about his room. I am told you walk well and firmly. I can only reach my garden, and that with sensible fatigue. I ride, however, daily. But reading is my delight. I should wish never to put pen to paper; and the more because of the treacherous practice some people have of publishing one's letters without leave. Lord Mansfield declared it a breach of trust, and punishable at law. I think it should be a penitentiary felony; yet you will have seen that they have drawn me out into the arena of the newspapers; although I know it is too late for me to buckle on the armor of youth, yet my indignation would not permit me passively to receive the kick of an ass.

To turn to the news of the day, it seems that the cannibals of Europe are going to eating one another again. A war between Russia and Turkey is like the battle of the kite and snake. Whichever destroys the other, leaves a destroyer the less for the world. This pugnacious humor of mankind seems to be the law of his nature, one of the obstacles to too great multiplication provided in the mechanism of the universe. The cocks of the henyard kill one another. Bears, bulls, rams, do the same. And the horse, in his wild state, kills all the young males, until worn down with age and war, some vigorous youth kills him, and takes to himself the harem of females. I hope we shall prove how much happier for man the Quaker policy is, and that the life of the feeder is better than that of the fighter; and it is some consolation that the desolation by these maniacs of one part of the earth is the means of improving it in other parts. Let the latter be our office, and let us milk the cow, while the Russian holds her by the horns, and the Turk by the tail. God bless you, and give you health, strength, and good spirits, and as much of life as you think worth having,

TH: JEFFERSON

To Benjamin Waterhouse

June 26, 1822   *Monticello*

The doctrines of Jesus are simple, and tend all to the happiness of man.

1. That there is only one God, and he all perfect.
2. That there is a future state of rewards and punishments.
3. That to love God with all thy heart and thy neighbor as thyself, is the sum of religion. These are the great points on which he endeavored to reform the religion of the Jews. But compare with these the demoralizing dogmas of Calvin.
1. That there are three Gods.
2. That good works, or the love of our neighbor, are nothing.
3. That faith is everything, and the more incomprehensible the proposition, the more merit in its faith.
4. That reason in religion is of unlawful use.
5. That God, from the beginning, elected certain individuals to be saved, and certain others to be damned; and that no crimes of the former can damn them; no virtues of the latter save.

Now, which of these is the true and charitable Christian? He who believes and acts on the simple doctrines of Jesus? Or the impious dogmatists, as Athanasius and Calvin? Verily I say these are the false shepherds foretold as to enter not by the door into the sheepfold, but to climb up some other way. They are mere usurpers of the Christian name, teaching a counter-religion made up of the *deliria* of crazy imaginations, as foreign from Christianity as is that of Mahomet. Their blasphemies have driven thinking men into infidelity, who have too hastily rejected the supposed author himself, with the horrors so falsely imputed to him. Had the doctrines of Jesus been preached always as pure as they came from his lips, the whole civilized world would now have been Christian.* I rejoice that in this blessed country of free inquiry and belief, which has surrendered its creed and conscience to neither kings nor priests, the genuine doctrine of one only God is reviving, and I trust that there is not a young man now living in the United States who will not die a Unitarian.

But much I fear, that when this great truth shall be reestablished, its votaries will fall into the fatal error of fabricating formulas of creed and confessions of faith, the engines which so soon destroyed the religion of Jesus, and made of Christendom a mere Aceldama; that they will give up morals for mysteries, and Jesus for Plato. How much wiser are the Quakers, who, agreeing in the fundamental doctrines of the gospel, schismatize about no mysteries, and, keeping within the pale of common sense, suffer no speculative differences of opinion, any more than of feature, to impair the love of their brethren. Be this the wisdom of Unitarians, this the holy mantle which shall cover within its charitable circumference all who believe in one God, and who love their neighbor!

---

* See Jefferson's letter to Charles Clay, January 29, 1815, and the footnote.

To Samuel Benjamin H. Judah *

June 27, 1822   *Monticello*

Th: Jefferson returns thanks to Mr. Judah for the poem of Odofriede, of which he has been so kind as to send him a copy. The chill of eighty winters has so completely extinguished his sensibility to the beauties of poetry, as to leave him no longer competent either to enjoy or judge them. He transfers therefore to the younger members of his family, a pleasure which their more susceptible imaginations may feel and relish and with his thanks, he presents to Mr. Judah his respectful salutations.

To Benjamin Waterhouse

July 19, 1822   *Monticello*

Dear Sir, A long ago dislocated, and now stiffening wrist, makes writing an operation so slow and painful to me, that I should not so soon have troubled you with an acknowledgment of your favor of the eighth, but for the request it contained of my consent to the publication of my letter of June the 26th. No, my dear sir, not for the world. Into what a nest of hornets would it thrust my head! The *genus irritable vatum,* on whom argument is lost, and reason is, by themselves, disclaimed in matters of religion. Don Quixote undertook to redress the bodily wrongs of the world, but the redressment of mental vagaries would be an enterprise more than Quixotic. I should as soon undertake to bring the crazy skulls of Bedlam

---

* Judah (1799-1876) was a New York author and playwright. His work, *Odofriede, the Outcast,* which he sent to Jefferson, has been described as a "lugubrious dramatic poem."

to sound understanding, as inculcate reason into that of an Athanasian. I am old, and tranquillity is now my *summum bonum*. Keep me, therefore, from the fire and faggots of Calvin and his victim Servetus.

To David Bailie Warden *

October 30, 1822   *Monticello*

I have received your letters, dear sir, at different times with pamphlets and other favors without specific acknowledgments. Not that I have not been duly sensible and thankful for these kind attentions, but that I am become all but unable to write. Besides the weight of eighty years pressing heavily on me, a wrist and fingers which have nearly lost their joints render writing so slow and painful that I have been obliged to withdraw from all correspondence but the most indispensable. It is therefore long since I have written to my European friends, to whom I owe apologies: and if you will be my apologist to any who may complain it will be an additional favor.

I need say nothing to you about the affairs of Europe, such as the Holy Alliance, the suffering Greeks . . . of whom you know so much more than I do, and really you know as much of ours as I do, retired as I am in the mountains, going nowhere, and scarcely reading a newspaper. These vehicles of everything good and bad begin already to agitate us about the next president. It seems we have some dozens of characters fit for that office. I am glad we are so rich, although I shall not live to see its proof. Our Spanish neighbors have established their independence beyond the reach of their mother country,

* Warden, an exile from Ireland, came to the United States in 1799 and was made American consul at Paris in 1810; dismissed four years later, he spent the rest of his life in France.

and even of the Holy Alliance, its secret as well as avowed members. I wished them success because they wished it themselves; but I fear they have much to suffer until a better educated generation comes on the stage, one formed to the habits of self-government. They have already begun to disgrace our hemisphere with emperors and kings, and will, I fear, fall under petty military despotisms. Our age will present two remarkable contrasts in history: the birth of political liberty, and death of political morality. For certainly the modern sovereigns, from Bonaparte and the Holy Alliance to George IV and Castlereagh, are rival scelerats to the successors of Alexander and of the Borgias. Our University of Virginia is nearly finished, the style of the buildings is purely classical and we shall endeavor, with the aid of both sides of the Atlantic, to make it by its professors more than rival any other establishment of the United States. My aching hand refuses to follow me in this ramble further than to assure you of my great attachment and respect and of my best wishes for your health and happiness,

TH: JEFFERSON

To Edward Everett *

February 24, 1823   *Monticello*

By analyzing too minutely we often reduce our subject to atoms, of which the mind loses its hold. Nor am I a friend to a scrupulous purism of style. I readily sacrifice the niceties of

---

* Everett (1794-1865) was professor of Greek at Harvard, 1819-25. Later he became a member of Congress from Massachusetts (1825-35), Governor of his State (1836-40), president of Harvard (1846-49), U. S. Secretary of State (1852-53), and Senator (1853-54). As a commentary on the dramatic continuity of history, it is interesting to note that Everett, with whom Jefferson corresponded, was the orator whose long speech at Gettysburg received more contemporary attention than Lincoln's short and immortal address.

syntax to euphony and strength. It is by boldly neglecting the rigorisms of grammar, that Tacitus has made himself the strongest writer in the world. The hypercritics call him barbarous; but I should be sorry to exchange his barbarisms for their wise-drawn purisms. Some of his sentences are as strong as language can make them. Had he scrupulously filled up the whole of their syntax, they would have been merely common. To explain my meaning by an English example, I will quote the motto of one, I believe, of the regicides of Charles I, "Rebellion *to* tyrants is obedience to God." Correct its syntax, "Rebellion *against* tyrants is obedience to God," it has lost all the strength and beauty of the antithesis.

To John Adams

February 25, 1823   *Monticello*

I have just finished reading O'Meara's Bonaparte. It places him in a higher scale of understanding than I had allotted him. I had thought him the greatest of all military captains, but an indifferent statesman, and misled by unworthy passions. * The flashes, however, which escaped from him in these conversations with O'Meara, prove a mind of great expansion, although not of distinct development and reasoning. He seizes results with rapidity and penetration, but never explains logically the process of reasoning by which he arrives at them. This book, too, makes us forget his atrocities for a moment, in

---

* Jefferson had long held a low opinion of Napoleon Bonaparte. He wrote to George Logan, in October 1813: "No man on earth has stronger detestation than myself of the unprincipled tyrant who is deluging the continent of Europe with blood. No one was more gratified by his disasters of the last campaign." In his correspondence he referred to Napoleon as the "scourge," "tyrant" and "maniac." In a letter to John Adams, July 1814, he called the Emperor "the ruthless destroyer of ten millions of the human race, whose thirst for blood appeared unquenchable, the great oppressor of the rights and liberties of the world."

commiseration of his sufferings. I will not say that the authorities of the world, charged with the care of their country and people, had not a right to confine him for life, as a lion or tiger, on the principle of self-preservation. There was no safety to nations while he was permitted to roam at large. But the putting him to death in cold blood, by lingering tortures of mind, by vexations, insults and deprivations, was a degree of inhumanity to which the poisonings and assassinations of the school of Borgia, and the den of Marat never attained. The book proves, also, that nature had denied him the moral sense, the first excellence of well-organized man. If he could seriously and repeatedly affirm that he had raised himself to power without ever having committed a crime, it proves that he wanted totally the sense of right and wrong. If he could consider the millions of human lives which he had destroyed, or caused to be destroyed, the desolations of countries by plunderings, burnings, and famine, the dethronements of lawful rulers of the world without the consent of their constituents, to place his brothers and sisters on their thrones, the cutting up of established societies of men and jumbling them discordantly together again at his caprice, the demolition of the fairest hopes of mankind for the recovery of their rights and amelioration of their condition, and all the numberless train of his other enormities; the man, I say, who could consider all these as no crimes, must have been a moral monster, against whom every hand should have been lifted to slay him.

To John Adams

April 11, 1823   *Monticello*

Dear Sir, The wishes expressed in your last favor, that I may continue in life and health until I become a Calvinist, at least in his exclamation of, *"mon Dieu! jusqu'à quand!"* would make me immortal. I can never join Calvin in addressing *his God*. He was indeed an atheist, which I can never be; or rather his religion was daemonism. If ever man worshipped a false God, he did. The being described in his five points, is not the God whom you and I acknowledge and adore, the Creator and benevolent Governor of the world; but a daemon of malignant spirit. It would be more pardonable to believe in no God at all, than to blaspheme Him by the atrocious attributes of Calvin. Indeed, I think that every Christian sect gives a great handle to atheism by their general dogma, that, without a revelation, there would not be sufficient proof of the being of a God. Now one-sixth of mankind only are supposed to be Christians: the other five-sixths then, who do not believe in the Jewish and Christian revelation, are without a knowledge of the existence of a God!

To James Monroe

June 11, 1823   *Monticello*

On the question you propose, whether we can, in any form, take a bolder attitude than formerly in favor of liberty, I can give you but commonplace ideas. They will be but the widow's mite, and offered only because requested. The matter which now embroils Europe, the presumption of dictating to an independent nation the form of its government, is so arrogant, so atrocious, that indignation, as well as moral sentiment, enlists all our partialities and prayers in favor of one, and our equal execrations against the other. I do not know, indeed, whether all nations do not owe to one another a bold and open declaration of their sympathies with the one party, and their detestation of the conduct of the other. But farther than this we are not bound to go; and, indeed, for the sake of the world, we ought not to increase the jealousies, or draw on ourselves the power of this formidable confederacy [Holy Alliance]. I have ever deemed it fundamental for the United States, never to take active part in the quarrels of Europe.

To John Adams

September 4, 1823   *Monticello*

Dear Sir, Your letter of August the 15th was received in due time, and with the welcome of everything which comes from you. With its opinions on the difficulties of revolutions from despotism to freedom, I very much concur. The generation which commences a revolution rarely completes it. Habituated from their infancy to passive submission of body and mind to their kings and priests, they are not qualified when called on to think and provide for themselves; and their inexperience, their ignorance and bigotry make them instruments often, in the hands of the Bonapartes and Iturbides, to defeat their own rights and purposes. This is the present situation of Europe and Spanish America. But it is not desperate. The light which has been shed on mankind by the art of printing, has eminently changed the condition of the world. As yet, that light has dawned on the middling classes only of the men in Europe. The kings and the rabble, of equal ignorance, have not yet received its rays; but it continues to spread, and while printing is preserved, it can no more recede than the sun return on his course. A first attempt to recover the right of self-government may fail, so may a second, a third. . . . But as a younger and more instructed race comes on, the sentiment becomes more and more intuitive, and a fourth, a fifth, or some subsequent one of the ever renewed attempts will ultimately succeed. In France, the first effort was defeated by Robespierre, the second by Bonaparte, the third by Louis XVIII and his Holy Allies; another is yet to come, and all Europe, Russia excepted, has caught the spirit; and all will attain representative government, more or less perfect. This is now well understood to be a necessary check on kings, whom they will probably think it more prudent to chain and tame, than to exterminate. To attain all this, however, rivers of blood must yet flow, and years of desolation pass over; yet the object is worth rivers of blood, and years of desolation. For what inheritance so valuable, can man leave to his posterity?

To James Monroe *

October 24, 1823   *Monticello*

Dear Sir, The question presented by the letters you have sent me, is the most momentous which has ever been offered to my contemplation since that of Independence. That made us a nation, this sets our compass and points the course which we are to steer through the ocean of time opening on us. And never could we embark on it under circumstances more auspicious. Our first and fundamental maxim should be, never to entangle ourselves in the broils of Europe. Our second, never to suffer Europe to intermeddle with cis-Atlantic affairs. America, North and South, has a set of interests distinct from those of Europe, and peculiarly her own. She should therefore have a system of her own, separate and apart from that of Europe. While the last is laboring to become the domicile of despotism, our endeavor should surely be, to make our hem-

* This letter led to the adoption, by President Monroe, of what has since been known as the "Monroe Doctrine." In this communication Jefferson reversed a lifelong policy when he advocated an alliance with Great Britain.

isphere that of freedom. One nation, most of all, could disturb us in this pursuit; she now offers to lead, aid, and accompany us in it. By acceding to her proposition, we detach her from the bands, bring her mighty weight into the scale of free government, and emancipate a continent at one stroke, which might otherwise linger long in doubt and difficulty. Great Britain is the nation which can do us the most harm of anyone, or all on earth; and with her on our side we need not fear the whole world. With her, then, we should most sedulously cherish a cordial friendship; and nothing would tend more to knit our affections than to be fighting once more, side by side, in the same cause. Not that I would purchase even her amity at the price of taking part in her wars. But the war in which the present proposition might engage us, should that be its consequence, is not her war, but ours. Its object is to introduce and establish the American system, of keeping out of our land all foreign powers, of never permitting those of Europe to inter-meddle with the affairs of our nations. It is to maintain our own principle, not to depart from it. And if, to facilitate this, we can effect a division in the body of the European powers, and draw over to our side its most powerful member, surely we should do it. But I am clearly of Mr. Canning's opinion, that it will prevent instead of provoking war. With Great Britian withdrawn from their scale and shifted into that of our two continents, all Europe combined would not undertake such a war. For how would they propose to get at either enemy without superior fleets? Nor is the occasion to be slighted which this proposition offers, of declaring our protest against the atrocious violations of the rights of nations, by the interference of any-one in the internal affairs of another, so flagitiously begun by Bonaparte, and now continued by the equally lawless alliance, calling itself holy.

But we have first to ask ourselves a question. Do we wish to acquire to our own confederacy any one or more of the Spanish provinces? I candidly confess, that I have ever looked on Cuba as the most interesting addition which could ever be made to our system of states. The control which, with Florida Point, this island would give us over the Gulf of Mexico, and the countries and isthmus bordering on it, as well as all those whose waters flow into it, would fill up the measure of our political well-being. Yet, as I am sensible that this can never be obtained, even with her own consent, but by war; and its independence, which is our second interest, (and especially its independence of England), can be secured without it, I have no hesitation in abandoning my first wish to future chances, and accepting its independence, with peace and the friendship of England, rather than its association, at the expense of war and her enmity.

I could honestly, therefore, join in the declaration proposed, that we aim not at the acquisition of any of those possessions, that we will not stand in the way of any amicable arrangement between them and the mother country; but that we will oppose, with all our means, the forcible interposition of any other power, as auxiliary, stipendiary, or under any other form or pretext, and most especially, their transfer to any power by conquest, cession, or acquisition in any other way. I should think it, therefore, advisable, that the Executive should encourage the British government to a continuance in the dispositions expressed in these letters, by an assurance of his concurrence with them as far as his authority goes; and that as it may lead to war, the declaration of which requires an act of Congress, the case shall be laid before them for consideration at their first meeting, and under the reasonable aspect in which it is seen by himself.

I have been so long weaned from political subjects, and have so long ceased to take any interest in them, that I am sensible I am not qualified to offer opinions on them worthy of any attention. But the question now proposed involves consequences so lasting, and effects so decisive of our future destinies, as to rekindle all the interest I have heretofore felt on such occasions, and to induce me to the hazard of opinions, which will prove only my wish to contribute still my mite towards anything which may be useful to our country. And praying you to accept it at only what it is worth, I add the assurance of my constant and affectionate friendship and respect,

TH: JEFFERSON

To ——— *

December 16, 1823   *Monticello*

Dear Sir, Your letter of November 5, if it were not a mistake for December 5, has been strangely delayed, as it did not reach me till yesterday. You could not have applied to a worse hand for an inscription on the tombstone of our friend. I have no imagination. And an epitaph is among the most difficult of things. It requires brevity, point and pith. Were such a task enjoined on me, as an imposition on a schoolboy for a fault, my barren brains might hammer out some such bald thing as this.

William A. Burwell †
of Virginia
His Body Here
His Spirit with it's Kindred,
The Just, the Good, the Beloved of Men,
In the Bosom of his God.

Born [at such a time]
Died [at such a time]
At His Post in Congress
At Washington.

But how tame is such stuff as this alongside of the "siste Viator, Heroem calcas" over Marshal Saxe, or the "Hic cinis, ubique fama," over the great Frederick.

---

* Addressee unknown.
† He was a member of Congress from Virginia for fourteen years; for a short time he was secretary to Jefferson during his Presidency.

To Thomas Jefferson Grotjan

January 10, 1824 *Monticello*

Your affectionate mother requests that I would address to you, as a namesake, something which might have a favorable influence on the course of life you have to run. Few words are necessary, with good dispositions on your part. Adore God; reverence and cherish your parents; love your neighbor as yourself, and your country more than life. Be just; be true; murmur not at the ways of Providence—and the life into which you have entered will be one of eternal and ineffable bliss. And if to the dead it is permitted to care for the things of this world, every action of your life will be under my regard. Farewell,

TH: JEFFERSON

To Francis Adrian van der Kemp

January 11, 1824 *Monticello*

I have been lately reading a most extraordinary book, that of M. Flourens on the functions of the nervous system, in vertebrated animals. He proves by too many, and too accurate experiments, to admit contradiction, that from such animals the whole contents of the cerebrum may be taken out, leaving the cerebellum, and the rest of the system uninjured, and the animal continue to live, in perfect health, an indefinite period. He mentions particularly a case of ten and one-half months survivance of a pullet. In that state the animal is deprived of every sense of perception, intelligence, memory and thought of every degree; it will perish on a heap of corn unless you

cram it down its throat. It retains the power of motion, but
feeling no motive it never moves unless from external excitement. He demonstrates in fact that the cerebrum is the organ
of thought, and possesses alone the faculty of thinking. This is
a terrible tub thrown out to the Athanasians. They must tell
us whether the soul remains in the body in this state, deprived
of the power of thought? Or does it leave the body, as in death?
And where does it go? Can it be received into heaven while its
body is living on earth? These and a multitude of other
questions it will be incumbent on them to answer otherwise
than by the dogma that everyone who believeth not with them,
without doubt shall perish everlastingly. The materialist,
fortified by these new proofs of his own creed, will hear with
derision these Athanasian denunciations. It will not be very
long before you and I shall know the truth of all this, and in
the meantime I pray for the continuance of your health,
contentment and comfort,

TH: JEFFERSON

To Ira H. Taylor, Benjamin F. Nourse and John C. Tidball

March 8, 1824   *Monticello*

I pray you to accept for yourselves and to communicate
to the Franklin literary society of the College * which has
honored me in the choice of its name, my thanks for the proof
of their respect in naming me a member of their society. I
receive it as an evidence of their good will, the more disinterested as little could be expected from an octogenary
associate. The weight of years, and wane of mind inseparable
from that withdraw me from serious applications and leave me

---

* Jefferson College, at Canonsburg, Pennsylvania, which was organized in 1802.

nothing to contribute to the rising institutions of my country but blessings on their efforts, prayers for their success, and exhortations to perseverance. The cultivation of science is an act of religious duty to the Author of our being who gave us the talent of superior mind not to be hid under a bushel, but to raise us to that eminence of intellect which may prepare us for the future state of blessedness which he destines to those who render themselves worthy of it. With my best wishes accept the assurance of my high respect,

TH: JEFFERSON

To John Cartwright *

June 5, 1824   *Monticello*

Dear and Venerable Sir: I am much indebted for your kind letter of February the 29th, and for your valuable volume on the English constitution. I have read this with pleasure and much approbation, and think it has deduced the constitution of the English nation from its rightful root, the Anglo-Saxon. It is really wonderful, that so many able and learned men should have failed in their attempts to define it with correctness. No wonder, then, that Paine, who thought more than he read, should have credited the great authorities who have declared, that the will of parliament is the constitution of England. So Marbois, before the French Revolution, observed to me, that the Almanac Royal was the constitution of France. Your derivation of it from the Anglo-Saxons, seems to be made on legitimate principles . . . And although this constitution was violated and set at naught by Norman force, yet

---

* Cartwright, born in 1740, was an English political writer and reformer who had championed the cause of the American colonies. He died in London on September 23, 1824, possibly before or just about at the time this letter reached him.

force cannot change right . . . It has ever appeared to me, that the difference between the Whig and the Tory of England is, that the Whig deduces his rights from the Anglo-Saxon source, and the Tory from the Norman. And Hume, the great apostle of Toryism, says, in so many words, note AA to chapter 42, that, in the reign of the Stuarts, "it was the people who encroached upon the sovereign, not the sovereign who attempted, as is pretended, to usurp upon the people." This supposes the Norman usurpations to be rights in his successors. And again, C 159, "the commons established a principle, which is noble in itself, and seems specious, but is belied by all history and experience, *that the people are the origin of all just power.*" And where else will this degenerate son of science, this traitor to his fellow men, find the origin of *just* powers, if not in the majority of the society? Will it be in the minority? Or in an individual of that minority?

Our revolution commenced on more favorable ground. It presented us an album on which we were free to write what we pleased. We had no occasion to search into musty records, to hunt up royal parchments, or to investigate the laws and institutions of a semi-barbarous ancestry. We appealed to those of nature, and found them engraved on our hearts . . .

We have not yet so far perfected our constitutions as to venture to make them unchangeable. But still, in their present state, we consider them not otherwise changeable than by the authority of the people, on a special election of representatives for that purpose expressly: they are until then the *lex legum*.

But can they be made unchangeable? Can one generation bind another, and all others, in succession forever? I think not. The Creator has made the earth for the living, not the dead. Rights and powers can only belong to persons, not to things, not to mere matter, unendowed with will. The dead are not even things. The particles of matter which composed their bodies, make part now of the bodies of other animals, vegetables, or minerals, of a thousand forms. To what then are attached the rights and powers they held while in the form of men? A generation may bind itself as long as its majority continues in life; when that has disappeared, another majority is in place, holds all the rights and powers their predecessors once held, and may change their laws and institutions to suit themselves. Nothing then is unchangeable but the inherent and unalienable rights of man.

To Henry Lee *

August 10, 1824   *Monticello*

I am no believer in the amalgamation of parties, nor do I consider it as either desirable or useful for the public; but only that, like religious differences, a difference in politics should never be permitted to enter into social intercourse, or to disturb its friendships, its charities or justice. In that form they are censors of the conduct of each other, and useful watchmen for the public.

Men by their constitutions are naturally divided into two parties. First those who fear and distrust the people, and wish to draw all powers from them into the hands of the higher classes. Secondly those who identify themselves with the people, have confidence in them, cherish and consider them as the most honest and safe, although not the most wise depository of the public interests. In every country these two parties exist, and in every one where they are free to think, speak, and write, they will declare themselves. Call them therefore liberals and serviles, Jacobins and Ultras, Whigs and Tories, Republicans and Federalists, aristocrats and democrats or by whatever name you please, they are the same parties still and pursue the same object. The last appellation of aristocrats and democrats is the true one, expressing the essence of all.

---

* Lee (1758-1846) was a Kentucky surveyor and pioneer.

To Thomas Jefferson Smith *

February 21, 1825   *Monticello*

This letter will, to you, be as one from the dead. The writer will be in the grave before you can weigh its counsels. Your affectionate and excellent father has requested that I would address to you something which might possibly have a favorable influence on the course of life you have to run, and I too, as a namesake, feel an interest in that course. Few words will be necessary, with good dispositions on your part. Adore God. Reverence and cherish your parents. Love your neighbor as yourself, and your country more than yourself. Be just. Be true. Murmur not at the ways of Providence. So shall the life into which you have entered, be the portal to one of eternal and ineffable bliss. And if to the dead it is permitted to care for the things of this world, every action of your life will be under my regard. Farewell,

TH: JEFFERSON

[Accompanying the letter was]

A Decalogue of Canons for Observation in Practical Life

1. Never put off till tomorrow what you can do today.
2. Never trouble another for what you can do yourself.
3. Never spend your money before you have it.
4. Never buy what you do not want because it is cheap; it will be dear to you.
5. Pride costs us more than hunger, thirst, and cold.
6. We never repent of having eaten too little.
7. Nothing is troublesome that we do willingly.
8. How much pain have cost us the evils which have never happened.
9. Take things always by their smooth handle.
10. When angry, count ten before you speak; if very angry, a hundred.

---

* Son of Samuel Harrison Smith (see Jefferson's letter to him, Sept. 21, 1814).

<h1 style="text-align:center">To ——— *</h1>

October 25, 1825   *Monticello*

Dear Sir, I know not whether the professors to whom ancient and modern history are assigned in the university have yet decided on the course of historical reading which they will recommend to their schools. If they have, I wish this letter to be considered as not written, as their course, the result of mature consideration, will be preferable to anything I could recommend. Under this uncertainty, and the rather as you are of neither of these schools, I may hazard some general ideas, to be corrected by what they may recommend hereafter.

In all cases I prefer original authors to compilers. For a course of ancient history, therefore, of Greece and Rome especially, I should advise the usual suite of Herodotus, Thucydides, Xenophon, Diodorus, Livy, Caesar, Suetonius, Tacitus, and Dion, in their originals if understood, and in translations if not. For its continuation to the final destruction of the empire we must then be content with Gibbons, a compiler, and with Segur, for a judicious recapitulation of the whole. After this general course, there are a number of particular histories filling up the chasms, which may be read at leisure in the progress of life. Such is Arrian, Curtius, Polybius, Sallust, Plutarch, Dionysius, Halicarnassus, Micasi. . . . The ancient universal history should be on our shelves as a book of general reference, the most learned and most faithful perhaps that ever was written. Its style is very plain but perspicuous.

In modern history, there are but two nations with whose course it is interesting to us to be intimately acquainted, to wit: France and England. For the former, Millot's General History of France may be sufficient to the period when I Davila commences. He should be followed by Perefixe, Sully, Voltaire's Louis XIV and XV, la Cretelle's XVIIIme siècle,

---

* Addressee unknown.

Marmontel's Regence, Foulongion's French Revolution, and Madame de Stael's, making up by a succession of particular history, the general one which they want.

Of England there is as yet no general history so faithful as Rapin's. He may be followed by Ludlow, Fox, Belsham, Hume and Brodie. Hume's, were it faithful, would be the finest piece of history which has ever been written by man. Its unfortunate bias may be partly ascribed to the accident of his having written backwards. His maiden work was the History of the Stuarts. It was a first essay to try his strength before the public. And whether as a Scotchman he had really a partiality for that family, or thought that the lower their degradation, the more fame he should acquire by raising them up to some favor, the object of his work was an apology for them. He spared nothing, therefore, to wash them white, and to palliate their misgovernment. For this purpose he suppressed truths, advanced falsehoods, forged authorities, and falsified records. All this is proved on him unanswerably by Brodie. But so bewitching was his style and manner, that his readers were unwilling to doubt anything, swallowed everything, and all England became Tories by the magic of his art. His pen revolutionized the public sentiment of that country more completely than the standing armies could ever have done, which were so much dreaded and deprecated by the patriots of that day.

Having succeeded so eminently in the acquisition of fortune and fame by this work, he undertook the history of the two preceding dynasties, the Plantagenets and Tudors. It was all-important in this second work, to maintain the thesis of the first, that "it was the people who encroached on the sovereign, not the sovereign who usurped on the rights of the people." And again, chapter fifty-three, "the grievances under which the English labored [to wit: whipping, pillorying, cropping, imprisoning, fining . . .] when considered in themselves, without regard to the constitution, scarcely deserve the name, nor were they either burthensome on the people's properties, or anywise shocking to the natural humanity of mankind." During the constant wars, civil and foreign, which prevailed while these two families occupied the throne, it was not difficult to find abundant instances of practices the most despotic, as are wont to occur in times of violence. To make this second epoch support the third, therefore, required but a little garbling of authorities. And it then remained, by a third work, to make of the whole a complete history of England, on the principles on which he had advocated that of the Stuarts. This would comprehend the Saxon and Norman conquests, the former exhibiting the genuine form and political principles of the people constituting the nation, and founded in the rights of man; the latter built on conquest and physical force, not at all affecting moral rights, nor even assented to by the free will of the vanquished. The battle of Hastings, indeed, was lost, but the natural rights of the nation were not staked on the event of a single battle. Their will to recover the Saxon consti- tution continued unabated, and was at the bottom of all the unsuccesful insurrections which succeeded in subsequent times. The victors and vanquished continued in a state of living hostility, and the nation may still say, after losing the battle of Hastings,

> "What though the field is lost?
> All is not lost; the unconquerable will
> And study of revenge, immortal hate
> And courage never to submit or yield."

The government of a nation may be usurped by the forcible intrusion of an individual into the throne. But to conquer its will, so as to rest the right on that, the only legitimate basis, requires long acquiescence and cessation of all opposition. The Whig historians of England, therefore, have always gone back to the Saxon period for the true principles of their constitution, while the Tories and Hume, their Coryphæus, date it from the Norman conquest, and hence conclude that the continual claim by the nation of the good old Saxon laws, and the struggles to recover them, were "encroachments of the people

on the crown, and not usurpations of the crown on the people."
Hume, with Brodie, should be the last histories of England
to be read. If first read, Hume makes an English Tory, from
whence it is an easy step to American Toryism. But there is a
history, by Baxter, in which, abridging somewhat by leaving
out some entire incidents as less interesting now than when
Hume wrote, he has given the rest in the identical words of
Hume, except that when he comes to a fact falsified, he states
it truly, and when to a suppression of truth, he supplies it,
never otherwise changing a word. It is, in fact, an editic
expurgation of Hume. Those who shrink from the volume of
Rapin, may read this first, and from this lay a first foundation
in a basis of truth.

For modern continental history, a very general idea may be
first aimed at, leaving for future and occasional reading the
particular histories of such countries as may excite curiosity at
the time. This may be obtained from Mollet's Northern Antiquities, Vol. Esprit et Mœurs des Nations, Millot's Modern
History, Russell's Modern Europe, Hallam's Middle Ages, and
Robertson's Charles V.

You ask what book I would recommend to be first read in
law. I am very glad to find from a conversation with Mr.
Gilmer, that he considers Coke Littleton, as methodized by
Thomas, as unquestionably the best elementary work, and the
one which will be the text book of his school. It is now as agreeable reading as Blackstone, and much more profound. I pray
you to consider this hasty and imperfect sketch as intended
merely to prove my wish to be useful to you, and that with it
you will accept the assurance of my esteem and respect,

TH: JEFFERSON

To Thomas Jefferson Randolph

February 8, 1826   *Monticello*

My dear Jefferson, I duly received your affectionate
letter of the 3d, and perceive there are greater doubts than
I had apprehended, whether the legislature will indulge my
request to them.* It is a part of my mortification to perceive
that I had so far overvalued myself as to have counted on it
with too much confidence. I see in the failure of this hope,
a deadly blast of all peace of mind, during my remaining days.
You kindly encourage me to keep up my spirits; but oppressed
with disease, debility, age, and embarrassed affairs, this is
difficult. For myself I should not regard a prostration of
fortune, but I am overwhelmed at the prospect of the situation
in which I may leave my family. My dear and beloved daughter,
the cherished companion of my early life, and nurse of my
age, and her children, rendered as dear to me as if my own
from having lived with me from their cradle, left in a comfort-
less situation, hold up to me nothing but future gloom; and I
should not care were life to end with the line I am writing,
were it not that in the unhappy state of mind which your
father's misfortunes have brought upon him, I may yet be
of some avail to the family. Their affectionate devotion to me
makes a willingness to endure life a duty, as long as it can be
of any use to them. Yourself, particularly, dear Jefferson, I
consider as the greatest of the Godsends which heaven has
granted to me. Without you, what could I do under the
difficulties now environing me? These have been produced, in
some degree, by my own unskillful management, and devoting
my time to the service of my country, but much also by the
unfortunate fluctuation in the value of our money, and the
long continued depression of the farming business. But for

---

* Jefferson requested the Legislature of Virginia for permission to sell his lands
at auction in order to pay pressing debts.

these last I am confident my debts might be paid, leaving me Monticello and the Bedford estate; but where there are no bidders, property, however great, is no resource for the payment of debts; all may go for little or nothing. Perhaps, however, even in this case, I may have no right to complain, as these misfortunes have been held back for my last days, when few remain to me. I duly acknowledge that I have gone through a long life, with fewer circumstances of affliction than are the lot of most men—uninterrupted health—a competence for every reasonable want—usefulness to my fellow-citizens—a good portion of their esteem—no complaint against the world which has sufficiently honored me, and, above all, a family which has blessed me by their affections, and never by their conduct given me a moment's pain. And should this, my last request, be granted, I may yet close with a cloudless sun a long and serene day of life. Be assured, my dear Jefferson, that I have a just sense of the part you have contributed to this, and that I bear you unmeasured affection,

TH: JEFFERSON

To Roger Weightman *

June 24, 1826   *Monticello*

Respected Sir, The kind invitation I received from you, on the part of the citizens of the city of Washington, to be present with them at their celebration of the fiftieth anniversary of American Independence, as one of the surviving signers of an instrument pregnant with our own, and the fate of the world, is most flattering to myself, and heightened by the honorable accompaniment proposed for the comfort of such a journey. It adds sensibly to the sufferings of sickness, to be deprived by it of a personal participation in the rejoicings of

---

* Weightman (1786-1876) was a librarian in the Patent Office and mayor of Washington. This is Jefferson's last letter. He died three weeks later.

that day. But acquiescence is a duty, under circumstances not placed among those we are permitted to control. I should, indeed, with peculiar delight, have met and exchanged there congratulations personally with the small band, the remnant of that host of worthies, who joined with us on that day, in the bold and doubtful election we were to make for our country, between submission or the sword; and to have enjoyed with them the consolatory fact, that our fellow-citizens, after half a century of experience and prosperity, continue to approve the choice we made. May it be to the world, what I believe it will be (to some parts sooner, to others later, but finally to all), the signal of arousing men to burst the chains under which monkish ignorance and superstition had persuaded them to bind themselves, and to assume the blessings and security of self-government. That form which we have substituted, restores the free right to the unbounded exercise of reason and freedom of opinion. All eyes are opened, or opening, to the rights of man. The general spread of the light of science has already laid open to every view the palpable truth, that the mass of mankind has not been born with saddles on their backs, nor a favored few booted and spurred, ready to ride them legitimately, by the grace of God. These are grounds of hope for others. For ourselves, let the annual return of this day forever refresh our recollections of these rights, and an undiminished devotion to them.

I will ask permission here to express the pleasure with which I should have met my old neighbors of the city of Washington and its vicinities, with whom I passed so many years of a pleasing social intercourse; an intercourse which so much relieved the anxieties of the public cares, and left impressions so deeply engraved in my affections as never to be forgotten. With my regret that ill health forbids me the gratification of an acceptance, be pleased to receive for yourself, and those for whom you write, the assurance of my highest respect and friendly attachment,

TH: JEFFERSON

JEFFERSON'S OWN INSCRIPTION FOR HIS TOMBSTONE

HERE WAS BURIED

THOMAS JEFFERSON

AUTHOR

OF THE DECLARATION OF

AMERICAN INDEPENDENCE

OF

THE STATUTE OF VIRGINIA

FOR RELIGIOUS FREEDOM AND

FATHER OF THE UNIVERSITY

OF VIRGINIA

BORN APRIL 2D *

1743 O.S.

DIED [JULY 4]

[1826]

---

* April 2d, Old Style, is April 13, New Style.

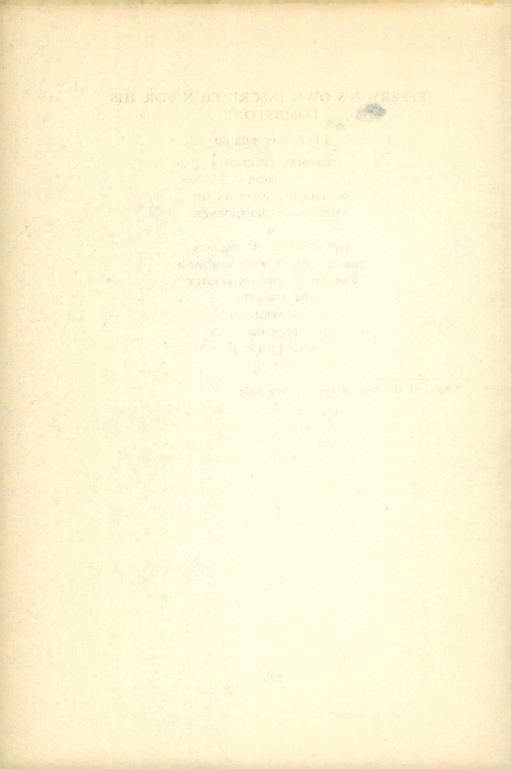

CHRONOLOGY OF THOMAS JEFFERSON

1743	April 13	Born, Shadwell, Albemarle Co., Va.
1757	August 17	Death of his father, Peter Jefferson
1760	March to April 1762	Attended William and Mary College
1762	April	Entered George Wythe's law office at Williamsburg
1766	May	Travelled to Philadelphia and New York
1767		Admitted to bar
1769		Began building Monticello
1769	March	Elected to House of Burgesses
1770	November 26	Moved to Monticello
1772	January 1	Married Martha Wayles Skelton
1772	September 27	Birth of daughter Martha
1773	October	Appointed surveyor of Albemarle County
1774	April 3	Birth of second daughter, Jane Randolph
1774	August	Published his *Summary View of the Rights of British America*
1775	March	Elected delegate to Continental Congress
1775	June 21 to July 31	Attended Continental Congress at Philadelphia
1775	October 2 to December 28	Attended Continental Congress at Philadelphia
1776	June 11	Appointed on committee to draft the Declaration of Independence
1776	June 28	Submitted draft of Declaration
1776	October 11 to December 14	Attended Virginia Assembly at Williamsburg
1776	November 5	Appointed on committee to revise Virginia laws
1778	August 1	Birth of third daughter, Mary
1779	June 1	Elected Governor of Virginia
1780	June 1	Re-elected Governor of Virginia
1781	June 1	Resigned as Governor

347

1781	June 14	Appointed Peace Commissioner to Europe
1781	June 30	Declined appointment
1781	November 5	Attended Virginia Assembly
1781	November 30	Elected delegate to Congress
1782	September 6	Death of Mrs. Jefferson
1783	June 6	Elected delegate to Congress
1784	March 12	Elected chairman of Congress
1784	May 7	Appointed Minister to France
1784	August 6	Arrived in Paris
1789	September 25	Nominated Secretary of State
1789	September 26	Left Paris
1789	December	Arrived at Monticello
1790	February 24	Accepted Secretaryship of State
1793	December 31	Resigned as Secretary of State
1796	November	Elected Vice-President of the United States
1797	January	Elected President, American Philosophical Society
1797	March 4	Took oath of office as Vice-President
1798	October	Drafted Kentucky Resolutions
1800	May	Nominated candidate for President
1801	February 17	Elected President
1804	November	Re-elected President
1807	December 22	Signed Embargo Act
1809	March 4	Retired from Presidency
1826	June 25	Wrote his last letter
1826	July 4	Died at Monticello

SELECTED BIBLIOGRAPHY

Jefferson's writings, including his letters, have been published in three major collections:

H. A. Washington's *The Writings of Thomas Jefferson* (9 vols., 1853-54).
P. L. Ford's *The Writings of Thomas Jefferson* (10 vols., 1892-99).
A. A. Lipscomb and A. E. Bergh's *The Writings of Thomas Jefferson* (20 vols., 1903).

These collections are now being superseded by *The Papers of Thomas Jefferson,* under the editorship of Julian P. Boyd, in association with Mina R. Bryan and others, which Princeton University Press is bringing out at the rate of about four a year, beginning with 1950. The total number of volumes will be well over fifty, and the work is expected to be completed sometime in the 1960's.

Other collections, containing mostly letters, are the following:

N. F. Cabell, *Early History of the University of Virginia, As Contained in the Letters of Thomas Jefferson and Joseph C. Cabell, Hitherto Unpublished* (1856).
G. Chinard, *The Commonplace Book of Thomas Jefferson: A Repertory of His Ideas on Government* (1926).
—— *The Correspondence of Jefferson and du Pont de Nemours* (1931).
—— *Houdon in America: A Collection of Documents in the Jefferson Papers in the Library of Congress* (1930).
—— *The Letters of Lafayette and Jefferson* (1929).
—— *Trois amitiés françaises de Jefferson d'après sa correspondance inédite avec Madame de Bréhan, Madame de Tessé et Madame de Corny* (1927).
W. D. Johnson, *History of the Library of Congress* (vol. I, 1904).
R. J. Honeywell, *The Educational Work of Thomas Jefferson* (1931).
C. F. Jenkins and W. J. Campbell, *Jefferson's Germantown Letters* (1906).
Magazine of History, "Letters of Thomas Jefferson" (1915).
D. Malone, *Correspondence between Thomas Jefferson and Pierre Samuel du Pont de Nemours, 1798-1817* (1930) .
Massachusetts Historical Society, Collections, *The Jefferson Papers* (ser. 7, vol. I, 1900).
Missouri Historical Society, "Correspondence of Thomas Jefferson, 1788-1826," (vol. III, 1936).
New York Historical Society, Collections, *The Papers of Charles Thomson.*

Secretary of the Continental Congress, 1765-1816 (vol. I, 1878)—about 100 letters exchanged between Jefferson and Thomson.

Saul K. Padover, *Thomas Jefferson and the National Capital* (1946).

T. J. Randolph, *Memoir, Correspondence and Miscellanies, from the Papers of Thomas Jefferson* (4 vols., 1829).

Jefferson's official messages are to be found in:

J. D. Richardson's *A Compilation of the Messages and Papers of the Presidents* (vol. I, 1897), 306-446.

Other writings, primarily letters, are scattered in various historical publications. The reader is referred to the Bibliography by R. H. Johnson in the Lipscomb and Bergh edition of Jefferson's *Writings,* vol. XX, and to Saul K. Padover's *Jefferson* (1942), pp. 435-47.

Index